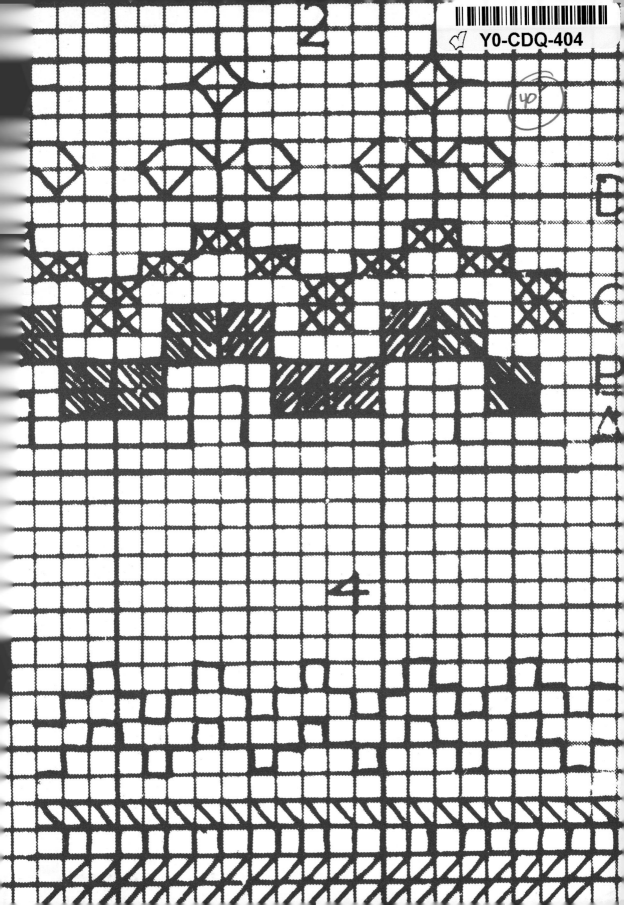

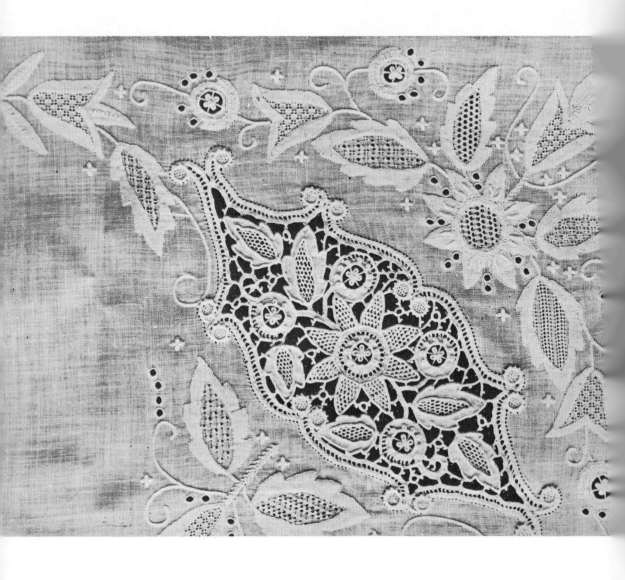

The corner of a tea-cloth where more than one medium were used, i.e.: shadow work, drawn fabric work and Venetian point. DM: Author.

EMBROIDER NOW

Hetsie van Wyk

Foreword by Mrs Betsie Verwoerd

Perskor

Perskor Publishers, Johannesburg and Cape Town
Copyright © 1977
All rights reserved
First edition, first impression 1977
Second edition, first impression 1982
Third edition, first impression 1987

ISBN 0 628 01129 6
ISBN 0 628 02314 6
ISBN 0 628 03197 1

Set in 10 on 12 pt. Times Roman/VIP
Cover design and concept: Marc Achleitner
Cover and illustrations: Author
Photos: M.T. Steyn
Set, printed and bound by
Perskor Book Printers, Doornfontein, Johannesburg (B9507)

EMBROIDER NOW
is a translation by
Esther Geldenhuys
of the book BORDUUR SO

To my husband

Contents

Foreword

To all those who are interested in embroidery this book is not only a treasure box of beautiful designs; it also provides the necessary tuition in this special branch of art.

It is a commonplace fact that we are living in an age of materialism and industrialisation; that we rarely have the leisure to devote to the finer things of life. Hence the remark is often heard that embroidery is a sheer waste of time; that work as beautiful can be machine-produced, cutting out considerable loss of time as well as undue eye-strain.

Such a viewpoint is a total negation of the very nature of embroidery. Would the same argument be raised with reference to the painter or the sculptor or any other handicraft artist? In their case it is taken for granted that the innate artistic urge seeks and finds satisfaction in the art practised. To be sure, there is a tendency (or is it a fashion?) for these visual arts to become abstract, to portray ideas and emotions rather than actualities, **thus becoming intelligible only to the initiated.**

Be that as it may, the process, as well as the result, serves to satisfy the creative impulse and is the expression of the artist's innermost being, no matter what others may say or think.

In the same way the art of embroidery is the expression of an innate urge, and I venture to say that it is less prone to becoming abstract and unintelligible to the masses than most other arts. As presented in this book, it is the creative work of a fine artist – work that is not only the result of careful training and years of experience, but essentially the expression of her innermost being.

This by itself would be reason enough for the publication in hand, as in the case of a collection of paintings or sculptures. But the book is far more: for the woman interested in hand embroidery it is a manual based on years of both study and practice. After obtaining the B.Sc. (Domestic Science) degree, with distinction for needlework, including embroidery, at the University of Stellenbosch, Mrs van Wyk spent three years studying in Cambridge and Birmingham, England, and gained the City and Guilds of London Institute Diploma in Hand Embroidery in the First Class. She also took a six months' course in the same subject in Geneva, Switzerland, and has for years been giving embroidery lessons in Bloemfontein.

The course of training starts at the beginning, as shown by the illustrations of specimens worked by the little girl of nine. It progresses gradually with complete and precise directions to the most complicated, most interesting combinations of stitches and patterns and the most exquisite designs, every **one of them original. Almost without realizing it, the amateur becomes an artist.**

The value of the book lies in the fact that it is a labour born of a great love and thereby acting as an inspiration to others. Of that there can be no doubt. And for this reason its contribution to the civilisation of a nation is important, for any appreciation of beauty, no matter what outward form it takes, is a sure aid to cultural development.

The field covered by this publication is specifically feminine, thereby serving to refine the atmosphere of the home. And it is the refinement in the home which distinguishes a civilised nation from an uncivilised one.

Because of its comprehensiveness and the great number of indispensible illustrations, this book will necessarily be expensive. I am nevertheless convinced that owing to its completeness and its rich variety of pattern and design, it will prove to be such a thorough guide and such a source of pleasure that it will be welcomed by all who are interested in embroidery.

It is a pleasure to give my full support to a publication of outstanding merit which will supply a long-felt want.

E. Verwoerd

Introduction

For centuries embroidery has played a major role in the life of man. In Exodus, for example, the descriptions of the hangings in the Temple indicate that they were elaborately embroidered by hand. The oldest piece of embroidery known to us was made in the 4th century B.C. and excavated in the Crimea. Similarly many other very old pieces, dating from the earliest centuries A.D., have been salvaged from Egyptian tombs. During the Middle Ages the standard of embroidery reached brilliant heights and played an important part in many spheres, especially in the Church, in clothing, and in the interiors of the homes. In England it developed into a particularly fine art during the 10th and 13th centuries, of which the famous church embroideries, the ''Opus Anglicanum'', bear witness. Until the end of the 17th century the European monarchs, their courtiers and the nobility were well-known, not only for their extravagant and richly embroidered clothes, but also in the palaces and homes, the walls, upholstery and the floors were lavishly adorned with embroidery.

The greatest inspiration for embroidery emanated from the beautiful relics of these glorious centuries. These museum pieces should, however, never be imitated, but serve as a source of inspiration and study only, to develop a particular trend characteristic of the 20th century.

The mechanised era tended to obscure hand-embroidery, but industries today supply beautifully finished materials and other aids for the modern embroideress. There are easily handled linen or cotton embroidery materials of all kinds, widths and colours to satisfy all her needs. There is cotton, wool and silk for every possible kind of embroidery and the wide selection of needles and embroidery frames further facilitates her task.

Already since the beginning of the 20th century a revival of this old art-form could be observed and it has grown steadily to the present stage of development. In the hurried tempo of life of the modern woman this art-form offers tranquility and satisfaction because she is able to create something which is not only lovely and useful, but could also be a source of enjoyment to her descendants. Embroidery in the home creates an atmosphere of genuine values and portrays the personality of the creator.

The purpose of this book is mainly to give technical aid, inspiration, ideas and designs to those for whom personal instruction is unavailable. It has been written for young and old, for the beginner as well as for the advanced student. For the latter there are also ideas that may lead into new directions and may bring new possibilities to their attention. It has been planned especially with a view to practical embroidery for the home. May it serve to encourage originality and freshness in the work of those who wish to experiment with the old well-known media, and may it help to let this beautiful time-honoured art-form regain its rightful place in our daily lives.

Nearly half of the book has been devoted to drawn fabric work. It is a practical, striking, reasonably quick and hard-wearing kind of embroidery, which has been proved by experience to be especially suitable for this hurried age of ours. Its rudiments are simple enough for children to grasp and to work correctly, and special attention has been given to them. At the same time it offers numerous possibilities for the advanced em-

broideress and it will continually be a challenge for her to discover new avenues.

Many of the plates used in this book are of work done by South African embroideresses. These designs are not given, but other similar, original designs, which the reader will be able to tackle with confidence, are supplied. The different stitches, especially in the first four chapters, are often introduced to the reader through these designs. Every chapter deals with new stitches, the names of which are listed in the Index.

How to read the codes in this book

Every chapter is divided into paragraphs, each with its own number, e.g. Chapter 3 has paragraphs 3.1, 3.2, 3.3 etc. Chapter 8 has 8.1, 8.2, 8.3 etc.

Every chapter has diagrams, also numbered according to the chapter to which they apply, e.g. the diagrams of chapter 10 are Fig. 10.1, Fig. 10.2, Fig. 10.3 etc.

The designs are numbered in the same way, but prefixed with the letter D to distinguish them from the other diagrams, e.g. the designs in chapter 9 are D9.1, D9.2 etc. On these designs and in the text letters are used as keys so that the text can be consulted for descriptions.

I am deeply indebted to Judge M. T. Steyn for his untiring application and patience with the taking of the photographs over a long period. I also want to thank Mrs Yvonne Steyn and Mrs J. van Heerden for their help. Mrs K. Uys gave excellent advice and criticism when she revised the manuscript and I am deeply grateful. To Mrs Esther Geldenhuys a special word of thanks for translating the book from Afrikaans into English. A very special word of thanks to all my pupils who so kindly put their embroidery at my disposal for many of the photographs in this book. I want to thank them and other friends too for their inspiration and encouragement.

Drawn Fabric Embroidery

1.1 Introduction

Drawn fabric embroidery, or pulled work, as the name indicates, is a type of embroidery in which the threads of the material are pulled together in different directions and in different ways in order to achieve a lacy effect with many open spaces without weakening the material in any way. It therefore differs basically from drawn thread work which requires the removal of threads from the material.

This type of embroidery is very striking and has many practical advantages. It is strong, because threads are not removed from the material and it is easy on the eyes as the embroideress is free to choose the material, either coarse or fine, of which she is able to count the threads easily. It is a neat and accurate type of embroidery based on the counting of the threads of the fabric and therefore even a child or a beginner can be successful from the start. With a few stitches, or even only one, a pretty and effective article can be made. The work remains interesting and a challenge even to the advanced embroideress because it offers innumerable possibilities. One stitch and one filling can lead to a new stitch and a new filling. While she is working, new ideas will constantly occur to the worker. What is, therefore, described on the following pages could never be the last word on drawn fabric work.

Drawn fabric work is most attractive in white and cream shades of material and thread. However very interesting results can also be achieved in pastel shades. The work is not as striking in darker colours because the lacy effect does not show up as well as on the lighter fabrics. Similarly a dark thread on a lighter fabric will be less effective as the dark thread draws the attention away from the holes which should form the actual design. During the 17th and 18th centuries this very old type of embroidery was worked on the finest cambric and became famous as "Dresden Work" which closely resembled needlepoint lace.

1.2 Materials and designs

Evenly woven linen is used for drawn fabric work, e.g. evenly woven linen with approximately 20 threads to 2½ cm in both directions (course), evenly woven linen with approximately 30 threads to 2½ cm in both directions (fine), Evenweave (fairly fine and loosely woven) as well as many Scandinavian linens obtainable in this country. Tapestry needles are used. These needles have blunt points and are supplied from No. 18 (thick) to No. 26 (fine). A linen thread was used originally and still is today, but Pearl Cotton — D.M.C. or Anchor or other similar thread — No. 12 (fine), No. 8 (medium) and No. 5 (coarse) — is suitable. Popular shades of cotton in the D.M.C. range are No. 642 (fairly dark) and No. 644 (lighter), but other ecru shades can be used on white, ecru or ivory linens. Where No. 12 is not available, use D.M.C. Brillanté D'Alsace No. 30 on fine linen and No. 8 on coarse linen for the pulled work. A tambour embroidery frame, 15 cm or 18 cm in diameter, is necessary and an extra smaller one can be very useful.

Some designs, built up on the counted thread and worked from squared paper, can be geometrical or free in style. Freehand designs, however, are outlined on the material by tacking-threads, (See Par. 1.3, hint No. 15) and surface stitches are worked as outlines

PLATE 1.1
Drawn fabric embroidery in white on ecru linen with approximately 35 threads to 2½ cm in both directions. Size: 86 cm diam.
DM: Author

for the drawn fillings. Geometrical and freehand designs can be used together on one article, an example of which is the cloth on Plate 1.2.

1.3 Practical hints

1. Use an embroidery frame so that an even tension of the stitches can be maintained.

2. Always pull the thread perpendicular to the material. In the case of eyelets and star stitch, however, the thread must be pulled away from their centres along the surface of the material.

3. When finishing off a thread on the wrong side, care must be taken that it does not cross an open space.

4. Finishing off on the wrong side must be done very firmly. With a few exceptions, the finishing off of stitches is not discussed again, but left to the discrimination of the worker.

5. Use a needle suited to the thread. E.g. No. 22 needle for No. 5 cotton, No. 24 needle for No. 8 cotton, No. 26 needle for No. 12 cotton, etc.

6. Buy graph paper and keep it at hand while working. Ideas and problems can be planned and solved on it, expecially when one line of the graph paper denotes one thread of the material.

7. Geometric satin stitch, which is often combined with drawn fabric work, must be finished off on the wrong side as follows: Pass the needle underneath the stitches already worked, hook it around the end stitch, and pass it through the stitches again. Repeat once more.

8. In the case of geometric satin stitch the number of stitches made will be one more than the number of threads that have to be covered according to the design. If the design indicates that 6 threads of the material have to be covered, then 7 stitches have to be worked. (Two stitches cover one thread of the material, one on either side of the thread, because it is not worked through the thread. In the same way 3 stitches cover 2 threads, 13 stitches cover 12 threads, etc.)

9. The direction of the geometric satin

PLATE 1.2
Drawn fabric embroidery on white linen with approximately 35 threads to 2½ cm in both directions. Good examples of free and geometrical designs. See also **Plate 3.1. Tea-cosy D: Author M: Mrs S. Venter**

stitches is indicated by the lines on the design.

10. It is sometimes necessary to join the material for a tablecloth as the linens are mostly only 140 cm or 170 cm wide. See Par. 1.6 for methods of joining. The following hints concern the execution of the instructions given on the design. Note that every square of the design indicates 3 threads of the material, unless otherwise stipulated.

tions: Tack a thread along the length of the material and one along the breadth near the edge as described above under 11. Cut the surplus material away, or enlarge the design as may seem necessary. Should the material be too small for the design, the latter must be altered, or a different piece of material used. See Fig. 1.3.

13. To make sure that the four corners of a border will be identical: Start working

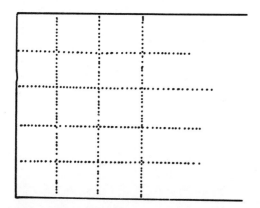

Figure 1.1

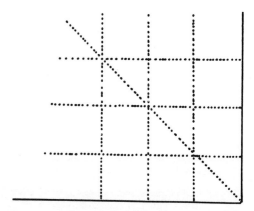

Figure 1.2

11. To make sure that no mistakes are made in the counting of the threads it is advisable to make a network of tacking threads on the material. Tack in both directions according to lines that can easily be marked on the design. As the work progresses the design can be controlled at every tacking thread. This thread must be tacked over and under every 3 threads and must be in a contrasting colour. It is recommended to tack at intervals of 150 threads of the material. See Fig. 1.1.

When a corner motif is worked it is also advisable to tack a thread diagonally from the corner, again over and under 3 threads. See Fig. 1.2.

12. To make sure that a piece of material will have enough threads to accommodate a given design, follow these direc-

on a corner, allowing enough threads for the hem. Work until the second corner has been completed identically with the first. Now start again at the first corner and work along the other side. The hem should not be put in until at least three corners have been completed. See Par. 2.2.

14. Where Pearl Cotton is used only the number, indicating the thickness, will be given, e.g. No. 5, No. 8 or No. 12.

15. The best way to transfer a freehand design into the material is by tacking. Place firm transparent paper over the design and trace all the lines with a pencil. Now place this design on the material in exactly the right position and pin along the sides. Using a sharp needle, dark blue, black or green machine-cotton and with a substantial knot, start

Figure 1.3

running stitches along all the lines of the design in stitches of about 6 mm long on the right side and smaller on the wrong side. Where the lines are curved, the stitches should be smaller. Finish off firmly with a few backstitches. When the whole design has been completed, pull the needle gently along all the tacked lines on the paper so that the paper tears and can easily be lifted from the material.

16. When the embroidery has been completed, iron on the wrong side with a damp pressing-cloth on a thick and soft ironing-sheet. Never iron on the right side.

1.4 Mitred corners
The corners of all hems, wide or narrow, must be made as follows: See Fig. 1.4

    (i) Pull out the threads where the hem must be sewn except for the two ends

tacking anywhere on the design. Commence with a small backstitch and work

Figure 1.4

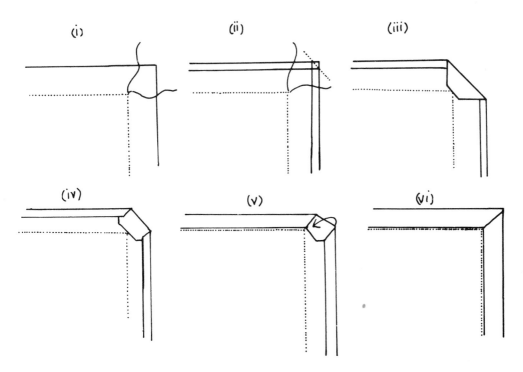

(i)   (ii)   (iii)

(iv)   (v)   (vi)

PLATE 1.3
Drawn fabric embroidery on a cream tea-cloth where repetition of motifs and stitches give a pleasing result. Note decorative hem. Size: 1,80 m × 2,75 m . D: Author, M: Mrs. C. Tidmarsh.

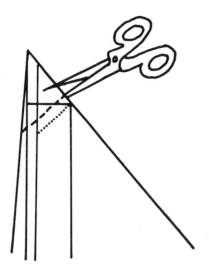

Figure 1.5

(the width of the hem) at each corner as shown in Fig. 1.4(i) leaving about 25 mm of the thread hanging, which

will later be hidden inside the hem.

(ii) Fold over once on both sides, mark the new corner, and cut away as indicated.

(iii) Fold this crosswise cut edge to where the short loose threads are and push them under the hem.

(iv) Now tack the first fold of the hem if necessary.

(v) Then fold the hem to the drawn thread on both sides of the corner and tack down.

(vi) Sew the mitred corner with small, invisible slipstitches on the wrong side. Preferably a thread of the material should be used.

When the hem is very wide, the corner must be machine-stitched diagonally on the wrong side up to the first fold of the hem. The extra material must be cut away, the corner pressed open and turned over. See Fig. 1.5.

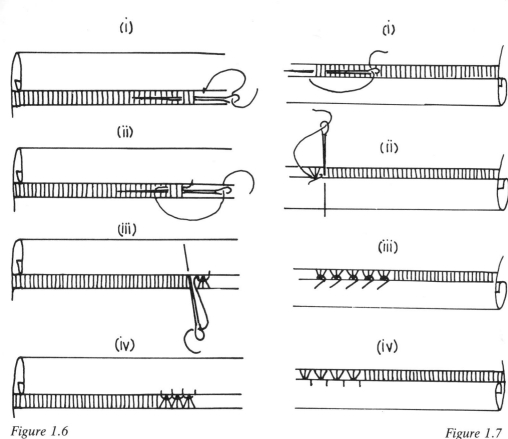

(i)

(ii)

(iii)

(iv)

Figure 1.6

(i)

(ii)

(iii)

(iv)

Figure 1.7

1.5 Hems

A few stitches for securing hems.

1. Punching. See Fig. 1.6

Pull out one thread where the hem is to be secured and tack the hem down. Using No. 12 cotton, work on the wrong side from right to left. Secure the thread to the hem with a tiny backstitch.

(i) Pick up 3 threads in the space where the thread has been drawn out.

(ii) Pick up the same 3 threads again but with the working thread under the needle.

(iii) Then make a tiny vertical stitch into the edge of the fold of the hem directly above the position of the working thread.

(iv) Repeat from (i).

2. Hemstitching. See Fig. 1.7

One or more threads are drawn. Using No. 12 cotton and holding the hem towards the worker, work on the right side from left to right.

(i) Pick up 3 threads from right to left.

(ii) Now pass the needle straight down through both the hem and the material and repeat.

3. Double hemstitching. See Par. 1.9 No. 10 for a full description. Used with punching, it forms a delightful finish to the hem.

4. Open Italian hemstitching. See Fig. 1.8, and Plate 2.4

Allow enough threads for the hem, then pull out one thread, leave 3 threads, pull out 5 threads, leave 3 threads and finally pull out one thread. Use No. 12 cotton.

(i) Firstly secure the hem by punching on the wrong side where the first thread was drawn out.

(ii) Then work a row of double hemstitch over the first horisontal group of 3 threads.

(iii) Repeat double hemstitch over the second group of 3 threads, but with the following variation: Work double

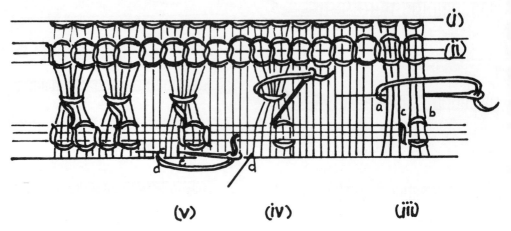

Figure 1.8

hemstitch over one group. Then the needle comes up at a and goes down at b, 6 threads to the right of a. The needle comes up at a again keeping the thread under the needle.

(iv) Now the needle goes down between the 2 groups of 3 threads at c and comes up at d.

(v) Bind the bottom group d e, keeping the thread under the needle. Work the next group as for double hemstitch and repeat from (iii).

The corner for Italian hemstitching: See Fig. 1.9.

Commence at a and overcast 4 times over the 3 threads. Bring the needle back to the hem on the wrong side and secure the hem by overcasting 4 times up to b. Overcast 4 times over 3 threads, bring the needle through to c and overcast around the little square according to the darts to cover the open threads of the material. Overcast again up to d and secure the hem by overcasting 4 times. Overcast 4 times over the 3 threads again at e, secure the hem and finish off.

5. Brick stitch over the hem. See Par 1.9 No. 6 for a full description and Plate 2.3 where it is worked over the hem.

Fold a narrow hem (e.g. 15 threads) and pull out one thread next to it. Using No. 12 cotton work brick stitch on the right side in the space

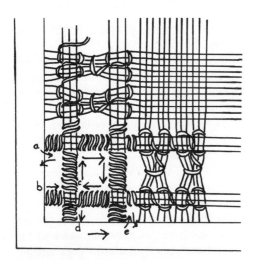

Figure 1.9

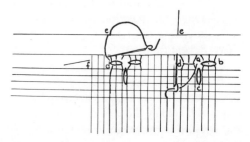

Figure 1.10

8

PLATE 1.4
Drawn fabric embroidery in 3 shades of blue on white linen with approximately 30 threads to 2½ cm in both directions. Brick stitch used on hem. D: Author, M: Esthé van Wyk (11 years)

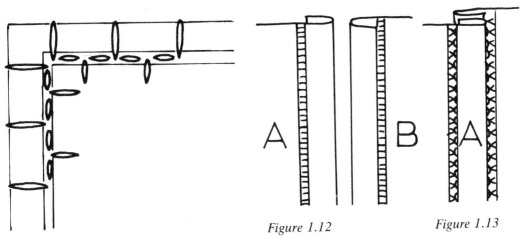

Figure 1.12

Figure 1.13

Figure 1.11

where the thread has been removed. See Fig. 1.10. Bind stitch d e twice over the hem to form a scalloped edge.

The corner: See Fig. 1.11. Work a mirror-image around the corner. This stitch can also be used as a filling.

1.6 Joining of material

When making large articles, it is often neces-

sary to join the material. Various methods can be used, but the following have specific advantages:

1. By punching. See Fig. 1.12
Fold A a 6 mm to the wrong side and pull out a thread where the raw edge of the material now lies, i.e. 5 or 6 threads away from the fold. Fold B to the right side and repeat. See Fig. 1.13. Place A on B so that the two

9

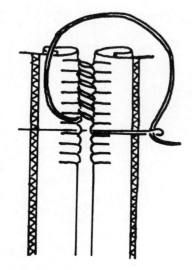

Figure 1.14

hems lie on top of each other. A is now joined to B by punching on the right side and in the same way B is joined to A on the wrong side. This gives a particularly firm result. Embroidery can be done on either side to disguise and decorate the join.

2. Hedebo buttonhole stitch. See Fig. 1.14 Fold a narrow hem to the wrong side of both

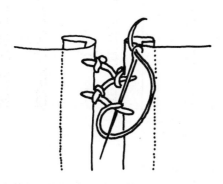

Figure 1.15

pieces of material and secure each by punching. Now work Hedebo buttonhole stitch using No. 8 cotton, over the edge of each hem so that the stitches cover about half of the width of the hem. The two pieces of material

are now joined by overcasting with No. 5 cotton through the loops of the stitches.

3. Knotted insertion stitch. See Fig. 1.15 Make two narrow hems in both pieces of material as in 2. Tack the two hems on to firm paper about 3 mm apart. Using No. 8 cotton, work to and fro from the one hem to the other and secure each stitch with a coral knot as is clearly shown on the diagram.

1.7 Basic stitches

The following are a few basic stitches continually used in drawn fabric work. One line on the diagram represents one thread of the material unless otherwise stated.

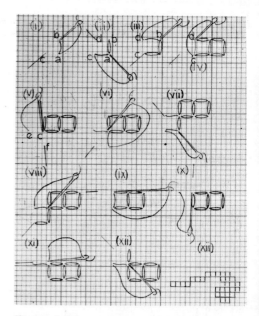

Figure 1.16

1. Four-sided stitch. See Fig. 1.16 and Plate 1.5
This is a very useful and versatile stitch and often forms the basis on which a design is built — see Plate 1.6.

Use No. 12 cotton and work from right to left.

(i) The needle comes up at a and goes down at b, 3 threads higher than a.

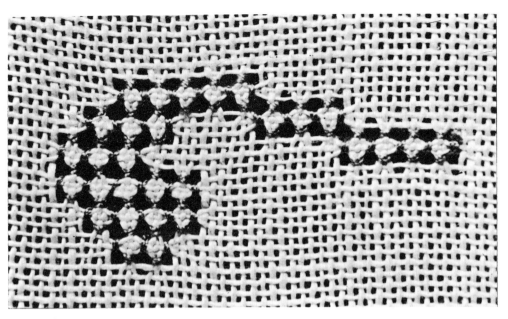

PLATE 1.5
Four-sided stitch

Bind a b twice and bring the needle out at c, 3 threads to the left of a.

(ii) Bind c a twice, bring the needle out at d and bind d b twice.

(iii) Bring the needle out at c and bind c d twice, which has been worked like a b.

Repeat according to the design.

This stitch is worked in 3 stages, always in the same order: Bind the right side of the square first, then below and then at the top and repeat. If this sequence is followed, the stitch will always appear fresh and neat and the holes will be clearly defined.

Fig. 1.16 Nos. (v) — (viii) indicate how to proceed from one row to the next. No. (v) shows how the thread is taken around a group of 3 threads at e c to get a perfect little hole. If the needle is taken directly to f, where the next row begins, the thread will show. Bind e c then only once (viii) because it has been bound once before (v). The same principle applies when crossing to a row on the opposite side, as indicated in Fig. 1.16 No. (ix) — (xii). (xiii) Shows how the stitch is indicated on all designs. When rows of four-sided stitch are worked next to one another, mutual sides must be bound only once, so that when com-

PLATE 1.6
Four-sided stitch used as a framework for design. Section of a table-cloth. D: Author, M: Mrs. C. Tidmarsh

11

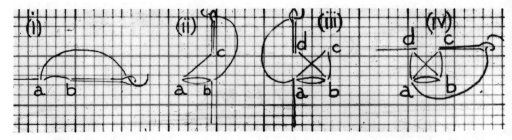

Figure 1.17

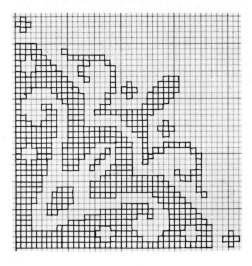

D 1.1
A simple design

pleted all the stitches will have been bound twice.

The experienced embroideress will find that four-sided stitch can be worked faster and with greater ease on the wrong side. It also ooks neater because the two binding threads are not inclined to cross, but lie neatly side by side.

See Fig. 1.17 for the different stages of this method. Note that in No. (iv) stitches d c and a b are both worked in the same way.

A simple design
In design D 1.1 only four-sided stitch is used.
Scale: One square equals 3 threads.

2. Double faggot. See Fig. 1.18 and Plate 1.7.

Although double faggot closely resembles four-sided stitch, it is worked quite different-ly. A row of double faggot is always worked

Figure 1.18

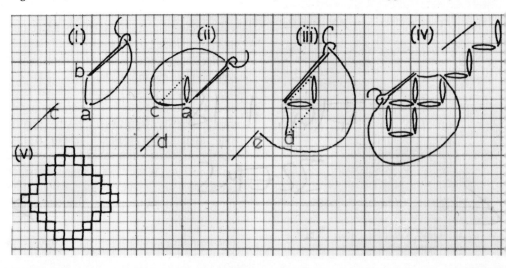

only diagonally while a row of four-sided stitch can be worked diagonally as well as parallel to the thread of the material.

Double faggot is usually worked in two successive rows, but a single row gives a light and pretty effect. Use No. 12 cotton.

(i) The needle comes out at a and goes in

wrong side so that the diagonal stitches appear on the right side. See Fig. 7.3.

3. Algerian eyelets. See Fig. 1.19 and Plate 1.8.

As in the case of four-sided stitch this stitch is particularly suitable to give the effect of sof-

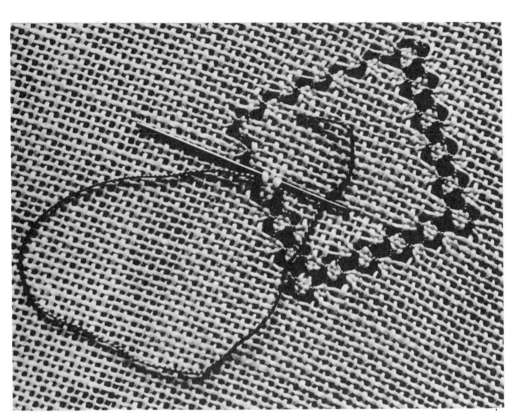

PLATE 1.7
Double faggot stitch

at b, 3 threads above a. Bind a b twice and bring the needle out at c, 3 threads to the left of a.

(ii) Bind c a twice and bring the needle out at d, 3 threads below c.

(iii) Bind d c twice and bring the needle out at e, 3 threads to the left of d, etc.

Fig. 1.18 No. (v) (Scale: One square equals 3 threads) shows how this stitch is indicated throughout on all the designs.

Sometimes double faggot is worked on the

ter, flowing lines in a drawn fabric design. Use No. 12 cotton.

(i) Commence at a and insert the needle at b, which lies diagonally over 3 threads from a. Bind a b twice and bring the needle out at c, 3 threads below b.

(ii) Bind c b twice and bring the needle out at d, 3 threads to the right of c.

(iii) Bind d b twice and bring the needle out at e, 3 threads above d. d b is worked like a b.

13

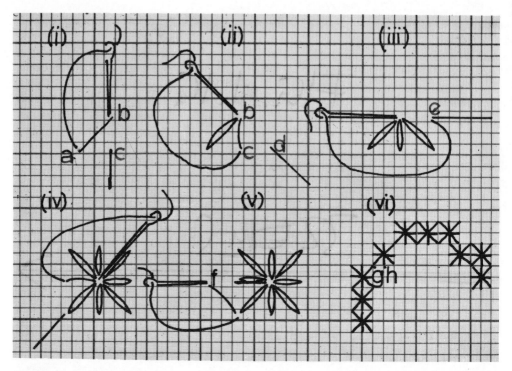

Figure 1.19

PLATE 1.8
Algerian eyelets

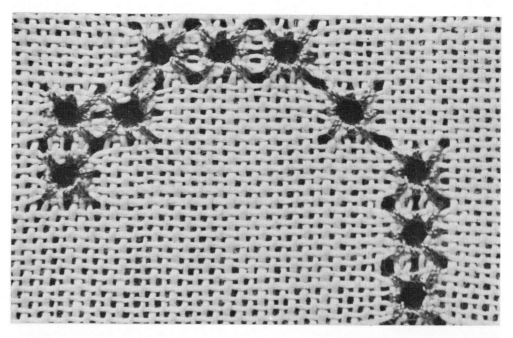

(iv) Repeat until the eyelet has been completed.

(v) Bring the needle again out in the corner at a and insert at f, diagonally over 3 threads from a. a f is worked like a b. Repeat. Fig. 1.19 No. (vi) (Scale: One square equals 3 threads) shows how the stitch is indicated throughout on all the designs.

When the eyelets on the design meet only at the corners, as in No. (vi) g, do not start the next eyelet at the corner as this stitch will then appear longer than the other corner stitches.

In this case the eyelet must be started at h. It is sometimes necessary to darn the needle through a few stitches on the wrong side to get it to the best position from which to start the next eyelet.

4. Eyelets. See Fig. 1.20 and Plate 1.9.
The value of eyelets in any design cannot be stressed too strongly. When placed singly, the

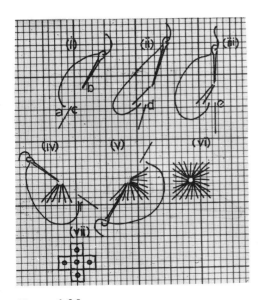

Figure 1.20

(i) The needle comes out at a and goes in at b, the centre of the eyelet, which lies diagonally over 3 threads from a. It comes out at c in the space next to a.

(ii) Insert the needle at b again and bring it

PLATE 1.9
Eyelets

out at d, which is directly next to c.

(iii) Insert at b again and bring out at e, which is next to d.

(iv) Work the next stitch one thread to the right and in this way 7 stitches must be worked from one corner to the other. f b, the 7th stitch, is again diagonal over 3 threads.

(v) From here the needle is brought out along the second side, which is worked exactly like the first side. Repeat for the 3rd and 4th sides, until

(vi) the eyelet has been completed. Fig. 1.20 No. (vii) (Scale: one square equals 3 threads) shows how the stitch is indicated throughout on all the designs.

1.8 The First practical steps

Although drawn fabric work is basically very simple, it is advisable to choose something small for the first attempt. A small and simple

effect is lighter and when grouped, they give an attractive lacy effect. The tension of the stitches must be firm and even so that the holes of the eyelets will be of the same size. See Hint No. 1 and 2 in Par. 1.3. Use No. 12 cotton.

design executed successfully will give the worker confidence and courage to attempt a larger article, e.g. a tea-cloth or a table-cloth. Experience gained by working a few small articles first will enable the worker to understand the designs on the squared paper more easily and she may even be able to change them according to her own taste or to adjust them according to the available material etc. Experience, in the long run, remains the best teacher and gradually the embroideress becomes acquainted with the pitfalls and learns to be on the alert.

Therefore it is advisable for a young girl or a beginner to start on a few tray-cloths until she feels she is really familiar with the nature of drawn fabric work. She will see the different textures develop in her hands and will later be able to feel almost intuitively which should be combined to give the work repose and artistic unity.

A firm, even tension must be maintained when using No. 12 cotton. In the case of satin stitch, however, when working with No. 5 cotton, the tension must be the same as that of the material.

1.9 Narrow borders

For the worker who does not yet feel confident enough to tackle a design, simple but effective narrow borders are recommended. A few ideas are listed below. Note that a few of these borders can be worked adjoining to form a wide border. The scale throughout is one line equals one thread, unless otherwise stated.

Dl. 2 No. 1
See Fig. 3.33 and Plate 3.36 where it is used as a filling.
A. Work one row four-sided stitch, using no. 12 cotton.
B. Using No. 5 cotton, work a satin stitch vertically over 6 threads into an opening of the four-sided stitch, then 2 satin stitches over 2

PLATE 1.10
Tea-cosy in drawn fabric work using ecru cottons on cream linen. D: Author, M: Esthé van Wyk (9 years)

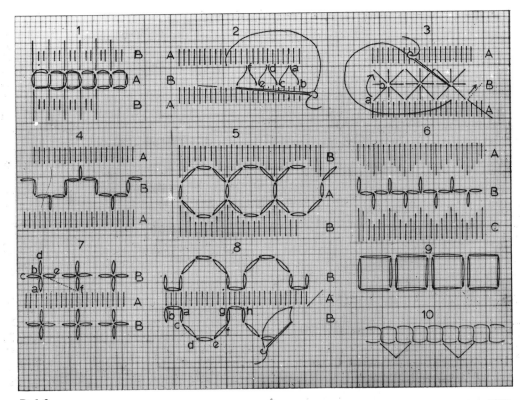

D 1.2

Figure 1.21

threads, again one over 6 threads into an opening of the four-sided stich, etc. Work the same row of satin stitches on the other side of the four-sided stitch.

Dl. 2 No. 2

See Plate 1.11. Use No. 12 cotton throughout.

A. Pulled lines. See Fig. 1.21

  (i) Scale: One square equals 3 threads. Pull upright stitches, each over 3 threads, between every thread of the material to form a straight line.

  (ii) To make a corner, 7 stitches are worked into one space above while the stitches fan round the corner below with the 4th stitch exactly on the corner and diagonally over 3 threads. Work 2 pulled lines 4 threads apart.

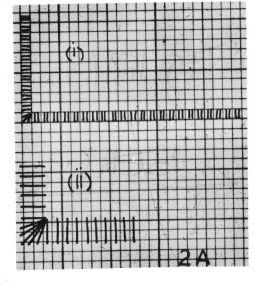

B. Now work a row of wave stitch in the space between the two lines as follows:

  (i) Bring the needle out at a and insert at b, 4 threads below and 2 threads to the right of a. Bring the needle out at c, 4

PLATE 1.11
Narrow borders

threads to the left of b.

(ii) Insert again at a and emerge at d, 4 threads to the left.

(iii) In again at c and out at e, in at d and out at f, etc. Maintain a medium tension. When used as a filling (see Fig. 3.64) the rows are worked adjoining, picking up the same groups of threads of the previous rows.

Dl. 2 No. 3

See Plate 1.11

A.   Using No. 5 cotton, work 2 rows satin stitch 6 threads apart over 3 threads of the material. The method is the same as for pulled lines, except that the tension must now be the same as that of the material.

B.   Work one row Algerian eyelets with No. 8 cotton in the space between the 2 rows of satin stitch, but bind each stitch only once instead of twice. Commence with stitch a b and follow the dart. The dotted line shows the way of passing from one eyelet to the next.

Dl. 2 No. 4

See Plate 1.11. Use No. 12 cotton only.

Figure 1.22

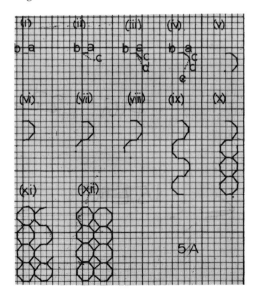

A.   Work 2 pulled lines, 9 threads apart.

B.   Work a zig-zag row of double faggot between A.

Dl. 2 No. 5

See Plate 1.11

A.   First work one row of eight-sided stitch as follows: See Fig. 1.22.

Use No. 12 cotton. Scale: one square equals 3 threads.

(i) Bring the needle out at a, and in at b, 3 threads from a. Bind a b twice.

(ii) Come out at c, which is diagonally 3 threads from a.

(iii) Bind c twice, and bring the needle out 3 threads below c at d.

(iv) Bind d c twice, and bring the needle out at e, which is diagonally 3 threads from d.

(v) — (ix) Continue in this way — one stitch on the straight and one on the diagonal, each bound twice to form a S-pattern.

(x) Repeat for the 2nd journey to complete the rings, and bind only once where stitches overlap.

(xi) — (xii) Work adjoining rows when used as a filling.

B.   Use No. 5 cotton and work one row of satin stitch over 3 threads of the material except where otherwise shown on the diagram, where one stitch lies over 4 threads, one over 5, and again one over 4. Note that one thread is left between A and B.

Dl. 2 No. 6

See Plate 1.11

A.   Use No. 5 cotton and work a row of satin stitch with all the stitches level at the top but different in length at the bottom, viz. over 3, 4, 5, 6 and again over 5, 4 threads. Repeat.

B.   Using No. 12 cotton, work a row of brick stitch so that the vertical stitches are placed 3 threads away and just opposite the shortest satin stitch.

Brick stitich: See Fig. 1.23

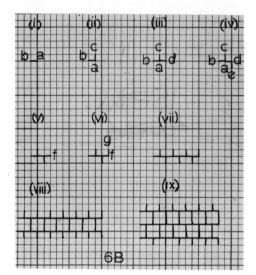

Figure 1.23

(i) Bring die needle out at a and insert at b. Bind a b twice.

(ii) Now insert the needle at c and emerge at a. Bind a c twice.

(iii) Insert at d, come out at a, in again at d, but then

(iv) out at e. Bind d e twice and bring the needle out at

(v) f. Position f is the same as position a.

(vi) and (vii) Repeat from (i) to the end of the row. Note that no diagonal stitch is made on the wrong side. When this stitch is used as a filling, work the rows successively with no intervening threads as in (viii) and (ix).

C. Repeat as in A but keep the stitches level below and see that the posision of the longer stitches remain correct.

Dl. 2 No. 7
See Plate 1.11
A. Using No. 12 cotton, work one pulled line.
B. Bring the needle out at a, right up against the pulled line and insert at b, 3 threads higher and bine a b twice. Emerge at c, 3 threads to the left of b, and bind c b twice. Similarly d b

and e b are each bound twice. Bring the needle out at f, 7 threads to the right of a, to start the next floret. Note that one thread is left between each floret. Work another similar row on the opposite side of the pulled line.

Dl. 2 No. 8
See Plate 1.11. Use No. 12 cotton throughout.
A. Work one pulled line.
B. Work two rows festoon stitch on both sides as follows:
Bring the needle out at a and insert at b, 3 threads to the left of a. Bind a b twice. Bring

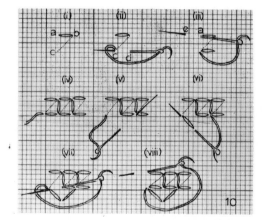

Figure 1.24

the needle out at c, 3 threads below a and bind c a twice. Bring the needle out at d, diagonally over 3 threads from c, and bind d c twice. Similarly e d, f e, g f are each bound twice. Repeat, as h g is worked like a b.

Dl. 2 No. 9
See Plate 1.11
This is really a very easy and extremely effective line stitch.
It consists only of detached four-sided stitch, but worked over 6 threads instead of over 3, and with one thread of the material left between each little square. Use No. 8 cotton.

20

Dl. 2 No. 10
See Plate 1.11 and Fig. 1.24

This is a very attractive stitch often encountered on Italian embroidery and especially effective along the hems of serviettes and tray-cloths. Use No. 12 or No. 8 cotton.

(i) Bring the needle out at a and insert at b, 3 threads from a. Bring the needle out at c, 3 threads directly below a.

(ii) Insert at d, 3 threads to the right of c and emerge again at c, keeping the thread under the needle.

(iii) Insert at a and out at e, 3 threads to the left of a. e a is worked like a b.

(iv) Repeat.

(v) — (viii) An extra trimming can be added on one or both sides by working a small V-shaped stitch as indicated on the diagram. When this stitch is used next to a hem, the V-stitch will hold the hem down.

1.10 Tray cloths
Design Dl. 3 offers 7 motifs suitable for tray-cloths or luncheon-mats Scale throughout: one square equals 3 threads.

Dl. 3 No. 1
See Fig. 1.25, Fig. 1.26, Fig. 1.27 and Fig. 1.28.

There are many ways in which this small design can be arranged on an article, as illustrated on the diagrams. The motif can be worked in 2 corners (Fig. 1.25) or in all 4 corners. If worked only in 2 corners, they can be connected by working 3 rows of pulled lines from motif to motif. Or work 3 adjoining pulled lines 76 mm or 7,6 cm from the hem right round the article, (10 cm on course linen), and place the motif as shown on the diagram, Fig. 1.26. Also place the motif adjoining 4 times with x as the centre and work 4 groups of 5 pulled lines towards the hem (Fig. 1.27). Or work the motif twice in each corner as in Fig. 1.28.

Key: A. Algerian eyelets. B. Pulled lines. C. Pulled square. See Fig. 1.29.

Figure 1.25

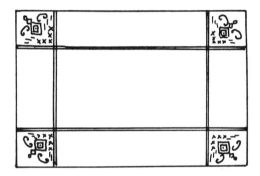

Figure 1.26

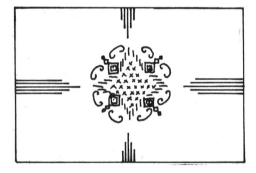

Figure 1.27

(i) Using No. 12 cotton, commence at a and make an ordinary eyelet.

(ii) Then bring the needle out at b and work a pulled line around the eyelet.

(iii) Work a second pulled line adjoining the first. In this way any number of pulled lines can be worked around an eyelet. Alternatively broken lines can be worked as in (iv) and (v). As a variation some lines can be worked

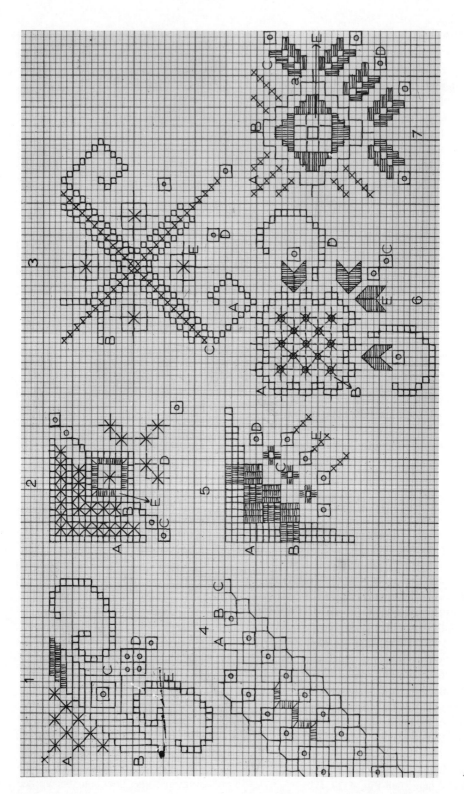

D 1.3

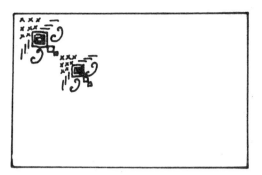

Figure 1.28

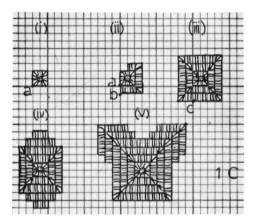

Figure 1.29

with No. 5 cotton. In the case of this particular motif, 6 broken lines are pulled on both sides of the pulled square.

D.   Eyelets. E.   Four-sided stitch.

Dl. 3 No. 2
See Fig. 1.30

This motif can be arranged in many different ways, e.g. as on the diagram. Find the centre of the short side of the cloth and work the motif on either side of the centre, right up against the hem, leaving 3 threads in between. Then connect the 2 short sides of the cloth with a row of four-sided stitch and work Algerian eyelets as shown in Fig. 1.30.

Key: A.   Four-sided stitch. B.   Algerian eyelets. C.   Eyelets. D.   Star stitch. See Fig. 1.31.

Use No. 12 Pearl cotton.

(i)   Bring the needle out at a, insert at b, 6 threads above a, bind a b twice, and emerge at c, diagonally over 3 threads from a.

(ii) Bind c b twice and emerge at d, 6 threads to the right of b.

(iii) and (iv) Bind d b twice and repeat around b as centre until the star has been completed. Pull die thread tightly so that a large hole is formed in the centre.

E.   Pulled line.

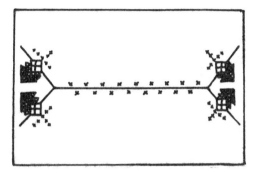

Figure 1.30

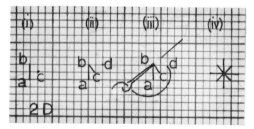

Figure 1.31

Dl. 3 No. 3 See Fig. 1.32

This motif can be used in many ways, e.g. as shown on the diagram. Work the motif in one corner, 3 threads away from the hem. Then work 2 rows of satin stitch in both directions and repeat the motif in the inside corner thus formed.

Key: A.   Double faggot stitch. B.   Four-sided stitch. C.   Diagonal raised band. See Fig. 1.33.

Use No. 12 Pearl cotton and keep the ten-

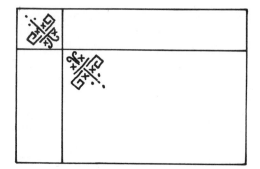

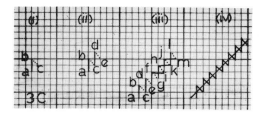

Figure 1.32

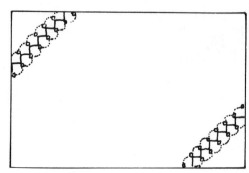

Figure 1.34

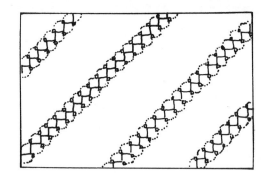

Figure 1.33

Figure 1.35

sion reasonably firm.

(i) Bring the needle out at a, insert at b, 6 threads above a, and bring it out at c, diagonally across 3 threads from b.

(ii) Now insert at d, 6 threads above c and emerge at e.

(iii) Repeat as far as necessary and then turn by emerging e.g. at m, inserting at j, out at k and in at h etc., until the row has been completed. The raised effect is formed in this way.

(iv) illustrates how this stitch is shown on the designs.

D. Eyelets. E. Star stitch, surrounded by a single row of double faggot over 6 threads.

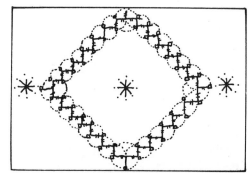

Figure 1.36

Dl. 3 No. 4

See Fig. 1.34, Fig. 1.35, Fig. 1.36 and Plate 1.12.

This diagonal band can be used in many different ways, some of which are shown on the diagrams.

Key: A. Using No. 12 Pearl cotton, work a pulled line along the middle of the design.
B. Eyelets. C. See Fig. 1.37.

Using No. 12 Pearl cotton, pull on the outside of A and B as follows:

(i) Bring the needle out at a, diagonally over 6 threads from the corner of the eyelet, insert at b, 6 threads higher. Bind a b twice, and bring the needle out at c, 6 threads to the left of a.

(ii) Bind c a twice.

(iii) Bind d b and c d twice. Then bring the needle out at e, which is 3 threads

24

diagonally from c and bind e c twice.

(iv) Bring the needle out at f, which is 6
threads below e. Bind f e twice. f e is
worked in the same way as a b. Repeat.

Dl. 3 No. 5
See Fig. 1.38

Work this design in all four corners and
lengthen the diagonal raised band begining at

and c.

(iv) Bring the needle out at d and work 3
similar vertical rows from right to left.
Repeat. This stitch can also be used as
a filling.

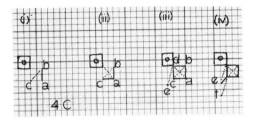

Figure 1.37

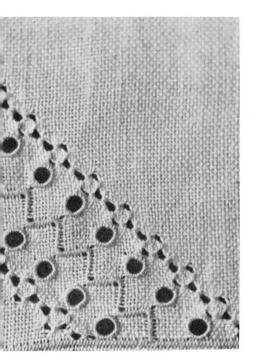

PLATE 1.12
Design D 1.3, no 4

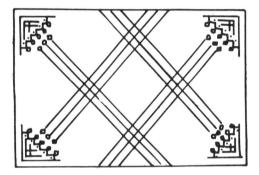

Figure 1.38

each eyelet and ending right up against the
hem on the opposite side.
Key: A. Four-sided stitch. B. Basket
stitch. See Fig. 1.39.

Use no 12 cotton

(i) — (iii) Bring the needle out at a and
work 3 pulled lines consisting of 10
stitches each over 3 threads of the material. Work each row from left to right
and pass the needle through the last 2
stitches on the wrong side of the work,
before starting the following rows at b

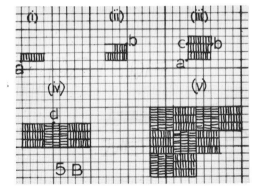

Figure 1.39

C. Mosaic stitch. See Fig. 1.40 and use No.
12 Pearl cotton.

(i) Bring the needle out at a and work 4
upright stitches over 3 threads. The last
stitch is c d.

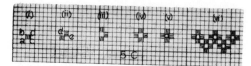

Figure 1.40

(ii) Now bring the needle out at e, 3 threads to the right of d, and work 4 stitches in the opposite direction. Insert the needle in the same hole on the corner to work the other two sides as in (iii) and (iv), completing the square around the centre of 3 threads by 3 threads.

(v) Work a four-sided stitch over these threads in the centre.

(vi) Use mosaic stitch as a filling.

D. Eyelets. E. Diagonal raised band.

Dl. 3 No. 6

See Fig. 1.41 and Plate 1.13

Work this design, either in the corners or slightly to the inside, and then work the lines on the diagram in four-sided stitch. Eyelets can then be worked as an allover pattern for the open spaces in the middle.

Key: A. Double faggot. B. Blanket stitch stars. See Fig. 1.42. Use No. 12 Pearl cotton.

Work 8 blanket stitches, with a as the centre and with the loops at the centre so that the stitches lie alternately over 6 threads (a b, a d, a f, and a h) on the straight of the material and diagonally over 3 threads (a c, a e, a g, and a i). When a i is completed, overcast all the

Figure 1.41

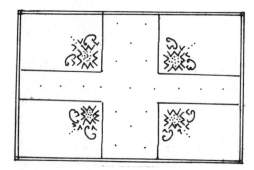

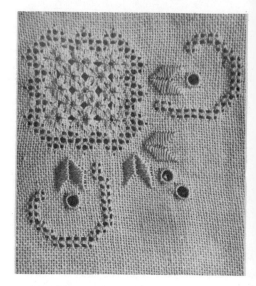

PLATE 1.13
Design D 1.3, no 6

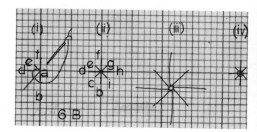

Figure 1.42

loops in the centre to form a firm ringlet. Work these blanket stitch stars where shown on the diagram and note that one line equals one thread for (iii).

(iv) Shows how this stitch is indicated on all designs.

C. Eyelets. D. Four-sided stitch. E. Diamond-shaped leaves in satin stitch. See Fig. 1.43 and use No. 5 Pearl cotton.

(i) Find position a on the material according to instructions on the design. Bring the needle out one thread to the right of this position. Keeping all the stitches level below, work the first satin stitch over one thread and every following stitch over one thread more until the 6th stitch is worked over 6 threads.

26

This will be position b.

(ii) Work 3 more stitches over 6 threads (4 in all): position c.

(iii) Keeping all the stitches level at the top, decrease every stitch by one thread until the last stitch is again worked over one thread. Note that the leaf ends one thread shorter at d than indicated on the diagram.

Dl. 3 No. 7

This motif will look lovely on the 4 corners of a tray-cloth. An enthusiastic embroideress, wanting to attempt more, could cover the 2

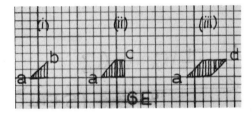

Figure 1.43

short sides with it completely as in Fig. 1.44. Key: A. Diagonal raised band. B. Double faggot over 6 threads. See Fig. 1.45.

Use No. 8 Pearl cotton and the same directions as for double faggot over 3 threads. The needle shows how to change direction.

C. Use No. 5 cotton. Commencing at a, work 3 adjoining satin stitches over 6 threads. The next 3 stitches are shorter by 3 threads at the bottom and longer by 3 threads at the top

Figure 1.44

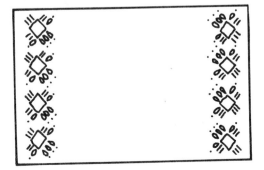

(thus also over 6 threads) Work 4 similar steps. Work the other 4 steps in the same way, but in die opposite direction and note that the stitches in the corners meet in the same holes.

D. Eyelets. E. Satin stitch motif. See Fig. 1.46.

Use No. 5 Pearl cotton.

(i) Bring the needle out at a. Keeping the stitches on the same level below, work 3 satin stitches over 3 threads, 3 over 6 threads, then 7 over 9 threads, again 3 over 6 and 3 over 3 threads. The last stitch is b c. Come out again at b and work the second side in the same way

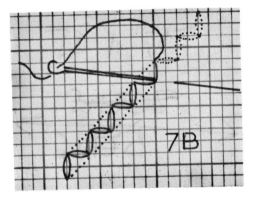

Figure 1.45

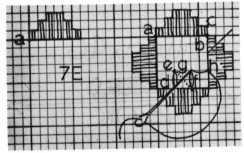

Figure 1.46

but in the opposite direction. Complete the other two sides. The inside of the flower is worked as follows: Use No. 12 Pearl cotton. Bring the needle out at d, 6 threads from the corner. Insert 6

PLATE 1.14
A border incorporating most of the stitches dealt with in this chapter. Design D 1.4

threads higher up at e, and bind d e twice. Come out at f, 6 threads to the right of d. Insert 6 threads higher up at g and bind f g twice. Come out at h, 6 threads to the right of g. h g is worked like d e. Repeat on all 4 sides. Work a four-sided stitch in the centre and finish off very firmly.

1.11 A border incorporating most of the stitches dealt with in this chapter

See D 1.4 and Plate 1.14
Scale: One square equals 3 threads.
Key: A. Satin stitch (See 6A of the narrow borders). B. Brick stitch. C. Pulled line using No. 12 cotton. D. 2 rows of wave stitch. E. Pulled line using No. 12 cotton. F. Eight-sided stitch. G. Satin stitch. H. Basket stitch. I. Foursided stitch. J. Sa-tin stitch motif. K. Eyelet. L. Double faggot. M. Star stitch. N. Satin stitch using no. 5 cotton. O. Pulled line using No. 12 cotton. P. Algerian eyelets. Q. Pulled line using No. 12 cotton. R. Festoon stitch. S. Diagonal raised band. T. Pulled square.

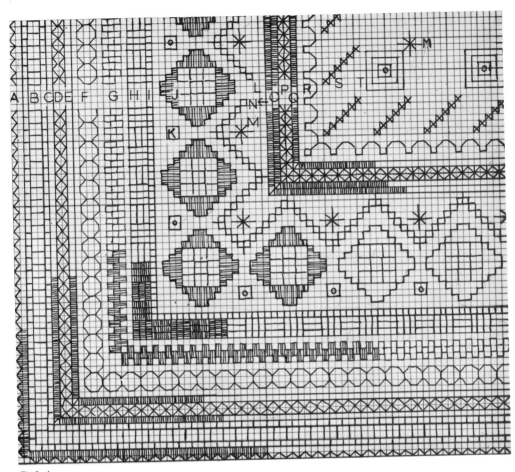

D 1.4

2.1 Borders

The border of an article is so important that it could make or mar a piece of embroidery. As it forms the frame for the article, it must not be something apart, but form a pleasing whole with the rest of the design. When composing a border for an article that already contains a variety of stitches, it is advisable to repeat some of these stitches in the border. Any border should not be given so much weight that it diverts the attention too much from the main design, as that could make the article appear overdone and unbalanced. On the other hand it should also not be so slight that it appears neglected. It is sensible to work the border last to prevent it being handled unnecessarily.

Borders and motifs in drawn fabric work

Figure 2.1

A border can be worked as the only decoration on an article, e.g. a tea-cloth or a table-cloth (Fig. 2.1) and then there is almost no limit to the richness of the design. A border is also suitable on a tea-cosy (Fig. 2.2), a cushion cover (Fig. 2.3) or a shopping bag (Fig. 2.4). Borders have been popular for a very long time, and are still today considered smart and striking.

2.2 Problems

There are a few problems likely to crop up when working a border. Hint No. 13, Par. 1.3 gives the method to ensure that all the corners will be similar. Cut off the extra material after completion of the embroidery which can vary in width from one to several inches. Another method is to tack along the edge of the material as described in hint No. 12, Par. 1.3. The number of squares for each repetition of the design as well as the number allowed for the corners, can be counted on the squared paper so that the worker will know exactly where the hem will be, before she starts to embroider. Although it is risky to work the hem first because one can so easily make a mistake in counting, some workers prefer this as it prevents fraying of the material. Often when the piece of material is already a little too small, or just wide enough for a certain purpose, and the worker is not prepared to risk cutting off any of the material, a border is then worked as follows: Work from the corners towards the centre of each side. Plan it so that the two borders meet as unobtrusively as possible or use a striking motif that will link up with the design of the border. Here the worker can apply her ingenuity and imagination. Some less experienced workers prefer to end the

Figure 2.2

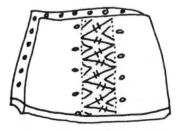

border in the corner where they meet. The open square thus formed can then be outlined and filled with a motif which matches the border.

2.3 Corners of borders

Effective or clumsy corners can be planned from one and the same border pattern. To find the most striking design for a corner, hold a small handbag mirror diagonally on the border, moving it to and fro until the most effective corner can be decided upon. Draw this design on squared paper.

2.4 Designs

The following are a few suggestions for wide borders suitable for tea-cloths, table-cloths, a panel across a cushion cover, a tea-cosy etc. Narrower borders for finishing off table-cloths on which a lot of embroidery has already been done, and very narrow borders for small articles will also be described. A few ideas are also given for the embroideress who wishes to adorn the hem of the article before it

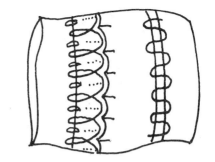

Figure 2.3   *Figure 2.4*

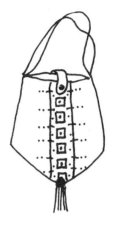

PLATE 2.1
A yellow table-cloth with a border and motif design. D: Author, M: Mrs. A. Brink

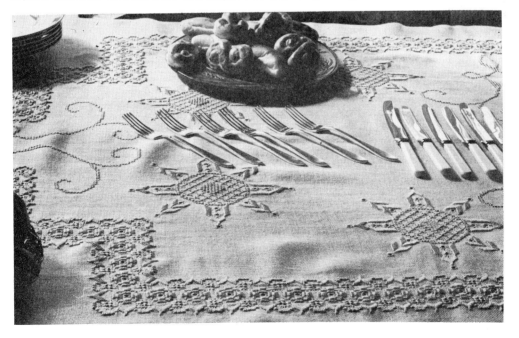

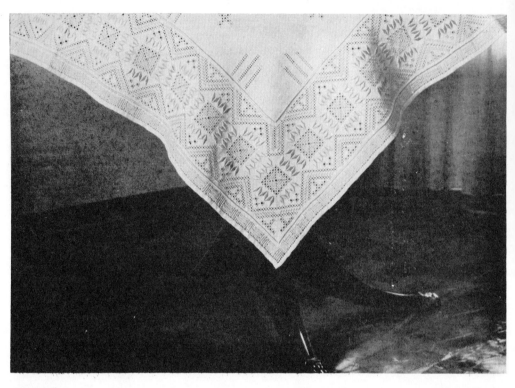

PLATE 2.2
A border in drawn fabric work. D: Author, M: Mrs C. B. Steyl

is folded and stitched.
Scale: One square equals 3 threads throughout, unless otherwise specified.

D 2.1

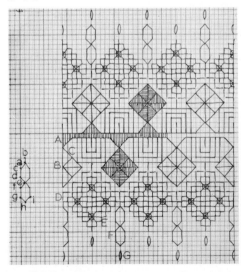

D 2. 1
Key: See Fig. 2.5.
A. Scale: One line equals one thread.

Using No. 5 Pearl cotton, work one row
satin stitch in the middle of the band as follows: Commencing at a, keep all the stitches
above and below level and work 7 stitches
over 3 threads. Then, keeping all the stitches
level below work one stitch over 4 threads,
one over 5, over 6, 7, 8 and 9 threads; and
then again one over 8, over 7, 6, 5, 4 and 3
threads. Continuing, work another 6 stitches
over 3 threads, then, keeping the stitches level
above, work one stitch over 4 threads and
again over 5, 6, 7, 8 and 9 threads and again
over 8, 7, 6, 5, 4 and 3 threads. Repeat.
B. See Fig. 2.5 (B). Using No. 5 Pearl
cotton work a group of 8 satin stitch triangles,
each consisting of 11 stitches, on each point
made in A. The first and last stitch is worked
over one thread of the material and the middle
stitch over 6 threads. The first triangle is not

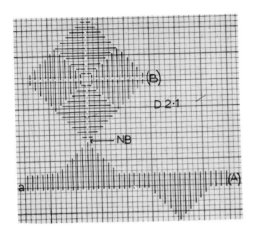

Figure 2.5

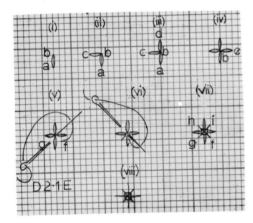

Figure 2.6

b, 6 threads higher and bind a b twice.

(ii) Bring the needle out at c, 6 threads to the left of b and bind c b twice.

(iii) and (iv) In the same way d b and e b are each bound twice over 6 threads.

(v) The needle, having been inserted at b, is now brought out at f, 3 threads diagonally across from b. Insert at g, 3 threads diagonally from b, and bring it out at b, with the thread under the needle (blanket stitch).

(vi) and (vii) Work 2 more blanket stitches

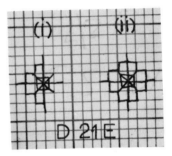

Figure 2.7

diagonally over 3 threads i.e. h b and i b. To complete the little square formed in the centre pass the needle under the thread coming from f. Take It over the same thread to the back of the work, whip around the last stitch made in the material and finish off by tacking in a circle a few times.

(viii) This shows how the stitches are indicated on the designs.

The outlined star is similar, but surrounded with a row of double faggot as shown in Fig. 2.7.

F. Using No. 12 cotton, and working on the principle of backstitch, two oblong shapes are pulled as indicated on the diagram. See detailed motif inserted on the diagram. Commence at a, bind a b twice, insert needle diagonally across at c and bind c a twice. Take needle straight to d and bind d c twice. Repeat this movement — e d, f e, g f, h g and i h etc., to complete the other half.

G. Detached buttonhole bars. See Fig. 2.8

begun in the same hole in which the point ended, but one thread higher. A square, 2 threads by 2, is left unworked in the centre of the motif.

C. Using No. 12 Pearl cotton, work pulled lines in the spaces between the satin stitch motifs and right up against the satin stitch band in the middle.

D. Adjoining the satin stitch motifs, work a single zigzag row of double faggot — 7 steps up and 7 down.

E. Work 4 Stars with blanket stitch centres outlined in double faggot in position as shown on the diagram. See Fig. 2.6.

Use No. 12 Pearl cotton.

(i) Bring the needle out at a, and insert at

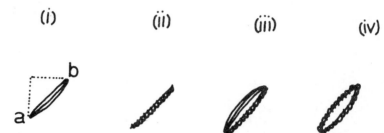

(i)   *(ii)*   *(iii)*   *(iv)*

Figure 2.8

and use No. 8 or No. 12 Pearl cotton.

This stitch consists of 2 detached bars of 3 threads each over which buttonhole stitch is worked with the loops on the outside.

   (i) Work 3 stitches diagonally over 6 threads from a to b.

  (ii) Bring the needle out slightly below a and cover the bar with firm buttonhole stitches. Insert the needle into the material slightly below b.

 (iii) Carry 3 threads from b to a.

 (iv) Repeat for the second bar. Finish off neatly on the wrong side. By weaving over the 6 loose threads. The detached buttonhole bars can also be worked straight over 6 threads or in any other position.

An alternative method of working the bars, is to carry the thread 6 times in stead of 3 times from a to b and to work over 3 of these threads as described in (ii). At the end of the bar the needle goes through the 6 threads where they meet at b to the other side of b. Now work buttonhole stitches over the remaining 3 threads going back to a. See Plate 2.7 for detached buttonhole bars.

D 2.2

Key: A. Diamond motifs: Diagonal raised band, using No. 12 cotton. Work fillings in these diamond-shapes, repeating only 2 alternately or use only one throughout. See Chapter 3.

B. Algerian eyelets, using No. 12 Pearl cotton.

C. Heart-shaped motif: Four-sided stitch, using No. 12 Pearl cotton.

D 2.2

D. The floret — in — a — heart shapes: Satin stitch, using No. 5 cotton. Commencing at a, work 10 stitches over 6 threads, each stitch one thread lower than the previous one. Then 9 stitches, each one thread higher, to form a V. Work 7 similar stitches at each end.

E. Eyelets, using No. 12 cotton.

F. Detached buttonhole bars.

G. Satin stitch motifs. Using No. 5 cotton, work the same V in satin stitch as described in D. Commencing in the centre of the V, bring the needle out one thread higher and one thread to the right of the centre and work a stitch over 2 threads to the left; then a stitch over 4 threads and one over 6 threads. Work 12 more stitches over 6 threads, then again one over 4 and one over 2 threads. Then work the detached buttonhole bars.

D 2.3

See Plate 2.3

Key: A. Satin stitch, using No. 5 cotton. Work the stitches over 6 threads in groups of 5 to the outside and of 7 to the inside so that the groups overlap with 3 threads.

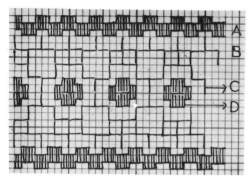

D 2.3

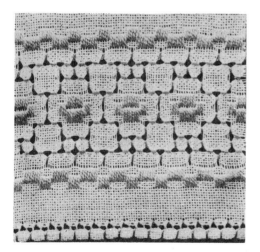

PLATE 2.3
Design D 2.3. Brick stitch hem (Par. 1.5 no 5)

B. Brick stitch over 6 threads.

C. Using No. 12 cotton, work a row of double faggot over 6 threads right up against the brick stitch — 5 steps up and 5 down.

D. The satin stitch motif in the centre: Work 3 stitches over 6 threads, 7 stitches over 6 threads (3 threads higher) and 3 stitches over 6

threads (3 threads lower) and then 7 stitches over 6 threads below and right up against the previous 7 stitches.

D 2.4

Key: A. The satin stitch flower: See Fig. 2.9 and use No. 5 Pearl cotton.

   (i) Bring the needle out at a and insert at b, 6 threads higher than a. Work 6 more similar satin stitches each stitch one thread higher above and below than the previous one. This will be position c d. Work 6 more satin stitches over 6 threads, keeping them level above and below (7 in all) and then again 6 over 6 threads, each stitch one thread lower than the previous one.

  (ii) The last stitch, which completes the

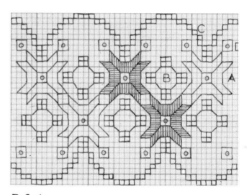

D 2.4

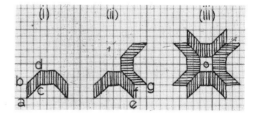

Figure 2.9

leaflet, is e f. Bring the needle out at g, 6 threads to the right of f. g f is similar to a b. Work a second leaflet in the same way and make sure that the first and the last 6 stitches of the two leaflets meet in the same holes in the centre.

(iii) Complete the 4 leaves of the flower and work an eyelet in the centre, using No. 12 cotton. Place the flowers as indicated on the diagram so that their corners meet in the same holes.

B. Using No. 12 cotton, work 4 four-sided stitches adjoining. Bind twice diagonally over 3 threads and then work the next 4 four-sided stitches etc. as shown on the diagram.

C. Four-sided stitches, using No. 12 Pearl cotton.

D. Eyelets, using No. 12 cotton.

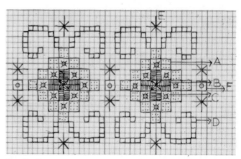

D. 2.6

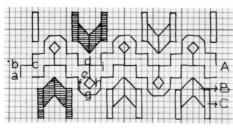

D. 2.5

D 2.5

Key: A. Using No. 12 cotton, and commencing at a, bind a b twice. Bring the needle out at c and bind c b twice. Work 3 more similar steps over 6 threads. Then work one stitch diagonally over 3 threads and one straight over 6 threads again one diagonally over 3 threads etc. up to e. Bind f e, g f, h g

and e h. Bring the needle diagonally across to i and bind i d, etc. Work the second row in the same way according to the diagram.

B. Work diamond-shaped leaves in satin stitch and use No. 5 Pearl cotton.

C. Using No. 12 cotton, work 2 pulled lines of 16 stitches each on both sides of the leaves.

D 2.6

See Plate 2.4

Key: A. Geometrical shadow work. See Fig. 2.10

Use No. 12 cotton and maintain a medium tension.

Scale: One line equals one thread.

(i) and (ii) Bring the needle out in the corner at a, insert at b, 2 threads to the right of a and bring it out at c, 2 threads below a.

(iii) Insert at a and bring out at d, 2 threads to the right of b.

PLATE 2.4
Design D 2.6. Note open Italian hem stitching. (Par. 1.5 no 4)

(iv) — (vii) Continue by following the diagram and the letters.

(viii) and (ix) Bring the needle out at m, 2 threads below l to proceed to the next square. The needle then goes in at l and comes out at n etc.

Figure 2.10

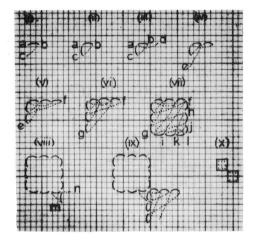

(x) Shows how the stitch appears on the designs.

B. Pulled lines, using No. 12 cotton.

C. Using No. 8 cotton work eyelets in the opening of 6 threads by 6 threads as follows: Work a stitch diagonally over 3 threads in the corner of the eyelet, work 3 more stitches along the side, each 2 threads apart and in the same centre hole. Complete on all 4 sides. These eyelets, having 4 stitches on each side, differ from Algerian eyelets, which have 3 stitches on each side and here each stitch is bound only once instead of twice.

D. Scrolls. Four-sided stitch using No. 12 cotton.

E. Stars. F. Eyelets.

2.5 Decoration of hems
The following are a few borders suitable for the decoration of hems. Work the designs near the edge of the material before the hem is put in, so that the embroidery will cover the

PLATE 2.5
Section of a lemon coloured table-cloth with white embroidery. Note the rich hem. D: Author, M: Mrs. C. Tidmarsh

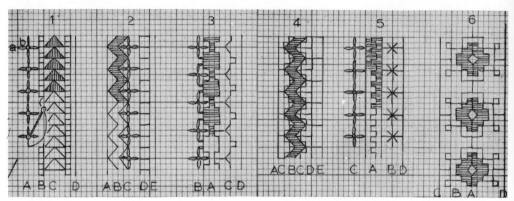

D. 2.7

whole breadth of the completed hem exactly. Enough threads must therefore be counted carefully from the raw edge for the first and second fold of the hem. The top part is then adorned with embroidery as desired.

D 2.7
See Plate 2.6. Scale: One square equals 3 threads throughout unless otherwise stated.

D 2.7 No. 1
Key: A. The middle of the eyelet is precisely on the second fold of the hem so that it forms a scallop on the edge. Using No. 12 cotton and commencing at a, bind 4 stitches each twice over 6 threads around the common centre b. The needle on the diagram shows how to progress to the next group of stitches. The long thread on the wrong side will be hidden when the hem is completed.
B. Four-sided stitch, using No. 12 cotton.
C. Using no. 5 cotton and commencing one thread away from the four-sided stitches, work 3 triangles, each consisting of 11 satin stitches. The first and last stitches are worked over one thread and the middle one over 6 threads.
D. Punch the hem.

D 2.7 No. 2
Key: A. The fold of the hem.

B. Using No. 5 cotton, work a zigzag row of satin stitch. Work each stitch over 6 threads and there are 7 stitches from point to point.
C. Using No. 12 cotton, work a row of eyelets as described in No. 1A.
D. Four-sided stitch over 6 threads, using No. 12 cotton.
E. Punch the hem.

D 2.7 No. 3
The fold of the hem is precisely in the middle of the stitches to be made in B.
Key: A. Using No. 5 cotton, work 5 satin stitches over 3 threads and 10 satin stitches over 9 threads alternately.
B. Using no. 12 cotton, work a row of eyelets as described in No. 1A but now bind 2 stitches twice each over 3 threads to the right between each eyelet.
C. Using No. 12 cotton, bind the stitches each twice on the principle of backstitch exactly as shown on the diagram.
D. Punch the hem.

D 2.7 No. 4
Key: A. The fold of the hem.
B. Using No. 5 cotton, work a zigzag row of satin stitch over 6 threads with 7 stitches from point to point.
C. Using no. 12 cotton work a row double faggot over 3 threads on both sides of the satin stitch.

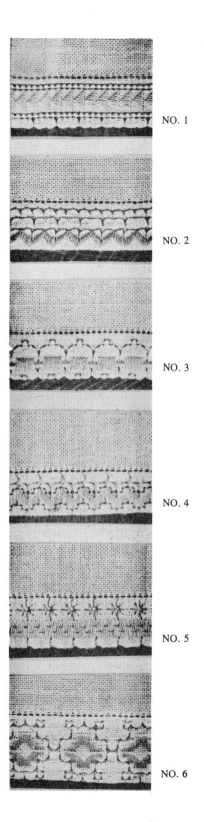

NO. 1

NO. 2

NO. 3

NO. 4

NO. 5

NO. 6

PLATE 2.6
Borders on hems

D. Brick stitch over 6 threads, using No. 12 cotton.

E. Punch the hem.

D 2.7 No. 5

Key: A. Using No. 5 cotton and keeping the satin stitches level on one side, work 3 stitches over 6 threads and 3 stitches over 3 threads alternately. Work a second row to fit into the first row.

B. Work a row of star stitch using no. 12 cotton.

C. Using No. 12 cotton, work a row of eyelets as described in No. 1 A.

D. Punch the hem.

D 2.7 No. 6

Key: A. Using No. 5 cotton, work satin stitch motifs 12 threads apart as follows: Work 3 satin stitches over 3 threads and 3 over 6 threads keeping all 6 stitches level at the bottom. Stitch No. 7 is over 8 threads, one thread shorter below and 3 threads longer above. Keep the following 6 stitches level with the previous one at the top, but shorter or longer below so that they will be over 7, over 6, 5, 6, 7 and over 8 threads. The following 6 stitches are again kept level at the bottom with the first 6, the first 3 over 6 threads and the last 3 over 3 threads. Repeat for the second half of the motif.

B. Using No. 12 cotton, bind the stitches twice each on the principle of backstitch, exactly as indicated on the diagram.

C. Fold of the hem.

D. Punch the hem.

2.6 Motifs

Motifs, lines and borders can be very useful to finish off an article which would otherwise seem incomplete or unbalanced. Motifs of different sizes can be worked on an article according to a definite plan to form a very

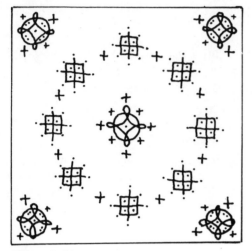

Figure 2.11

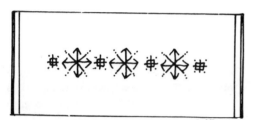

Figure 2.12

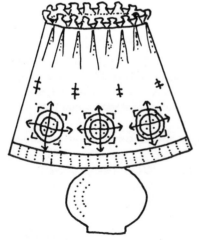

Figure 2.13

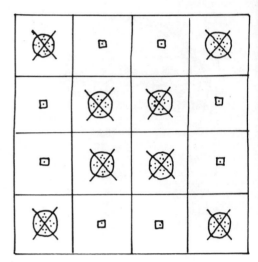

Figure 2.14

Figure 2.15

Fig. 2.13 shows how motifs can be used to decorate a lampshade successfully.

Related motifs worked on each luncheon mat will enhance the table, especially when a smaller motif is also worked on each serviette.

See Fig. 2.14 and Fig. 2.15 where the material is divided into squares in which big and small motifs are placed to form an allover design or a border.

Beautiful handbangs and workbags can be made by using several or only one motif, as

pleasing and interesting design.

See Fig. 2.11 for motifs on a cushion or Fig. 2.12 for motifs for the decoration of a runner.

Figure 2.16

Figure 2.17

Figure 2.18

shown in Fig. 2.16, Fig. 2.17 and Fig. 2.18. Use ecru coloured material or any other co-

lour for these articles, e.g. a blue bag with a design embroidered in white will be very striking. A few motifs in drawn fabric worked just above the hem of curtains will enhance a room. Serviette bags, besides keeping serviettes clean will make a laid table more attractive if they are embroidered with a pretty motif. In this case it is sensible to use a different motif on each bag so that each member of the family will be able to recognise his or her own. See Fig. 2.19.

With a little imagination many other uses can be found for these motifs.

Figure 2.19

2.7 **Designs**

D 2.8

Scale throughout: One square equals 3 threads.

D 2.8 No. 1

See Plate 2.7

Key: A. See Fig. 2.20. Using No. 12 cotton make a floret as follows:

  (i) Commencing at a, bind a b twice over 6 threads. Bring the needle out at c, bind c b twice and in the same way bind d c, e d and f e each twice. f e is worked like a b.

 (ii) Repeat till the floret is completed.

(iii) Work a star with a blanket stitch centre.

B. Using No. 12 cotton work two rows of diagonal raised band 6 threads apart around the floret.

C. Using No. 5 cotton, work a row of satin stitch steps 3 threads away. Now work 16 florets more as described in A.

D. Diamond-shaped leaves in satin stitch and using No. 5 cotton.

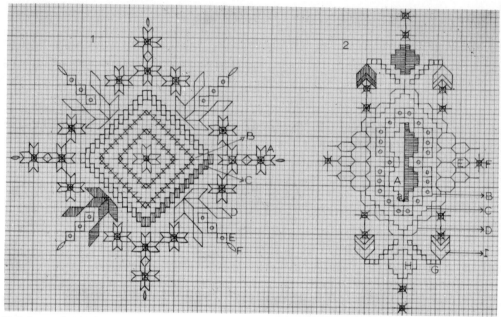

D 2.8 nos 1 and 2

E. Eyelets, using No. 12 cotton.
F. Detached buttonhole bars.

D 2.8 No. 2
Key: A. Using No. 5 cotton, commence at a
and proceed as follows: Keeping all the satin
stitches level below, work 6 stitches over 3
threads, 3 stitches over 6 threads, 10 over 9
threads, 3 over 6 threads and 5 over 3 threads.
Then 3 stitches over 6 threads, 10 over 9, 3
over 6 and 6 over 3 threads. Work the second
half.
B. Eyelets, using No. 12 cotton.
C. See Fig. 2.21
Using No. 12 cotton, bind each stitch twice on
the principle of backstitch as shown on **the**

Figure 2.20

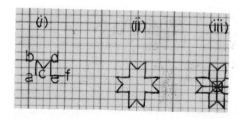

PLATE 2.7
Design D 2.8, no 1

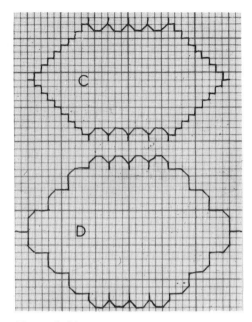

Figure 2.21

diagram.

D. See Fig. 2.21, the same as C.

E. Using No. 12 Cotton, bind on the principle of backstitch.

F. Star with a blanket stitch centre.

G. Four-sided stitch.

H. Using No. 5 cotton and keeping the stitches level below, work 3 stitches over 3 threads, 3 over 6, 7 over 9, 3 over 6 and 3 over 3. Repeat for second half.

I. Using No. 5 cotton, work 13 satin stitches over 6 threads to form a V, with the 7th stitch in the middle below. Using No. 12 cotton work a second row over 3 threads right up against the first, and work the 2 stars.

D 2.8 No. 3

Key: A. Using No. 8 Pearl cotton, commence in the centre and work 4 satin stitch squares diagonally. Each square consists of 11 diagonal stitches, the first and last stitch over one thread and the 6th diagonally over 6 threads.

B. Using No. 12 cotton, this motif is completed by binding each stitch twice on the principle of backstitch as follows: (See directions in D 4.2 A) Commence at a and bind a b twice. Insert the needle at c and bind c a twice, then d c, e d, f e, g f, h g, e h, i e, j i, k j etc. going right around and binding each twice. Note that the loose squares are worked over 4 threads.

C. The corners near the satin stitches in the centre are worked with No. 12 cotton on the same principle as described in B.

D 2.8 No. 4

Key: A. Use No. 5 Pearl cotton and com-

D 2.8 nos 3 and 4

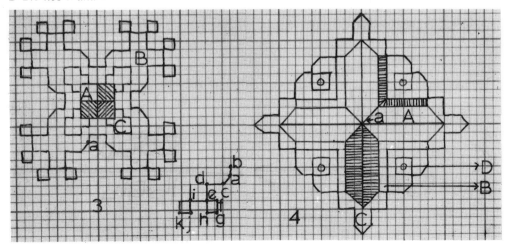

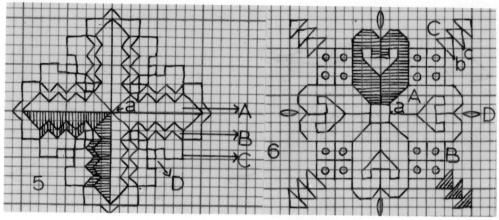

D 2.8 nos 5 and 6

mence in the centre. Find position a on the material, bring the needle out one thread to the right of a and work the area marked A first. Keeping all the stitches level below, work one stitch over one thread, one over 2, over 3, over 4, 5 and 6 threads. Work 18 stitches more over 6 threads (19 in all) then decrease by one thread till the last stitch is over one thread again. Work the other 7 sections of the satin stitch in the same way to complete the motif. A square of 2 by 2 threads will be open in the centre.

B. Pulled lines using No. 12 cotton.

C. Use No. 12 cotton and work the outside border by binding each stitch twice on the principle of backstitch.

D. Eyelets.

D 2.8 No. 5

See Plate 2.8

Key: A. Commence in the centre with No. 5 cotton. Find position a on the material and bring the needle out one thread to the right of a. Work the area marked A first as follows: One stitch over one thread, one over 2, 3, 4, 5 and 6 threads, then over 5, 4, 3, 4, 5 and 6 threads. Repeat to the 4th point and then work over 5, 4, 3, 2 and one threads. The second half, as well as the other 3 sections are worked in the same way.

B. Using no. 12 cotton, work a zigzag row of upright stitches right up against the satin

stitches over 3 threads.

C. Using No. 12 cotton, work the edge by binding each stitch twice on the principle of backstitch.

D. Using No. 12 cotton, work 4 short rows of double faggot in each corner.

D 2.8 No. 6

Key: A. Using No. 5 cotton, commmence at a and work A first. Keep the statin stitches level and work one stitch over 3 threads, one over 4, 5, 6, 7, 8 and 9 threads. Work 3 more stitches over 9 threads (4 in all). Then, keeping the stitches level above work one stitch over 8 threads, one over 7, 6, 5, 4 and 3 threads. Work 2 more stitches over 3 threads, then 4 stitches over 9, one over 7, 5 and 3 threads. Pass the needle through the back of the work and complete the point with 3 stitches over 3 threads. Complete the second half and the other sections.

B. Eyelets.

C. Using No. 8 cotton, bring the needle out at b, diagonally over 3 threads from the eyelet in the corner and work one stitch diagonally over 6, over 5, 4, 3, 2 and one thread. Bring the needle out at c, diagonally over 3 threads from b, and repeat twice.

D. Detached buttonhole bars.

D 2.8 No. 7

Key: A. Using No. 5 cotton and keeping the

satin stitches level below commence at a and work 7 stitches over 3 threads, one over 4, 5, 6, 7, 8 and over 9 threads, then again over 8, 7, 6, 5, 4 threads. Finally 7 stitches over 3 threads (25 stitches in all). Complete the other 3 sides taking care that the stitches on the corners meet in the same hole. The square in the centre will be 24 by 24 threads.

B. Using No. 5 cotton, and commencing 6 threads higher, work 7 stitches over 6 threads and then 6 stitches, each one thread higher than the preceding one. Repeat the mirror-image for the second half.

C. Work the edge. Use No. 12 cotton and bind each stitch twice on the principle of back-stitch.

D. Stars.

E. Work 4 four-sided stitches over 6 threads on each side of the square in the middle and one star stitch in the centre.

D 2.8 No. 8

Key: A. Using No. 5 cotton, commence at a and work one satin stitch a b, over 6 threads. Work a diagonal satin stitch band with each stitch one thread lower above and below up to the middle of the V, and then again each stitch one thread higher up to c d. The V will consist of 61 stitches with the 31st in the centre below. This completes the large V-shape. Now work the other 3 V's so that they all meet in the same hole in the centre.

B. Stars with blanket stitch centres, outlined, where the outline is bound over 6 threads.

C. Using no. 12 cotton work the edge right up against the satin stitch by binding each stitch twice on the principle of backstitch. Bind the detached squares over 4 threads.

PLATE 2.8
Design D 2.8 nos 5 and 13

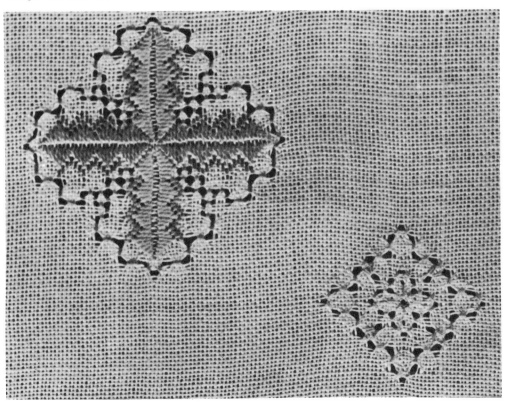

D 2.8 no 7

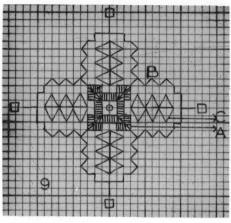

D 2.8 no 9

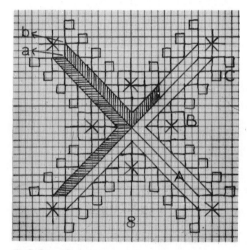

D 2.8 no 8

D 2.8 No. 9

Key: A. Using No. 12 cotton, commence in the centre and work a little pulled square with corners.

B. Use No. 12 cotton and work the edge by binding each stitch twice on the principle of backstitch. Remember that the detached squares must be worked at the same time, 2 threads higher than the stitch at the top and that the squares must be worked over 4 threads instead of 3.

C. Work short double rows of three-sided stitch in the 4 spaces as follows: See Fig. 2.22

(i)   Bring the needle out at a and insert at b, 6 threads lower and 3 threads to the right of a. Bind a b twice and bring the needle out at c, 6 threads to the left of a. Bind c b once only.

(ii) Bring the needle out at a and bind a c twice. Bring the needle out at d, 6 threads to the left of a and bind d a twice.

(iii) Bind d c twice and bring the·needle out at e. d c is similar to a b. Repeat. The next now is worked adjoining and in the same holes and therefore all the

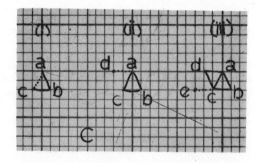

Figure 2.22

horizontal stitches will eventually also have been bound twice. See also Fig. 3.12 and Plate 3.17.

46

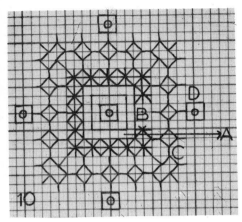

D 2.8 no 10

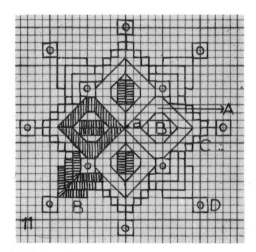

D 2.8 no 11

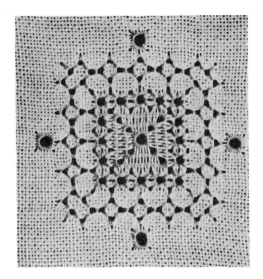

PLATE 2.9
Design D 2.8, no 10

of a. Work one satin stitch over one thread, one over 2, 3, 4, 5 and over 6 threads. Work the following 6 stitches over 6 threads, each one thread higher than the previous one. Now work 3 stitches over 6 threads on the same level as the last stitch (4 in all) and then again 6 stitches over 6 threads, each one thread lower than the previous one. Then one stitch over 5 threads, over 4, 3, 2 and one threads. Work the other half in the same way but reversed and complete the other 3 sections. In the centre a square of 2 by 2 threads will remain open.

B. Pulled lines using No. 12 cotton.

C. Double rows of double faggot using No. 12 cotton.

D. Eyelets.

D. 2.8 No. 12

See Plate 2.11

Key: A. Using No. 12 cotton, commence in the centre at a and make a star.

B. Pull one row of double faggot over 6 threads around the star.

C. Complete the design by binding each stitch twice on the principle of backstitch as shown on the diagram. The squares marked D must be worked at the same time.

D. 2.8 No. 10

See Plate 2.9.

Key: A. A Pulled square, using No. 12 cotton.

B. Algerian eyelets, using No. 12 cotton.

C. Bind the 2 rows on the principle of backstitch.

D. Eyelets.

D. 2.8 No. 11

See Plate 2.10

Key: A. Work the area marked A first. Using No. 5 cotton, find position a on the material and bring the needle out one thread to the right

PLATE 2.10
Design D 2.8 nos 11 and 16

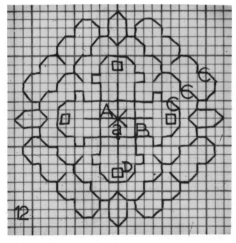

D 2.8 no 12

D. 2.8 No. 13
See Plate 2.8
Key: Use No. 12 cotton throughout. Commence in the centre with a blanket stitch star. Work the following two rows around it by binding each stitch twice on the principle of backstitch.

D. 2.8 No. 14
Key: A. Using No. 12 cotton, commence in

the centre and work a star with a blanket stitch centre.
B. Outline it with a row of double faggot over 3 and over 6 threads.
C. Work the outside row by binding each stitch twice on the principle of backstitch.

D. 2.8 No. 15
See Plate 2.11.
Key: Using No. 12 cotton work a star in the centre. Work the following 2 rows by binding each stitch twice on the principle of backstitch.

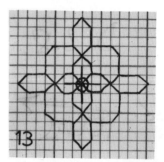

D 2.8 no 13

D. 2.8 No. 16
See Plate 2.10.
Key; Using No. 12 cotton, commence at a and bind a b twice over 6 threads. Bring the needle out at c and bind c a twice. Similarly d c, e c, f e, g e, h g and a g are each bound twice. Pass the needle through the back of the work and emerge at i. i d is worked like a b. Repeat. Make 4 similar pulled shapes that meet in the same hole f in the centre.

D. 2.8 No. 17
See Plate 2.10
Key: Italian stitch no. 12 cotton. See Par. 2.8, D 2.9.

D. 2.8 No. 18
Two rows brick stitch worked in a square, with No. 12 cotton.

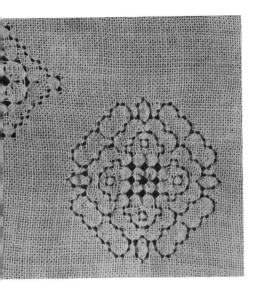

PLATE 2.11
Design D 2.8 nos 12 and 15

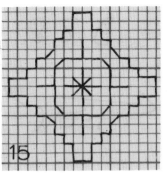

D 2.8 no 15

B. Diagonal raised band, No. 12 cotton.
C. Use No. 12 cotton and work the outside row by binding each stitch twice on the principle of backstitch. The detached squares must be worked at the same time, over 4 threads and 2 threads away.

D. 2.8 No. 21
Key: A. Use No. 12 cotton and work a floret as in No. 1. (See Fig. 2.20).
B. Work the outside row by binding each stitch twice on the principle of backstitch.
C. Eyelets, No. 12 cotton.

D. 2.8 No. 19
Key: A. Using No. 12 cotton, work a flower exactly as indicated on the diagram — first work 3 circles and then connect them.
B. Four-sided stitch.
C. A pulled line, No. 12 cotton.
D. Diamond-shaped leaves, with No. 5 cotton.

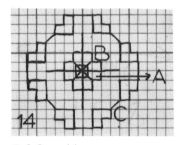

D 2.8 no 14

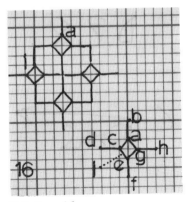

D 2.8 no 16

D. 2.8 No. 20
Key: A. Use No. 5 cotton and commence at a. Work 3 satin stitches over 3 threads, 4 over 6 threads, then one over 5, 4, 3, 2 and one thread. Work the second half so that the stitches meet in the corner and are perpendicular to the first half. Work the other corner.

D. 2.8 No. 22
Key: A. Using No. 12 cotton, commence at a and work 4 upright stitches over 3 threads. The following 12 stitches form the 2 corners with all the stitches meeting in one hole on the

inside and the centre and last stitches again straight over 3 threads. Work 3 more upright stitches over 3 threads up to a. Repeat on the other 3 corners.

B. Pulled line, using No. 12 cotton.

C. Eyelets.

D. Bind 4 stitches diagonally over 3 threads in the centre.

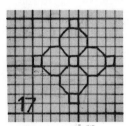

D 2.8 no 17

D. 2.8 No. 23

This motif repeated, results in an attractive border.

Key: A. Pulled line, using No. 12 cotton.

B. Bind all the stitches at the lower end twice on the principle of backstitch to form a small circle.

C. Using No. 5 cotton work satin stitch as follows: 3 stitches over 3 threads, 3 over 6, 4 over 9, 3 over 6 and 3 over 3 threads.

D. Double faggot.

D. 2.8 No. 24

Key: A. Double faggot or four-sided stitch.

B. Pulled line, using No. 12 cotton.

C. Satin stitch steps, No. 5 cotton.

D. Diagonally pulled lines, No. 12 cotton.

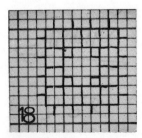

D 2.8 no 18

E. Detached buttonhole bars.

Repetition of this motif will result in a lovely border for tray-cloths and luncheon-mats.

D. 2.8 No. 25

Key: A. Use No. 5 cotton and commence at a.

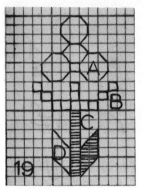

D 2.8 no 19

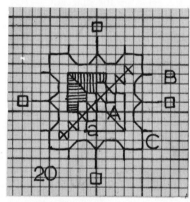

D 2.8 no 20

Work a V-shape in satin stitch. There will be 25 stitches in all with the 13th in the centre below.

B. Still using No. 5 cotton, commence in the centre of the V, but one thread higher and one thread to the right. Work one stitch over 2 threads, one over 4 and one over 6. Work 15 stitches more over 6 threads, then one over 4 and one over 2 threads.

C. Bring the needle out in the hole of the 2nd

satin stitch over 6 threads, and work across one thread, across 2, 3, 4, 5 and 6 threads. The needle is now in position b. Work 9 satin stitches more over 6 threads, one over 4 and one over 2.

D. Same as C.

E. Eyelets.

F. Work the edge by binding each stitch twice

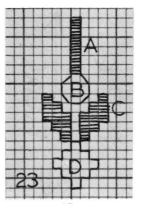

D 2.8 no 23

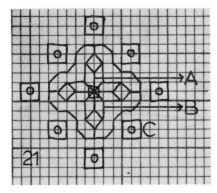

D 2.8 no 21

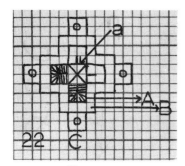

D 2.8 no 22

on the principle of backstitch, using No. 12 cotton. Note that all the squares are worked over 3 threads, except the last one which will be over 4 threads.

D. 2.8 No. 26

Key: A. Diamond-shaped leaflets in satin stitch, using No. 5 cotton.

B. Stars with blanket stitch centres.

C. Four-sided stitch.

D. Eyelets.

D. 2.8 No. 27

Key: A. Eyelets.

B. Diagonal satin stitch using No. 5 cotton.

C. Bind on the principle of eight-sided stitch.

D. 2.8 No. 28

Key: A. Find the middle of the motif on the material according to the diagram. Count up to a. Using No. 5 cotton, and keeping the stitches level below, work 3 satin stitches over 3 threads, 3 over 6, 7 over 9, 3 over 6 and 3 over 3 threads. Complete the satin stitches so that the stitches on the corners e.g. a, b and c, meet in the same hole.

B. Double faggot over 6 threads.

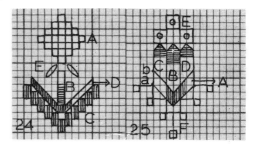

D 2.8 nos 24 and 25

C. Work the inside by binding each stitch twice on the principle of backstitch.

D. Double faggot over 6 threads on the outer edge with an extra stitch to the outside.

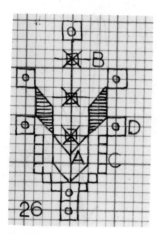

D 2.8 no 26

D. Using No. 12 cotton, work 8 detached squares in the centre and one thread away from the satin stitch. Those in the corners will be over 5 threads both ways. Skip one thread and make the centre square 5 threads high and 4 threads wide. Skip one thread again and make the square in the corner 5 by 5 threads. Complete the other 3 sides in the same way. Pull a stitch diagonally over 5 threads from every corner to the centre so that 2 threads form a cross in the centre.

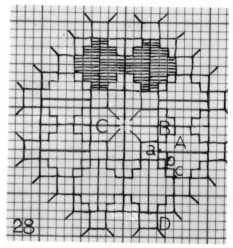

D 2.8 no 28

D. 2.8 No. 29

Key: A Use No. 5 cotton and commence at a. Work 4 satin stitches over 6 threads, each one thread lower than the preceding stitch. The following 6 stitches remain level below, but are longer or shorter at the top and are worked over 7, 8, 9, 8, 7 and 6 threads. The next 3 stitches are over 6 threads, each one thread higher than the previous one. Complete A by working a mirror-image of this. (25 stitches in all) The other 3 sides are done similarly and it must be noted that the first and last 4 stitches meet in the same holes in the corners.
B. Using No. 8 cotton, work a zigzag row of satin stitches over 3 threads to meet the points of A in the same holes.
C. Stars.

D 2.8 no 27

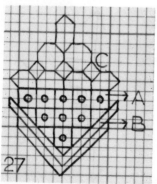

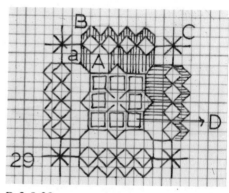

D 2.9 29

2.8 Combined motifs

It can be very interesting to combine a few smaller motifs to form a large design and this encourages the embroideress to give expres-

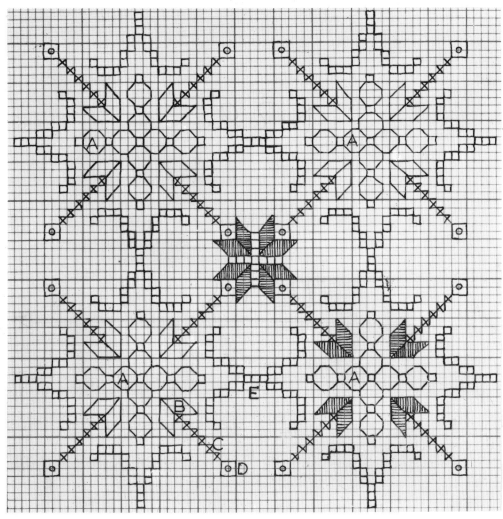

D 2.9

sion to her own ideas. By trying this she often finds the way to independent and original designing. See D 2.9 where a simple motif is used to compile a larger one.

It can be repeated to form an allover design e.g. to cover the whole area of a cushion cover.

Scale: One square equals 3 threads.

D. 2.9

Key: A. Italian stitch. See Fig. 2.23
Use No. 12 cotton.

  (i) Bring the needle out at a, insert at b and bind a b twice.

  (ii) Bring the needle out at c, bind c a twice and insert at d. Bind c d twice.

 (iii) — (vi) Similarly e c, f e, g f and h g are each bound twice.

 (vii) h g is worked like a b. Repeat till the required number of circles have been worked.

(viii) Complete the other half as shown on the diagram.

 (ix) Work the other section of the stitch also as indicated on the diagram.

B. Diamond-shaped leaves in satin stitch, using No. 5 cotton.

C. Diagonal raised band.

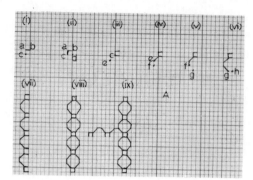

Figure 2.23

D. Eyelets.
E. Four-sided stitch.

2.9 Borders derived from motifs

Almost all the motifs can be used to design a border by repetition of one or more. It will be interesting to experiment with the preceding motifs to see what fascinating designs can result. The following are 4 examples of such combinations, narrow and wide and also an up-and-down effect.

D. 2.10
Scale: One square equals 3 threads.

D. 2.10 No. 1
Motif No. 25 is recognisable. Place it 3 threads apart and connect with a row of four-sided stitch, and double faggot. This border can also be reversed.

D. 2.10 No. 2
Use motif No. 22 and place it in a zigzag fashion.

D. 2.10 No. 3
Motif No. 17 is recognisable.

D.2.10 No. 4
Motif No. 6 is used here twice omitting the satin stitch triangles.

Key: A. Stars with blanket stitch centres.
B. Satin stitch over 3 threads, using No. 5 cotton.
C. Algerian eyelets.
D. Use No. 12 cotton and bind 2 rows on the principle of backstitch. This border alone will be very effective on a tea-cloth.
E. Detached buttonhole bars.

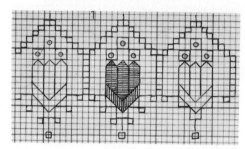

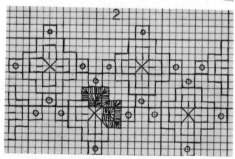

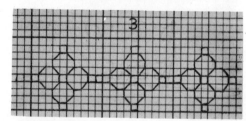

D 2.10 nos 1, 2 and 3

2.10 Check material

Sometimes a very pretty evenly-woven check linen can be obtained, mostly from Germany, Switzerland and Scandinavia. Often this hard-wearing linen is hand-woven. The squares are formed by using thicker threads or of contrasting colour for the warp and woof. They can be as big as 15 cm square or as small as a 20 mm square. Although the linen is often striking enough on its own, it can be

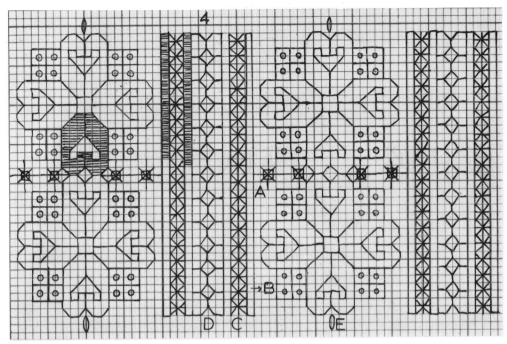

D 2.10 no 4

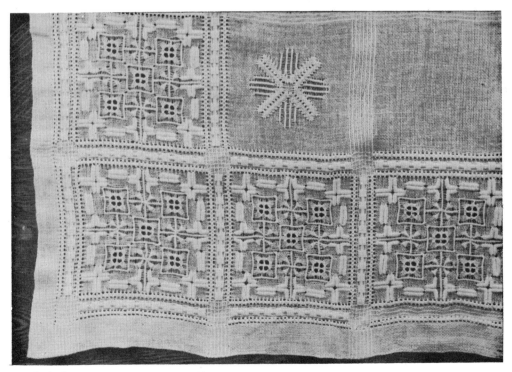

PLATE 2.12
Hand woven blue-grey check linen from Switzerland embroidered in white. D: Author, M: Mrs. Max van den Heever

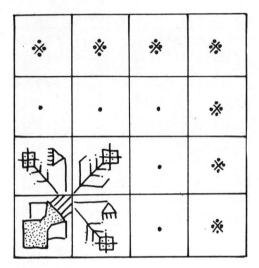

Figure 2.24

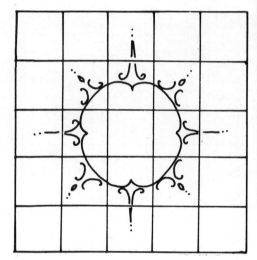

Figure 2.25

enriched with embroidery, and because it is mostly woven evenly and loosely, pulled work is pre-eminently suitable.

Some workers find a large article like a table-cloth cumbersome to handle, and this can be overcome by dividing the material into squares. After all the squares have been completed, they are joined with lace or a decorative stitch. It is advisable to plan the design with an odd number of squares in the length and in the breadth of the article, as this simplifies the placing of the design.

The use of check material will put the worker under some restraint and mostly the squares will determine the size and nature of the design.

Construct a border of squares (See Plate 2.12) or embroider every alternative square of the whole article, or only those in the corners, etc. It is also possible to ignore the outlines of the squares and to build up a free design over a number of squares See Plate 2.13. Such a design will tend to tone down the severe lines of a check design.

Figure 2.26

Figure 2.27

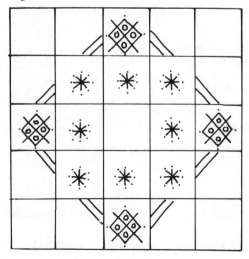

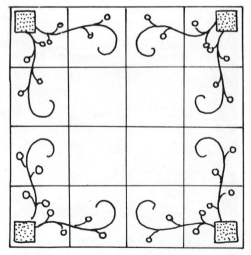

PLATE 2.13
25 Squares joined to make up this tea-cloth of cream evenweave linen, embroidered in ecru. Specially designed for a round table. Size 180 cm × 180 cm . D: Author, M: Mrs Lulu Theron.

PLATE 2.14
A corner of the same tea-cloth in Plate 2.13

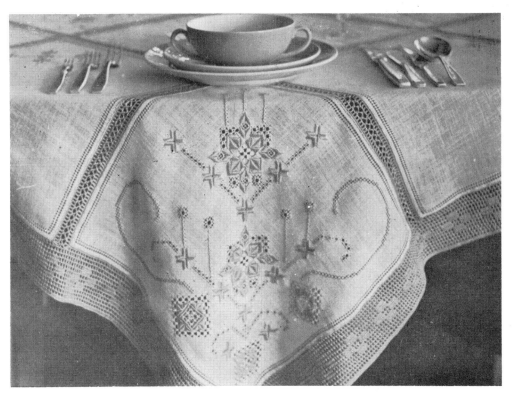

3.1 Introduction

The experienced embroideress in drawn fabric work will choose designs with scope for fillings. Sometimes she will be tempted to use a great variety of fillings on one article because these fillings are so exciting to execute. Too great a variety of these beautiful textures, however, could spoil the balance of the design and make it look restless. Repetition always has a soothing effect in a drawn fabric design, especially in the use of fillings. Each original filling developed by the embroideress will be a stimulus for further attempts. Some of these fillings look like lace. In museums in Europe one can see drawn fabric work of the 17th and 18th centuries, known as Dresden work and which was elaborately done on the finest cambric. The fillings closely resemble hand-made lace. From India beautiful examples of this work can also be seen. But even coarse linen acquires a light and elegant appearance when these lacy fillings are worked on it. In fact, experience has proved that there are few kinds of linen on which fillings can be worked as successfully as on linen with approximately 20 threads to 2½ cm in both directions. However, more kinds of drawn fabric fillings are possible on a fine, loosely woven linen, because groups of from 2 to 9 and 10 threads can be pulled together, whereas the variety is limited by a coarse linen, where not more than 6 threads can be pulled together successfully.

As indicated in Par. 3.4, a free design can be used for pulled fillings. The area outlined for a filling must, however, definitely be large enough to do justice to the filling. On a coarser linen, the areas for the fillings must be proportionately larger. In free designs different surface stitches are used to outline the fillings. This is not the only way in which fillings can be used. In the design D 4.6 there are 5 geometric shapes in the centre panel, which are ideal for fillings. Preferably the 2 outer squares should have the same filling, the 2 inner ones the same and the centre one can be different. Many workers will find it more satisfactory to use the same filling in all these

Fillings for drawn fabric work

Property Of:
Constellation Chapter
E. G. A.
Baltimore, Md.

5 squares because it gives greater unity. See also Plate 3.2

Fillings can also be used as a background as in design D 4.1. Here it is not outlined at all and gives the effect of a woven lace panel.

A tray cloth or luncheon-mats with only a filling in each of the 4 corners will look smart and sophisticated. See Plate 3.3 where the tile stitch is used as a filling in the corners. A variety of fillings can be used on a set of mats, but only one in each corner of every mat.

3.2 Choice of fillings

When a filling has to be chosen for an area, certain points have to be borne in mind. It stands to reason that a finer filling will be more suitable for a smaller area and vice versa. Similarly in a long and narrow shape a line filling will be better than an intricate flower design. Fillings placed at regular intervals on a design, must balance and be in effective contrast.

3.3 65 Different fillings

Scale: One square equals 3 threads throughout, unless otherwise stated. Use No. 12 Pearl cotton throughout, unless otherwise specified.

1. See Fig. 3.1 and Plate 3.6
   (i) Work rows of double faggot over 6

PLATE 3.1
Section of a tea-cloth, the whole of which depicts the 4 Provinces of the Republic of South Africa, its flora, abundant sunshine, some history etc. A wide variety of drawn fabric fillings enhance the article. Material: White evenly woven linen with approximately 35 threads to 2½ cm. Size: 81 cm x 81 cm. DM: Author

PLATE 3.2
A geometrical drawn fabric design on a table-cloth, with a great variety of fillings. Material: Cream evenweave. D: Author, M: Mrs. F. Olivier.

threads so that the parallel stitches of the different rows are 24 threads apart.

(ii) Do the same in the opposite direction and bind only once where the rows cross.

(iii) Then work double faggot over 3 threads in a diamond-shape in the open spaces.

2. See Fig. 3.2 and Plate 3.7

Work the diagonal rows exactly as indicated on the diagram by binding each group of threads twice on the principle of backstitch. The same row is repeated but the squares lie alternately to the top and to the bottom. Work blanket stitch stars in the spaces as indicated.

3. See Fig. 3.3 and Plate 3.8

(i) Work rows of double faggot over 6 threads so that the parallel stitches of

the different rows are 18 threads apart.

(ii) Do the same in the opposite direction and bind only once where the rows cross.

(iii) Now work stars with blanket stitch centres in rows in the open spaces.

4. See Fig. 3.4 and Plate 3.9

(i) Work the first row exactly as shown on the diagram by binding each group of threads twice on the principle of backstitch.

(ii) This row is repeated but alternately to the top and to the bottom so that the 2 rows meet in the same holes.

5. See Fig. 3.5 and Plate 3.10

(i) Work the first row exactly as shown on the diagram by binding each group of stitches twice on the principle of back-

PLATE 3.3
A table-mat decorated with drawn fabric corners. (Tile stitch)

PLATE 3.4
Section of a wall panel in drawn fabric work, depicting the development of the Gold Industry in South Africa. **Size:** 46 cm x 92 cm . M: Mrs. A. Wessels.

stitch. A second row is worked 6 threads away, but reversed. Cover the whole area in this way.

(ii) A. Work rows of Algerian eyelets in position.

B. Also work stars and two upright stitches over 6 threads, each bound twice, in the positions indicated.

6. See Fig. 3.6 and Plate 3.11

(i) Work a diagonal row of stars with blanket stitch centres, outlined with a row of double faggot over 6 threads and connected by 4 four-sided stitches as shown on the diagram. Subsequent rows are worked 24 threads apart.

(ii) Identical rows now cross these rows in the opposite direction at the 4 four-sided stitches.

7. See Fig. 3.7 and Plate 3.12

A. Work the first row exactly as indicated on the diagram by binding each group of stitches twice on the principle of backstitch. See also Par. 2.7 No. 3, which tells how the detached squares are worked.

B. Work a diagonal raised band right up against the first row.

C. Work another row like the first, but reversed. The 3 stages from A to C are now repeated.

8. See Fig. 3.8 and Plate 3.13

(i) — (iii) Work outlined stars with blanket stitch centres in diagonal rows that meet in the same holes.

9. See Fig. 3.9 and Plate 3.14

(i) Work a diagonal row of blanket stitch stars.

(ii) Work a diagonal pulled line over 3 threads by working each stitch one

62

thread higher or lower than the previous one. Note the direction of the stitches carefully. Repeat.

10. See Fig. 3.10 and Plate 3.15
Commence at a and work 7 upright stitches over 3 threads. Work the following 6 stitches all meeting in the same hole as the last one, so that a corner is formed and the last stitch is again straight over 3 threads. This is position b. To make the next corner the next 6 stitches must all meet at b at the top. Now 6 more upright stitches over 3 threads and then again 2 corners. Repeat. The second row lies reversed against the first and one four-sided stitch is worked in an open square of 6 by 6 threads as soon as it is formed.

PLATE 3.5
A wall panel with a great variety of drawn fabric fillings.
D: Author, M: Mrs. Louise Geldenhuys.

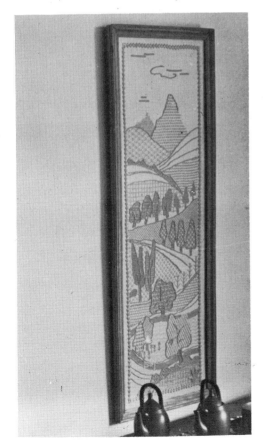

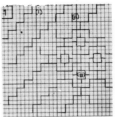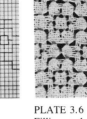

Figure 3.1

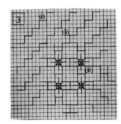

PLATE 3.6
Filling no 1

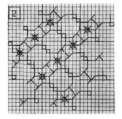

Figure 3.2

PLATE 3.7
Filling no 2

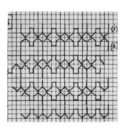

Figure 3.3

PLATE 3.8
Filling no 3

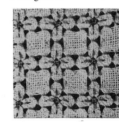

Figure 3.4

PLATE 3.9
Filling no 4

Figure 3.5

PLATE 3.10
Filling no 5

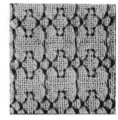

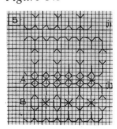

11. See Fig. 3.11 and Plate 3.16.

A. Commence by working 15 upright stitches over 3 threads. @ Work one four-sided stitch over 3 threads, followed by 14 vertical stitches and repeat from @. The rows meet in the same holes but the square is moved by 3 threads each time to form a diagonal line.

B. The same idea, but the squares are arranged differently.

12. See Fig. 3.12 and Plate 3.17

Three-sided stitch as a filling.

13. See Fig. 3.13 and Plate 3.18

This simple but effective filling consists of groups of 10 upright stitches worked over 3 threads, 3 threads left between each group and in rows 9 threads apart. Now work transverse rows to form a check design. Bind twice diagonally over 3 threads in the 4 corners of each square.

14. See Fig. 3.14 and Plate 3.19

(i) Pull a cross of straight stitches over 3 threads, each of the 4 parts consisting of 10 stitches, leaving an open square in the centre. Then pull triangles, consisting of 6 stitches made diagonally over one to 6 threads in each corner of the cross. Work a single row of double faggot around the cross.

(ii) The motif is worked in straight rows 3 threads apart.

15. See Fig. 3.15 and Plate 3.20

Work 11 stitches over 3 threads in a vertical position. Take 3 extra threads and bind the 6 threads 3 times. Bring the needle out in the middle and at the top of the 6 threads. Now pull 10 stitches over 3 threads in the opposite direction then bind thrice over 6 threads. Bring the needle out in the middle and at the bottom of the 6 threads, pull 10 stitches etc. Work one row of brick stitch and repeat.

16. See Fig. 3.16 and Plate 3.21

Commencing at a, first bind all the spokes and then the square in the centre clockwise. Finally the needle goes in at b and the dotted line

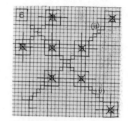

Figure 3.6

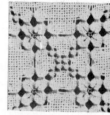

PLATE 3.11
Filling no 6

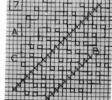
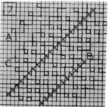

Figure 3.7

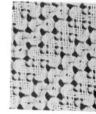

PLATE 3.12
Filling no 7

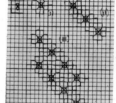
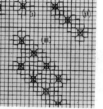

Figure 3.8

PLATE 3.13
Filling no 8

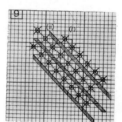

Figure 3.9

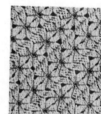

PLATE 3.14
Filling no 9

Figure 3.10

PLATE 3.15
Filling no 10

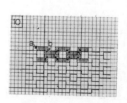

shows how to proceed from one motif to the next.

17. See Fig. 3.17 and Plate 3.22
Work pulled lines 6 threads apart. Then 2 rows hemstitch in the open spaces between the rows, the second row slightly different so that the stitches form little arrows, as follows: See Fig. 3.18.

For convenience' sake the threads are indicated in one direction only.

18. See Fig. 3.19 and Fig. 3.20 and Plate 3.23.
Work 4 groups of 2 blanket stitches diagonally over 3 threads with a common centre as follows: Bring the needle out at a, insert again at a. Bring it out diagonally across 3 threads at b, keeping the thread under the needle. Thus the first 2 stitches are made in one movement. Insert the needle diagonally over 3 threads in the other direction and bring it out in the centre with the first 2 stitches again with the thread under the needle. Work one more blanket stitch into the same position, and 2 pairs diagonally in the 2 remaining directions. Secure into the first stitch, and pass the needle through the centre at b to begin the second floret, as in Fig. 3.20.

Work rows of florets in adjoining rows.

19. See Fig. 3.21 and Plate 3.24
Work 2 vertical blanket stitches into the same holes over 3 threads facing upwards. Work the same facing down, but 3 threads away. Repeat. The rows meet in the same holes. Work florets in alternate openings between the rows by bringing out 4 straight blanket stitches over 3 threads in the same centre hole. See also Greek cross filling, Par. 4.3 S.

20. See Fig. 3.22 and Plate 3.25
Bound wave stitch. This is a variation of wave stitch as in D 1.2 No. 2. Bind 3 threads twice on the diagonal. Bring the needle out 6 threads away on the straight and again bind 3 threads on the diagonal and towards the first 2 stitches so that they meet in the same hole. Repeat. The rows meet in the same holes.

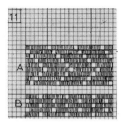

Figure 3.11

PLATE 3.16
Filling no 11

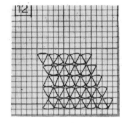

Figure 3.12

PLATE 3.17
Filling no 12

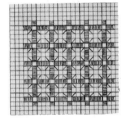

Figure 3.13

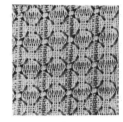

PLATE 3.18
Filling no 13

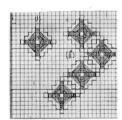

Figure 3.14

PLATE 3.19
Filling no 14

PLATE 3.20
Filling no 15

Figure 3.15

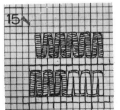

21. See Fig. 3.23 and Plate 3.26
Work 2 rows of blanket stitch over 3 threads so that the loops adjoin. Skip 6 threads and repeat. Work one row of three-sided stitch in the open space and bind all the stitches twice.

22. See Fig. 3.24 and Plate 3.27
Work a pulled line over 6 threads, skip 6 threads and repeat. Then work 2 rows wave stitch each over 3 threads in the open spaces.

23. See Fig. 3.25 and plate 3.28
Elongated eyelets. Work like ordinary eyelets except that 5 upright stitches on both sides connect the 2 halves of the eyelets. The length of the eyelets covers 12 threads and the width 6 threads. Note that the eyelets are placed alternately horizontally and vertically so that open squares of 3 threads by 3 threads are formed.

24. See Fig. 3.26 and Plate 3.29
(i) Pull 7 upright stitches over 3 threads in vertical rows 3 threads apart.
(ii) Bind around the groups in the same way as four-sided stitch.

25. See Fig. 3.27 and Plate 3.30
Work a row of four-sided stitch over 6 threads. Then a row of half-florets in blanket stitch over alternate four-sided stitches as follows: All the stitches meet in one hole and spread out like a fan — the first and last blanket stitches meet in the same hole as that of the four sided stitch and the position of the others are indicated on the diagram. The centre stitch lies over 9 threads. Pass the needle through the back of the four-sided stitch to the centre of the next floret where all the stitches will again meet. Repeat. Work in the same way on the other side of the four-sided stitches. The next row of four-sided stitch is 18 threads away from the first.

26. See Fig. 3.28 and Plate 3.31
(i) This filling is based on blanket stitches worked in diagonal rows. The stitches lie alternately straight over 6 threads and diagonally over 3 threads in groups

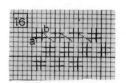

Figure 3.16

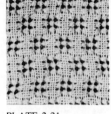

PLATE 3.21
Filling no 16

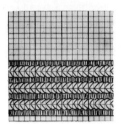

Figure 3.17

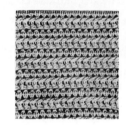

PLATE 3.22
Filling no 17

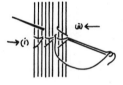

Figure 3.18

Figure 3.20

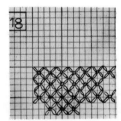

Figure 3.19

Figure 3.21

PLATE 3.23
Filling no 18

PLATE 3.24
Filling no 19

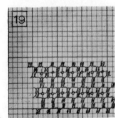

of 3 stitches into the same hole. Next they come out in another hole in groups of 3.

(ii) — (iv) The rows lie alternately back to back, with the loops adjoining.

27. See Fig. 3.29 and Plate 3.32
Commencing at a, work half an eyelet i.e. 13 stitches into one centre hole and end with a stitch over 3 threads on the straight. Instead of completing the eyelet, work another half an eyelet with the lower position of the last stitch, i.e. b, as the new centre. When this eyelet is half finished, the next one is commenced exactly like the first. The rows are 6 threads apart. In the open spaces detached squares are worked over 4 threads, with 2 threads between each square.

28. See Fig. 3.30 and Plate 3.33
(i) Work a single row of double faggot over 3 threads and the rows lie 6 threads apart.
(ii) Work one diagonal raised band between these rows.

29. See Fig. 3.31 and Plate 3.34
Work the first row as indicated on the diagram by binding each stitch twice on the principle of backstitch. The second row, 6 threads away, is the same, but reversed. Work the third row like the first but right up against the second. The fourth row is like the second. Work stars between the first and second rows and Algerian Eyelets between the second and third rows.

30. See Fig. 3.32 and Plate 3.35
The method for working this star with the blanket stitch centre is described in Par. 2.4, design D 2.1. Repeat them in diagonal rows as shown on the diagram. Be very careful when proceeding from one to the other as each stitch must be clearly defined and threads at the back of the work must not be visible on the right side. Commence the first and second stars at a, the third at b and the fourth at c, etc.

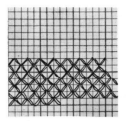

Figure 3.22

PLATE 3.25
Filling no 20

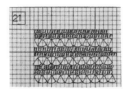

Figure 3.23

PLATE 3.26
Filling no 21

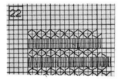

Figure 3.24

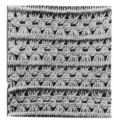

PLATE 3.27
Filling no 22

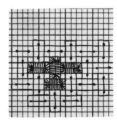

Figure 3.25

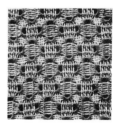

PLATE 3.28
Filling no 23

PLATE 3. 29
Filling no 24

Figure 3.26

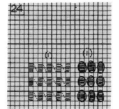

31. See Fig. 3.33 and design D 1.2 No. 1, and Plate 3.36
Scale: One line equals one thread. Using No. 12 cotton work rows of four-sided stitch over 3 threads, 6 threads apart. Using No. 5 cotton, work satin stitch as follows: From one square to the next make one long stitch over 6 threads (into the holes) and then 2 shorter stitches in the middle over 2 threads. Repeat.

32. See Fig. 3.34 and Plate 3.37
Scale: One line equals one thread.
   (i) Work one row double faggot over 3 threads.
   (ii) Work a second row of double faggot over 6 threads so that it meets the first row in alternate holes.
   (iii) Again a row of double faggot over 6 threads, so that the corners of the steps formed are diagonally one thread apart at a and a cross thread results.
   (iv) Again a row of double faggot over 3 threads to meet the previous row in alternate holes.
   (v) Work another row of double faggot over 3 threads so that the parallel stitches are 6 threads apart. This row is similar to the second row. Repeat.

33. See Fig. 3.35 and Plate 3.38
Scale: One line equals one thread. Use No. 8 Pearl cotton. First work two rows of bound wave stitch over 6 threads (see filling no. 20). Start opposite a hole of the wave stitch and work 3 upright satin stitches over 3 threads. Bring the needle out at the top instead of at the bottom of stitch No. 3. Now pass the needle underneath the 2 threads on either side of this space where the thread is hanging but 7 threads lower down. Insert again in the same hole at the top, work 5 upright stitches over 3 threads, repeat the long loop, work 5 stitches again, etc. The next row is reversed and right up against the first. Repeat.

34. See Fig. 3.36 and Plate 3.39
Scale: One line is one thread. Work an Algerian eyelet over 6 threads. Next to it, work a four-sided stitch over 4 threads, one thread to

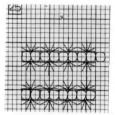

Figure 3.27

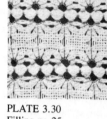

PLATE 3.30
Filling no 25

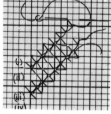

Figure 3.28

PLATE 3.31
Filling no 26

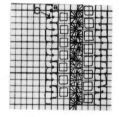

Figure 3.29

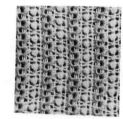

PLATE 3.32
Filling no 27

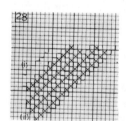

Figure 3.30

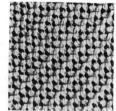

PLATE 3.33
Filling no 28

Figure 3.31

PLATE 3.34
Filling no 29

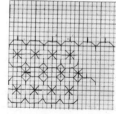

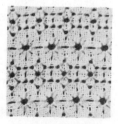

the right and one thread higher. Work another Algerian eyelet over 6 threads on the same level as the first one, then another four-sided stitch, etc. Place the next row alternately so that the Algerian eyelets meet at their corners.

35. See Fig. 3.37 and Plate 3.40
Scale: One line equals one thread. Work pulled lines over 3 threads and 6 threads apart. Work four-sided stitch over 6 threads in the open spaces, leaving one thread between each square.

36. See Fig. 3.38 and Plate 3.41
Scale: One line equals one thread. Bind 4 stitches twice each over 6 threads, viz. ab, cd, db and eb. Bring the needle out at f, 2 threads below e. Bind f g diagonally over 4 threads, twice. Pass the needle through to h, 2 threads to the right of d. Bind h i twice diagonally over 4 threads. Pass the needle through to j, 2 threads above c. Bind j k diagonally over 4 threads twice. Pass the needle through to l, 2 threads to the left of a. Bind l m diagonally over 4 threads twice. Pass the needle through the back of the stitches to n, 4 threads below f. Bind n f twice, then n g, o p, o q, r s, r t, u v and u w. Bind one four-sided stitch in the centre over 4 by 4 threads and pass the needle through the back of the work to x, 2 threads to the right of v. Bind x y like ab. Repeat these two little motifs to the end of the row. The other rows are similar and the positions of the stitches are clearly shown on the diagram.

37. See Fig. 3.39 and Plate 3.42
Scale: One line equals one thread. Work pulled lines 3 threads apart, and single rows of honeycomb stitch in the open spaces between the rows.

38. See Fig. 3.40 and Plate 3.43
Scale: One line equals one thread.
Here the principle is the same as for geometrical shadow work. The stitches swerve out twice to both sides to form a diamond shape, remain even for one stitch on both sides with 10 threads in between. Then

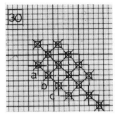

Figure 3.32

PLATE 3.35
Filling no 30

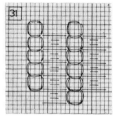

Figure 3.33

PLATE 3.36
Filling no 31

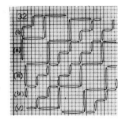

Figure 3.34

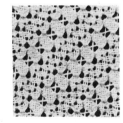

Plate 3.37
Filling no 32

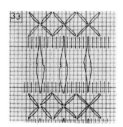

Figure 3.35

PLATE 3.38
Filling no 33

PLATE 3.39
Filline no 34

Figure 3.36

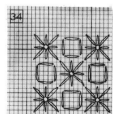

they swerve to the inside by 2 stitches on either side, remain even for 5 stitches with 2 threads in between and then swerve out again etc. The second row is similar and the centre stitch of the diamond shape lies right up against and in the same holes as the centre stitch of the 5 groups of stitches of the previous row.

39. See Fig. 3.41 and Plate 3.44
Scale: One line equals one thread. Work rows of festoon stitch 3 threads apart. Then, using No. 5 cotton, work satin stitch as indicated on the diagram.

40. See Fig. 3.42 and Plate 3.45
Scale: One line equals one thread. Make blocks of geometrical shadow work in groups of 4, 6 threads apart. Using No. 8 cotton make eyelets consisting of 4 stitches, each bound only once, on each side, in the spaces in between the blocks. (See Par. 2.4 design D 2.6 C).

41. See Fig. 3.43 and Plate 3.46
Scale: One line equals one thread. Work a small circle by binding each stitch twice over 2 threads on the principle of backstitch. Work a detached square, 2 threads away and level with the centre stitch of the circle. Then work another little circle etc. The second and subsequent rows are the same but are placed alternately.

42. See Fig. 3.44 and Plate 3.47
Scale: One line equals one thread. This filling consists only of hemstitched eyelets, each right up against the other. This is very effective for a small area.

43. See Fig. 3.45 and Plate 3.48
Scale: One line equals one thread. Commencing at a, work half a square or a triangle of geometrical shadow work with a diagonal stitch over 2 threads on the corner. At its widest the thread will be diagonally over 8 threads at the back of the work. Position b, which is starting point for the second triangle, can be found by consulting the diagram. Con-

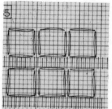

Figure 3.37

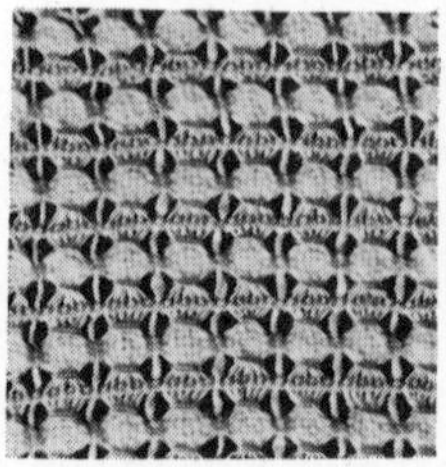

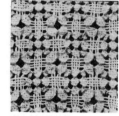

PLATE 3.40
Filling no 35

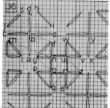

Figure 3.38

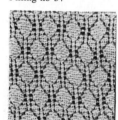

PLATE 3.41
Filling no 36

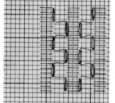

Figure 3.39

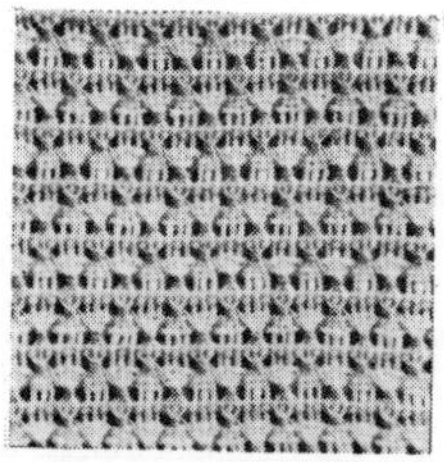

PLATE 3.42
Filling no 37

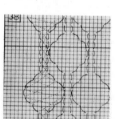

Figure 3.40

PLATE 3.43
Filling no 38

Figure 3.41

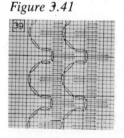

PLATE 3.44
Filling no 39

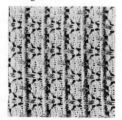

70

tinue thus. Now work 2 rows of double faggot over 4 threads right up against the triangles and repeat.

44. See Fig. 3.46 and Plate 3.49
Scale: One line equals one thread. Work from the top down. Commencing at a, insert the needle at b, out at c, in at d, out at e, in at a etc. All the stitches lie diagonally across 2 threads and the 3rd pair of stitches are two threads apart. Now word 3 four-sided stitches. Take the needle diagonally down to a and repeat. The second and subsequent rows are similar.

45. See Fig. 3.47 and Plate 3.50
Scale: One line equals one thread. Work a diagonal row of window eyelets each over a total of 7 threads. The following rows are 7 threads apart. Now bind twice diagonally over 3 threads in each corner of the open spaces so that one thread remains seperate in both directions in the centre.

46. See Fig. 3.48 and Plate 3.51
Scale: One line equals one thread.

Work a small band of shadow stitch, 4 threads wide and with 5 stitches on each side. Bring the needle out at a, insert at b, out at c, in at d, etc. to the end of the row. Skip 6 threads and repeat. Bind the threads twice in groups of 6 in the open space as shown on the diagram.

47. See Fig. 3.49 and Plate 3.52
See Par. 2.7, design D 2.8 No. 1A for the working method of this floret placed here in rows. Work a blanket stitch star in the open squares.

48. See Fig. 3.50 and Plate 3.53
Using No. 5 cotton, work a horizontal row of satin stitches over 6 threads in groups of 3, each stitch one thread higher than the previous one. The fourth is again on the same level as the first one, etc. Skip 6 threads and repeat the row, taking care that the highest points of the second row are in a line with the lowest points of the first row. Use No. 12 cotton and work a single row of brick stitch in the open spaces.

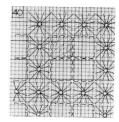

Figure 3.42

PLATE 3.45
Filling no 40

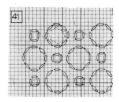

Figure 3.43

PLATE 3.46
Filling no 41

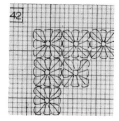

Figure 3.44

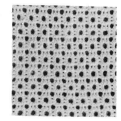

PLATE 3.47
Filling no 42

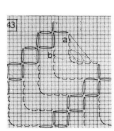

Figure 3.45

PLATE 3.48
Filling no 43

Figure 3.46

PLATE 3.49
Filling no 44

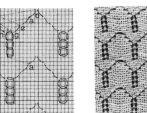

49. See Fig. 3.51 and Plate 3.54
Using No. 8 cotton work 4 adjoining triangles in diagonal satin stitch. The first stitch will be diagonally over one thread and the last diagonally over 6 threads. The diamonds meet to form diamond-shaped spaces in which detached squares are pulled over 4 threads, using no. 12 cotton.

50. See Fig. 3.52 and Plate 3.55
Use No. 5 cotton and work the satin stitch floret as follows: Work 4 leaves around an open square of 3 by 3 threads and work each section as follows: 10 satin stitches, all level at the top, the first over 3 threads, the second over 4, the third over 5 and the next 4 over 6 threads. Then again one over 5, over 4 and over 3 threads. Work the florets 3 threads apart. Using No. 12 cotton work four-sided stitch in the space between the rows.

51. See Fig. 3.53 and Plate 3.56
Use No. 5 cotton and work a zigzag row of satin stitch over 3 threads with 7 stitches from one point to the next. Use No. 12 cotton and pull an identical row right up against the first one. Repeat these double rows and take care that the lowest point of the first row fall in the same horizontal space as the highest point of the second row. Using No. 12 cotton, pull half a star in the open spaces below each row.

52. See Fig. 3.54 and Plate 3.57
Use No. 8 cotton and work 4 leaves each as follows: Work 7 stitches diagonally over 3 threads to form a corner, with the 4th stitch on the corner. The 4 corner-stitches of the 4 leaves meet in the same hole in the centre. Place the florets adjoining. Using No. 8 cotton again, bind over 3 threads on the straight in all 4 directions form the centre of each side of the open square formed by the leaves.

53. See Fig. 3.55 and Plate 3.66
Scale: One square equals 2 threads. Commencing at a, bind 6 threads twice each on the straight, with b as the centre. Bring the needle out at c, diagonally over 2 threads from a. Insert at d, 6 threads to the right of c and work

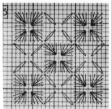

Figure 3.47

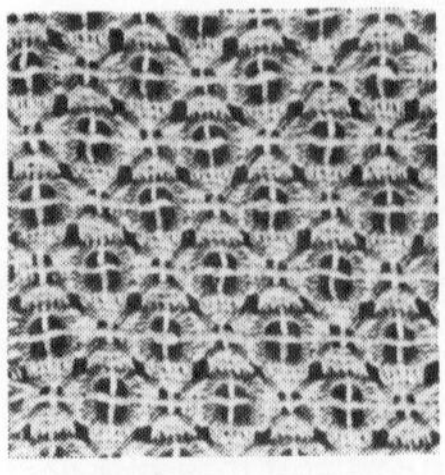

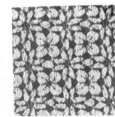

PLATE 3.50
Filling no 45

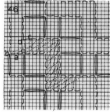

Figure 3.48

PLATE 3.51
Filling no 46

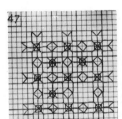

Figure 3.49

PLATE 3.52
Filling no 47

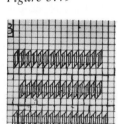

Figure 3.50

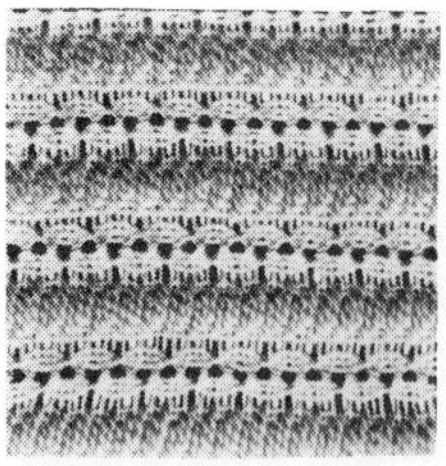

PLATE 3.53
Filling no 48

Figure 3.51

PLATE 3.54
Filling no 49

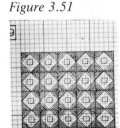

a second eyelet around d as centre. Repeat to form diagonal rows with a cross of 2 by 2 threads between each motif.

54. See Fig. 3.56 and Plate 3.66
Work diagonal raised bands 6 threads apart Repeat in the opposite direction so that the rows intersect on a little cross.

55. See Fig. 3.57 and Plate 3.66
   (i)   Work a row of double faggot over 6 threads.
   (ii) Work another row of double faggot over 3 threads adjoining the first.
   (iii) Again another row of double faggot over 6 threads and note that these stitches are in a line with the stitches of the first row.
   (iv) Another row over 3 threads, etc.

56. See Fig. 3.58 and Plate 3.58
Diagonal rows of stars, worked alternately with rows of diagonal raised band.

57. See Fig. 3.59 and Plate 3.59
Scale: One square equals 2 threads.
   (i)   Bring the needle out at a, insert at b, 6 threads above and 2 threads to the right of a. Bind a b twice.
   (ii) Bring the needle out at c, 4 threads to the right of a and bind c b twice.
   (iii) Bring the needle out at d, 6 threads to the right of b, and bind d b twice.
   (iv) Bring the needle out at e, 6 threads above and 2 threads to the right of b. Bind e b twice.
   (v)   Repeat in this way till the floret has been completed.
   (vi) Complete in the same way as the first and work adjoining rows.

58. See Fig. 3.60 and Plate 3.60
Work pulled lines over 3 threads and 6 threads apart. Work a row of bound wave stitch over 6 threads in the open spaces. See also Filling No. 20.

59. See Fig. 3.61 and Plate 3.61
Work pulled lines over 3 threads, 6 threads apart. Bring the needle out at a and insert at b, 3 threads diagonally across from a. Bind a b

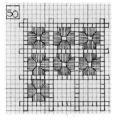

Figure 3.52

PLATE 3.55
Filling no 50

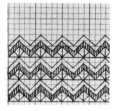

Figure 3.53

PLATE 3.56
Filling no 51

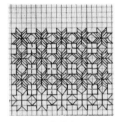

Figure 3.54

PLATE 3.57
Filling no 52

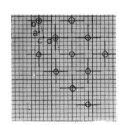

Figure 3.55

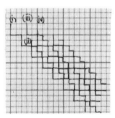

Figure 3.57

Figure 3.56

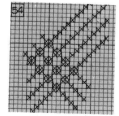

twice and again emerge at a. Bind a c twice on the straight over 6 threads, then a d twice diagonally over 3 threads and emerge at e, 6 threads below a. e d is the same as a b. Repeat.

60. See Fig. 3.62 and Plate 3.62
Work pulled lines 12 threads apart. Work Algerian eyelets between these rows as shown on the diagram. Note the way in which these eyelets are arranged in the second space in relation to those in the first space.

61. See Fig. 3.63 and Plate 3.63
Honeycomb stitch. Scale: 2 squares equal 3 threads. Use No. 8 cotton on coarser linen.
  (i)   Bring the needle out at a and insert at b, 3 threads above a. Bind a b twice and emerge at a.
  (ii) Insert at c, 3 threads to the left of a, and emerge at d, 3 threads below c. Bind dc thrice and emerge again at d.
  (iii) Insert at e, 3 threads to the right of d and emerge at f, 3 threads below e. Bind f e twice. Bind h g three times, j i twice, l k three times etc, to the end of the row.
  (iv) The second row: Bring the needle out at a and bind a b only once (bound three times in all). Insert at m, 3 threads to the right of a, and emerge at n, 3 threads below m. Bind m n twice, then f e again once (three times in all) o p twice, j i once, q r twice etc. Eventually all the groups will have been bound three times.

62. See D 1.2 No. 2, Fig. 3.64 and Plate 3.64
Scale: One square equals 2 threads. Rows of adjoining wave stitch are worked to form a filling.

63. Uneven double faggot. See Fig. 3.65 and Plate 3.65
Scale: One line equals one thread. Work rows of double faggot so that each row is diagonally one thread away from the previous one. Small crosses are formed between the rows in this way.

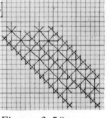

Figure 3.58

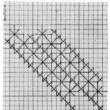

PLATE 3.58
Filling no 56

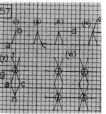

Figure 3.59

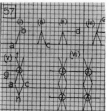

PLATE 3.59
Filling no 57

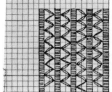

Figure 3.60

PLATE 3.60
Filling no 58

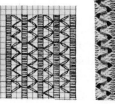

Figure 3.61

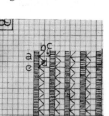

PLATE 3.61
Filling no 59

Figure 3.62

PLATE 3.62
Filling no 60

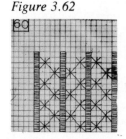

64. Uneven wave stitch. See Fig. 3.66 and Plate 3.66

Scale: One line equals one thread.

See Par. 1.9 design D 1.2 No. 2 for wave stitch. In this case the method is the same, except that 5 threads are taken instead of 4 and one thread is skipped between the groups. This thread is in fact the centre one taken up in the previous group. Work the rows one thread apart.

65. Tile stitch. See Fig. 3.67 and Plate 3.3
  (i) Bring the needle out at a and insert at b, three threads above a. Bind a b twice.
  (ii) Emerge at c, 3 threads diagonally from a. Bind c a twice.
  (iii) Emerge at d, 3 threads to the right of c and bind d c twice.
  (iv) Emerge at e, 3 threads diagonally from c, bind e c twice and emerge at f, exactly 3 threads below e.
  (v) Bind f e twice and emerge at g, 3 threads diagonally from e.
  (vi) Bind g e twice and emerge at h, 3 threads to the left of g.
  (vii) Bind h g twice, emerge at a and bind a g twice. This completes one motif.
  (viii) To proceed to the next one: Insert at g and at i, exactly 3 threads below d. i d is like a b and the whole process is repeated so that d and f are common holes for the first and second motifs.
  (ix) Work diagonal rows close together.

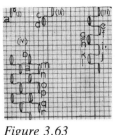

Figure 3.63

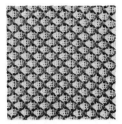

PLATE 3.63
Filling no 61

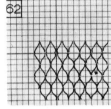

Figure 3.64

PLATE 3.64
Filling no 62

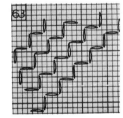

Figure 3.65

PLATE 3.65
Filling no 63

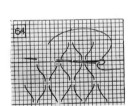

Figure 3.66

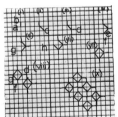

Figure 3.67

75

PLATE 3.66
Design D3.1. Section of the tray-cloth dealt with in Par 3.4. Fillings: Flower: no. 53, leaves: nos 54 and 55, serviette: no 63, pocket: no 64

3.4 A breakfast set with fillings

This set consists of a tray cloth, a tea cosy and a small serviette.

D 3.1*, D 3.2 and D 3.3

Schematic diagrams: See Fig. 3.68 and Fig. 3.69.

Size of tray cloth: 51 cm by 36 cm, of tea cosy: 19 cm by 27 cm, and serviette: 28 cm by 28 cm .

Scale of diagrams: 2,5 cm is 16 cm .

Hint: Preferably use Glenshee linen for this design. A beginner in drawn fabric work will find some difficulty with this design, especially working the fillings in the free hand motifs.

*Design at the back of the book in the envelope.

Figure 3.68

1. *The traycloth*

See Plate 3.66.

The traycloth is finished off with a narrow hem of 6 mm — 13 mm . Pull out one thread and punch or hemstitch to secure the hem. Cut a small square of linen, 15 cm by 15 cm . Pull out one thread of the material so that a hem of 6 mm wide can be folded to the right side on 2 sides and secured by hemstitching. The other 2 sides are folded only once to the wrong side, also 6 mm wide. The corner where the 2 hems were folded and worked towards the right side, will eventually be ironed over to the right side. See Fig. 3.70.

Method of work where the hem and the single fold meet:

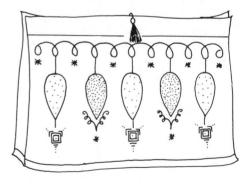

Figure 3.69

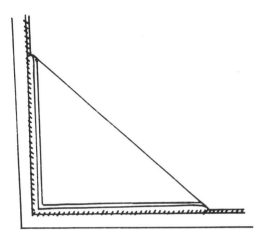

Figure 3.70

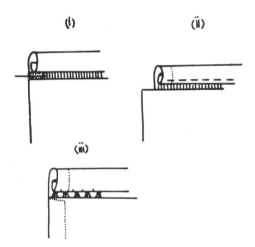

Figure 3.71

(i) See Fig. 3.71.
   Pull out the thread where the hem will be secured by hemstitching. Cut 6 mm from the raw edge into the space left by the drawn thread as shown by the arrow.

(ii) Fold this 6 mm under the hem and tack the hem.

(iii) Fold the rest of the raw edge to the wrong side. The corner of the square which will be ironed to the right side, can be decorated with a filling, e.g. uneven wave stitch. (See Filling No. 64) See Fig. 3.72.

If the motifs are not worked on the traycloth, a motif like the one on the serviette can be used on this corner of the square instead of a filling. (See Fig. 3.74)

Tack the 2 folded sides of the square onto the corner of the hemmed traycloth so that the 2 sides lie precisely up against the line on the traycloth where the thread has been removed. See Fig. 3.73

Secure by hemstitching around the same groups of threads of the hem of the traycloth. Iron the corner towards the right side. This

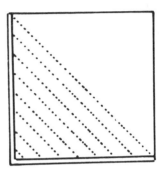

Figure 3.72

will be the pocket for the serviette. The design can also be placed as follows: See Fig. 3.74.

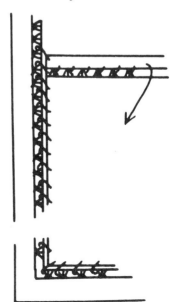

Figure 3.73

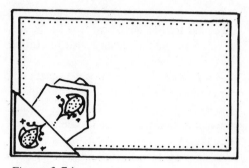

Figure 3.74

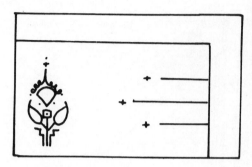

Figure 3.77

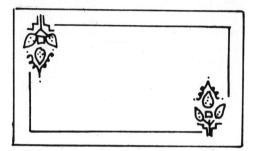

Figure 3.75

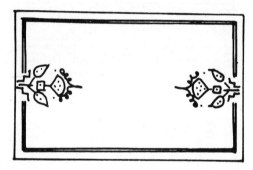

Figure 3.76

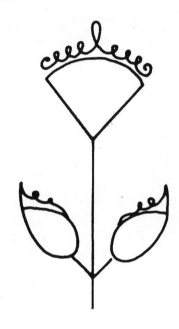

Figure 3.78

In this case a pretty, narrow border in drawn fabric work can be worked around the cloth. If preferred, the pocket need not be made, as e.g. in Fig. 3.75.

Here the motifs can also be arranged in many other ways as shown in Fig. 3.76 and Fig. 3.77.

For luncheon-mats it is also very effective to join the motifs with simple pulled stitches to form a narrow border.

To place the design on the material: Part of the design is worked by counting the threads and part is tacked onto the material. Fig. 3.78 shows which part must be tacked on to the material.

See Par. 1.3, hint no. 15 for the method of tacking.

Key for the traycloth:
D 3.1
Commence with the counted work after the free part of the design has been tacked on the material.
A. Using No. 12 cotton, work the pulled square first.
B. Then the eyelets, and
C. the detached buttonhole bars.

PLATE 3.67
A tea-cloth of evenly woven linen with approximately 30 threads to 2½ cm, decorated with drawn fabric embroidery with a great variety of fillings. Size: 127 cm x 127 cm. D. Author, M: Mrs. R. Pienaar

If the linen is very coarse the whole pulled square as on the design, will be too large and will have to be made smaller by e.g. pulling around the eyelet only twice instead of three times. Further by enlarging the corners only once instead of twice. It is also possible to work fewer eyelets. This applies to the pulled line underneath as well — the steps will possibly have to be shortened. The embroideress has to use her discretion when such a problem arises.

D. Using No. 12 cotton, work the pulled lines and the eyelents on both sides of the stem as indicated on the design. Do not work the eyelets near the flower just yet.

E. Using No. 5 cotton and a sharp needle, work the central stem in double knot stitch and note that the stem is broken by the pulled square.

Palestrina or Double knot stitch. See Fig. 3.79.

The straight line represents part of the design.

  (i) Bring the needle out just below the line and make a small stitch, about 3 mm long further along the line.

  (ii) Pass the needle through from the top down underneath this small stitch only.

  (iii) Repeat, but keep the thread under the needle this time. Do not pull too tightly.

  (iv) Insert again a little further along the line as in (i), and repeat as from (ii).

F. Using No. 5 cotton work the outline of the 2 leaves and the flower as follows: Portuguese stem stitch. See Fig. 3.80.

  (i) Bring the needle out on the line of the

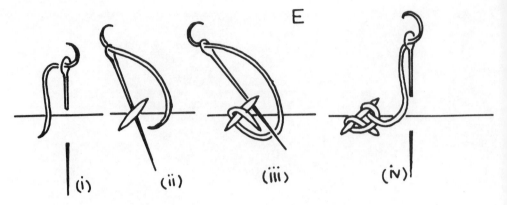

Figure 3.79

design. Make one small stem stitch forward and bring the needle out in the original position (Thread to the right of the needle).

(ii) Make a second stem stitch and bring the needle out at the top end of the first stitch. (Thread to the right of the needle).

(iii) Now insert the needle from right to left underneath the double thread. Repeat from (ii). It is necessary only at the beginning to make 2 successive stem stitches. Sometimes the stitch is made by working over the double stitch twice instead of only once.

G. Using no. 5 cotton on coarse linen and No.

8 on finer linen, work the scrolls on top of the flower and leaves in ordinary chain stitch, as is clearly shown in Fig. 3.81

Work the remaining eyelets above the H. flower and the outlined star, with blanket stitch centre above the motif on the right. All the tacking threads can now be removed. Now work the fillings as indicated. Any other fillings may also be used.

The flower on the left: Filling No. 53.

The flower on the right: Filling No. 30.

The 4 leaves: Fillings Nos. 54, 55, 56, and 57.

Figure 3.80

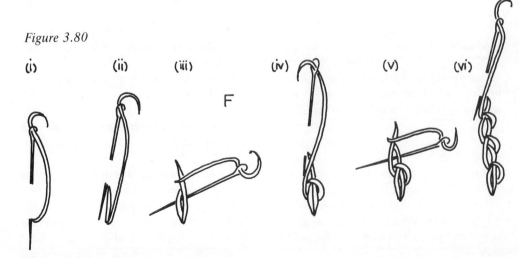

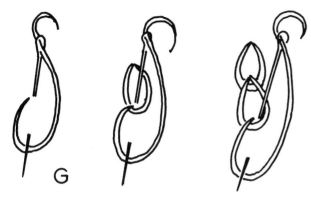

G

Figure 3.81

2. The tea cosy
D 3.2

Key: A. Work a row of four-sided stitch right across the breadth of the cosy and about 25 mm from the top. This will also serve as a guide for tacking the design on to the material. Tack the part of the design indicated in Fig. 3.82 on the material in the same manner as for the tray cloth.

Now work the part in counted thread.

B. Pulled square.

C. Outlined stars with blanket stitch centres.

D. Outline the leaves above the pulled square and the stem with Portuguese stem stitch.

E. Outline the other leaves with double knot.

F. Work the scrolls underneath the 2 leaves and under the four-sided stitch in chain stitch.

Fillings for the 5 leaves: No.'s 58, 59, 60. 61 and 62. Work a smaller motif on the other side of the tea cosy if preferred.

Finishing off the tea-cosy

See Fig. 3.83

Cut the 2 halves of the tea cosy, A and B.

Figure 3.82

about 34 cm or 36 cm by 27 cm or 28 cm and the gusset exactly the same height and 76 mm wide. Remove the 18th thread on the 2 short sides e.g. a c and b d, and on one long side e.g. a b, of A and B, but only up to the corners where they meet. Fold a wide hem along the other long side (remove the 40th thread). Make mitred corners at a and b as described in Par. 1.4. This cannot be done at c and d because the hems are not the same width. First fold the narrow hems and then the wide one at the bottom. Punch the hems. The gussets C and D are made in the same way. When the

Figure 3.83

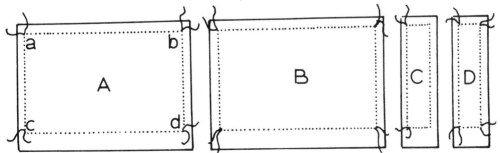

81

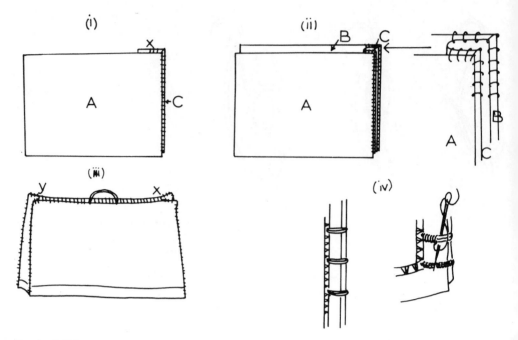

Figure 3.84

embroidery on the cosy has been completed, it is assembled as follows:

(i) Place A on C and tack together. Using No. 5 cotton, overcast 3 times through the first hole in the hems of A and C. See Fig. 3.84 (i). Pass the needle through the hem of A and emerge 4 holes higher up and repeat. Affix the strips A and C in this way, going around the corner and up to the middle of C. See Fig. 3.84 (i) x.

(ii) Affix B and C in the same way up to the middle of C at x.

(iii) On the other side D is affixed in the same way up to y, which is in the middle at the top of D. Now join up from y to x also.

(iv) Using No. 12 cotton, work firm buttonhole stitches around the bars, with the loops facing down.

A pretty little handle or tassel can be added on top.

To make a tassel: See Fig. 3.85

(i) Take a piece of cardboard about 76 mm square. Wind No. 8 Pearl cotton at least 50 times around it. Cut the cotton on the one side and carefully remove the threads from the cardboard. Secure these threads in the centre with a 15 cm thread folded double. The 2 loose ends are pulled through the loop, and tied into a firm knot.

(ii) Roll a small piece of cotton wool into a firm ball about the size of a large pea. Place it underneath the threads that have been secured by the loop and spread them out evenly so that the cotton wool is completely covered.

(iii) Now fold a 20 cm long thread double, wind it around the threads just below the little ball. Pull the 2 loose ends firmly through the loop and tie the ends into a knot. A needle can be used to pull these threads through the ball to the top to where the ends of the first double thread are. There will now be 4 threads by which the tassel will be secured to the tea cosy when finished.

(iv) Using No. 12 cotton, and with a firm knot, insert the needle from below

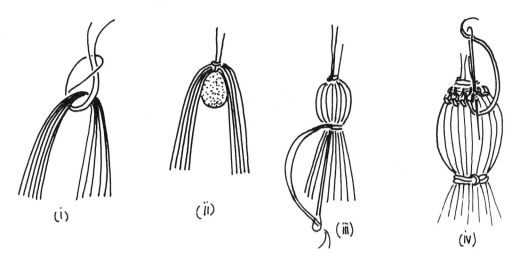

Figure 3.85

through the ball and emerge where the other 4 threads are. Wind the thread twice around the 4 threads and work buttonhole stitches over the latter. Work a second row by making 2 stitches into every loop formed by the first row. In this way the number of stitches is doubled to get the right shape. Proceed in this way in a circular movement, working buttonhole stitches in the loops of the previous row, and increasing the stitches where necessary. Decrease when the little ball is covered by working into every second stitch until it is firmly closed in at the bottom. The last row is worked over the thread that was used to hold the cotton wool ball in position. Trim the threads evenly at the bottom and affix to the tea-cosy with the 4 threads leaving a stem of about 25 mm. Finish this off by overcasting closely.

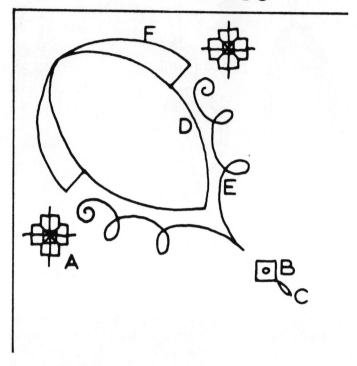

3. *The serviette*

D 3.3

Key: Almost the whole of this design is tacked on the material, except

A. the 2 stars with blanket stitch centres, outlined,

B. one eyelet and the

C. Detached buttonhole bar, which are worked after the design has been tacked in one corner of the serviette.

D. Outline the leaf in Portuguese stem stitch and the

E. scrolls in chain stitch and the

F. 2 extra lines below in double knot stitch.

Use filling No. 63

PLATE 3.68
A very dainty table-cloth of deep ecru linen richly embroidered in white with many contrasting fillings.
D. Author, M: Mrs. Ria Wessels

4.1 A table runner in drawn fabric work
D 4.1

Schematic diagram: See Fig. 4.1.

Size: 36 cm by 92 cm .

Scale of diagram: 21 mm equals 15 cm .

Scale of design: One square equals 3 threads.

Scale of figures: One square equals 3 threads unless otherwise specified.

This is a pure pulled work design for which only No. 12 Pearl cotton is used. A piece of work like this always gives an impression of fineness and delicacy. The cotton must be slightly darker than the material in order to get the best effect, although white on white will also look lovely and lacy. It is obvious that more work will have to be put into a design of this kind to make it striking enough.

See Plate 4.2

Key: A. Algerian eyelets.

B. Four-sided stitch.

C. Pulled lines.

D. Four hemstitched eyelets in the centre of the motif. See Fig. 4.2

Scale: One line equals one thread, except in No. (iii) where one square equals 3 threads.

  (i) Bring the needle out at a in the centre of the eyelet to be made and work 3 hemstitches from a, viz. b c, d b, and e d, over 2 threads each on the one side of the eyelet.

Designs for drawn fabric work

  (ii) In the same way, work 3 stitches on each of the other 3 sides so that 12 stitches in all have been made, radiating from a in the centre. The eyelet lies over 6 by 6 threads.

  (iii) This shows how the stitch is indicated on all designs. Make the other 3 eyelets in the same way and make sure that they are in the correct positions according to the diagram

E. See Fig. 4.3

  (i) Using No. 12 cotton, pull 2 rows on the principle of backstitch by binding each stitch twice. Commence at a, 3 threads

Figure 4.1

PLATE 4.1
M. Mrs. R. Pienaar

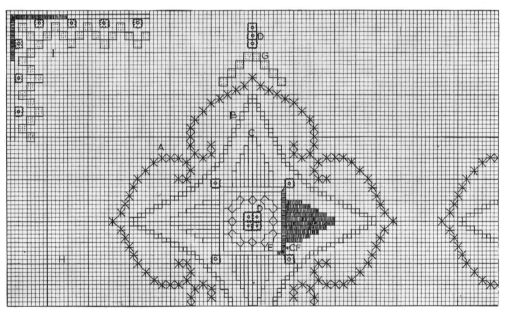

D 4.1

to the left and 6 threads higher than the corner of the top eyelet on the left. Bind a b, c a, d c, e d, f e, g e, h g, etc. until the first row has been completed.

(ii) Work the second row on the same principle. Commence by bringing the needle out at x, 6 threads above a, and inserting it at y, 3 threads higher. Bind x y twice, then c x, d c (bound once only because it had already been bound twice in the previous row), etc. till the second row has been completed.

F. Work a pulled line over 3 threads around the above rows with 4 hemstitched eyelets on each corner as shown on the diagram.

87

PLATE 4.2
Design 4.1. Section of the runner.

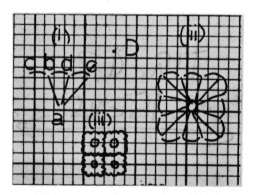

Figure 4.2

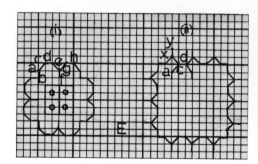

Figure 4.3

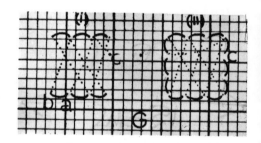

Figure 4.4

H. Work the following filling in the rectangular background. See Fig. 4.5.

Scale: One line equals one thread.

Note that this rectangle will not be outlined.

G. Geometrical shadow work. When using the method described in Par. 2.4, design D 2.6, the squares are inclined to become diamond-shaped which sometimes gives exactly the desired effect, as can be seen clearly on Plate 4.1. However to get them absolutely square, the alternative method is as follows: See Fig. 4.4

Scale: One line equals one thread.

(i) Commence in the corner and work to and fro from one side to the other, and

(ii) then similarly the last two sides, commencing at c. See also description of Fig. 4.5 (i).

(i) Using No. 12 cotton, bring the needle out at a, and insert at b, 2 threads above a. Then work c d, e a, f c, g e and h f. Bring the needle out at i, 2 threads to the right of g and pull 7 stitches over 2 threads. After the last stitch k l has been worked, bring the needle out at m, diagonally over 2 threads from k. Work m n like a b and repeat.

(ii) The second row is worked right up against the first, but the squares and the lines are arranged alternately. Fill in the background thus up to the Algerian eyelets.

I. The border is compiled by working a row of pulled stitches with hemstitched eyelets a cer-

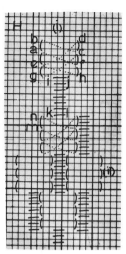

Figure 4.5

4.2 A luncheon set in drawn fabric work on the principle of backstitch

Few pulled work stitches as such are used here, but a lacy effect is obtained by pulling threads in groups into patterns which remind one of Holbein work. This is a particularly quick method for pulled work which gives very striking results. Beautiful bands can be made in this way to give the effect of lace insertions on table linen.

A few more ideas in this direction appear at the end of the paragraph. If the embroideress wishes to experiment she need not confine herself to groups of 3 or 6 threads, but she can bind groups of 4, 5 or 3 or 6 etc. to achieve the most effective results. Great care must be taken, however, when proceeding from one group to the next to ensure clearly defined open spaces without threads showing from the

tain distance from a zigzag row of geometrical satin stitch.

PLATE 4.3
Section of a cream table-cloth on coarse linen, worked in black, white and ecru embroidery cotton. All the openwork is made by the pulled back stitch method

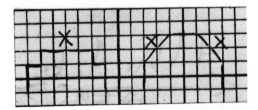

Figure 4.6

back. If one cannot progress from one stitch to the next in a neat way, the sequence of the stitches should be changed. Two stitches lying in the same direction must not be worked successively, as the thread on the wrong side of the work, will show through the hole. See Fig. 4.6

It is better not to pull over more than 4 threads diagonally or over more than 6 threads on the straight. The following design for a luncheon set with a runner, will illustrate this type of pulled work.

PLATE 4.4
Design D 4.2

1. *The luncheon-mat*
D 4.2
Schematic diagram: See Fig. 4.7

Figure 4.7

Size: 36 cm by 51 cm .
Scale of diagram: 6 mm equals, 5 cm .
Scale of design: One square equals 3 threads.
Scale of figures: One square equals 3 threads unless otherwise specified.
Hint: It is better to use a fine linen with approximately 30 threads to 2½ cm. If a coarser linen is used the design will have to be cut as in Fig. 4.8. See Plate 4.4
Key: Use the design as in Fig. 4.7, but other possibilities are as follows: See Fig. 4.9 — Fig. 4.14

Hem the mat and find the centre by counting the threads on the one short side. Tack along this line with a darker thread, under and over groups of 3 threads for about 13 cm . See Fig. 4.15
A. The outside row: Commence at a on the design, which will be about 13 mm from the hem and 3 threads from the tacked thread. See Fig. 4.16 and use No. 12 cotton.
  (i) Work one square over 6 threads by binding a b, c a, d c, and b d twice each, and bring the needle out at e, 6 threads to the right of d.
  (ii) Bind e f, diagonally over 3 threads, twice and bring the needle out at g. Bind g f, diagonally over 3 threads, twice and bring the needle out at h, 6 threads from g.

90

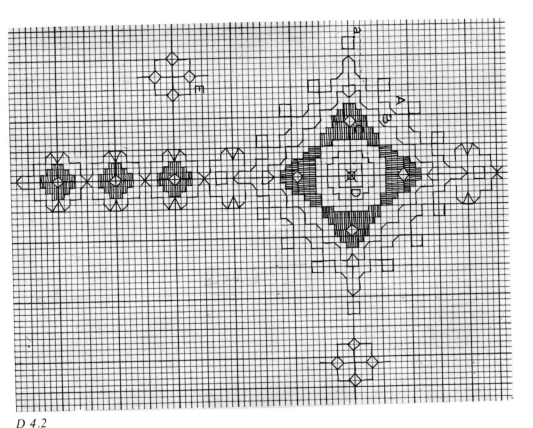

D 4.2

Figure 4.8

(iii) Bind h g twice.

(iv) Bind i h twice, diagonally over 3 threads.

(v) In the same way the following are each bound twice; j i on the straight over 3 threads, k j on the straight over 6 threads and l k, on the straight over 6 threads.

(vi) Bind clockwise around the square according to the letters.

(vii) This also shows the following stitches. It will be too cumbersome to describe the full round up to e, but the reader will be able to deduce the correct procedure from what has been given. Actually it consists only of backstitches worked successively and each bound twice. No mistake will be made if the design is copied carefully.

B. The second row: See Fig. 4.17

(i) — (v) Bring the needle out at a, 15 threads to the right of f. (See Fig. 4.16 (ii)). Insert the needle at b, 6 threads to the left of a and bind a b twice. The procedure, which is the same throughout, can easily be followed according to the diagram and the sequence of the letters.

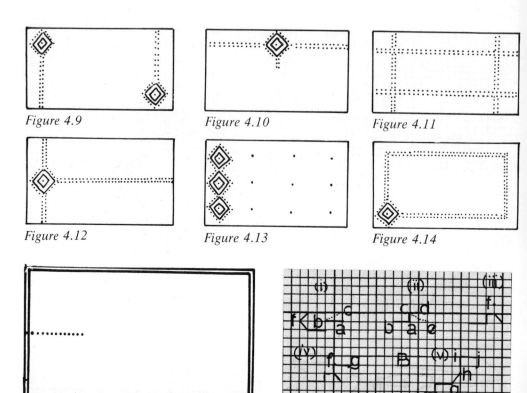

Figure 4.9

Figure 4.10

Figure 4.11

Figure 4.12

Figure 4.13

Figure 4.14

Figure 4.15

Figure 4.17

Figure 4.16

C. Now use No. 5 cotton and work satin stitch. See Fig. 4.18

See also Par. 2.5, D 2.7 No. 6A

(i) Find position a on the material according to the design. Bring the needle out at a and keeping the stitches level at the bottom, work 3 satin stitches over 3 threads and 3 over 6 threads. The next stitch is one thread shorter at the bottom and 3 longer at the top (over 8 threads). Keep the next 6 stitches level with the previous one at the top, but work over 7, over 6, 5, 6, 7 and over 8 threads. The next stitch is one thread longer at the bottom, but shorter by 3 threads at the top. (Over 6 threads). Keep the next 5 stitches level with the previous one at the bottom and work the first two over 6 threads and the last 3 over 3 threads.

(ii) Bring the needle out at c, 12 threads below and 6 threads to the left of a. Keeping the next 6 stitches level at the bottom, work 3 over 6 and 3 over 9 threads. The next stitch is 3 threads shorter at the bottom and 3 longer at the top (again over 9 threads). Keep the next 18 stitches level with the previous one at the bottom and work the first 5 stitches over 9 threads. Then one over 8, one over 7, one over 6, and over 5 threads, then again one over 6, 7, 8 and

92

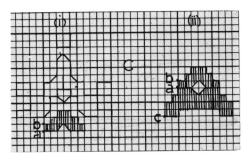

Figure 4.18

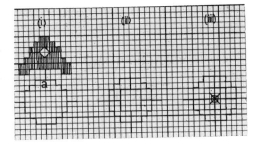

Figure 4.19

9 threads. Now work the last 5 stitches over 9 threads. The next 3 stitches are worked 3 threads longer than the previous one at the bottom and 3 shorter at the top (again over 9 threads). The last 3 stitches remain level at the bottom, but are 3 threads shorter at the top (over 6 threads). Now repeat this satin stitch

motif in the other 3 corners of the diamond-shaped motif.

D. See Fig. 4.19

Use No. 12 cotton.

(i) Commence at a and work on the same principle as described in A and B.

(ii) Work a row of double faggot over 6 threads just inside the first row.

(iii) Work a star with a blanket stitch centre in the middle.

This completes the diamond-shaped motif. The border compiled from this motif is made as follows: Use No. 5 cotton and work the satin stitch motifs in position. (See Fig. 4.18) Note that 2 of these motifs must be placed in juxtaposition. Using No. 12 cotton, work the little pattern all around on the same principle desribed in A and B. Pull the centres of all the satin stitch motifs by binding 4 straight stitches over 3 threads each twice round a common centre bole.

E. See Par. 2.7 No. 16.

F. This is only one quarter of the motif E.

2. *The runner*

D 4.3

Schematic diagram: See Fig. 4.20

Size: 36 cm by 92 cm .

Scale of diagram: 6 mm equals 5 cm .

Scale of design: One square equals 3 threads.

Scale of figures: One square equals 3 threads unless otherwise specified.

Figure 4.20

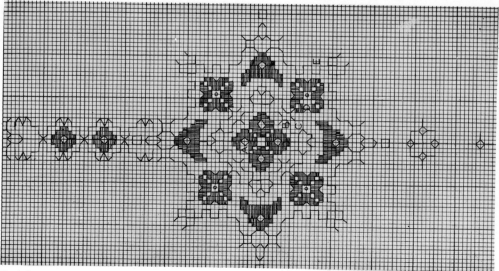

D 4.3

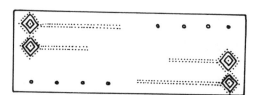

Figure 4.21

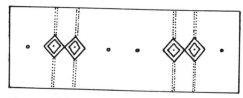

Figure 4.22

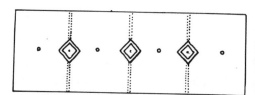

Figure 4.23

Key: In the case of the runner, the embroideress may also vary the position of the design on the material. The following are a few examples. The way in which the design fits in, depends on whether the linen is coarse or fine. See Fig. 4.21 — Fig. 4.23

A. Using No. 5 cotton, work the satin stitch in the centre as described in No. 1C.

B and C. See Fig. 4.24

Using No. 12 cotton, work 2 rows around the satin stitch on the principle described for the mat in A and B.

D. Using No. 5 cotton, work the other groups of satin stitches as indicated on the design. See Fig. 4.18

E. Using No. 12 cotton, work the outside row on the principle already used in the 2 centre rows.

This completes the motif. The band is the same as on the mat, as well as the 2 small motifs. If serviettes are desired, one or 3 or more of the motifs in the band can be used in the corners.

3. Borders

D 4.4

See Plate 4.5

Scale: One square equals 3 threads. The following are a few more ideas for this type of pulled work to use on other articles. Perhaps this will inspire the embroideress to develop a few original ideas.

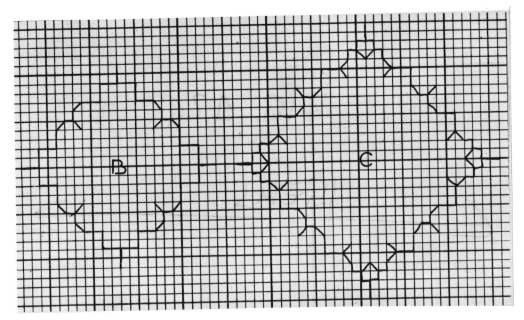

Figure 4.24

PLATE 4.5
Design D 4.4 nos 2, 5 and 6

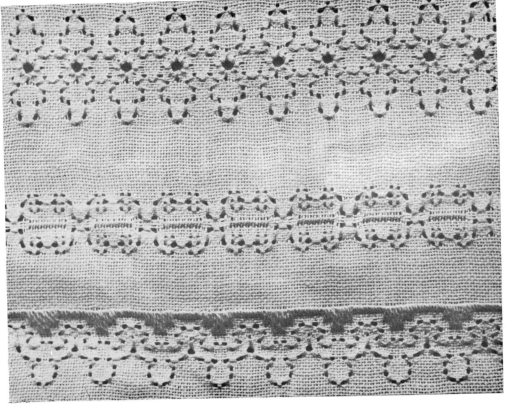

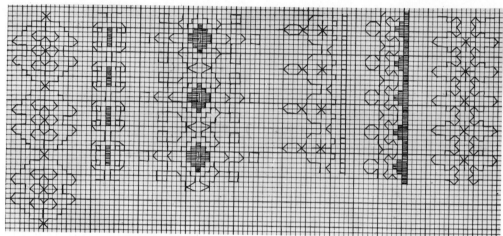

D 4.4

PLATE 4.6
Section of a tea-cloth in drawn fabric embroidery. Size 127 cm x 127 cm . D: Author, M: Mrs. R. Pienaar.

4.3 A tea cloth in drawn fabric work

D 4.5

Schematic diagram: See Fig. 4.25
Size: 127 cm by 127 cm .
Scale of diagram: 13 mm equals 25,5 cm .
Scale of design: One square equals 3 threads, unless otherwise specified.
Scale of Figures: One square equals 3 threads,

unless otherwise specified.
Other ways in which to use this design will be given at the end of the paragraph.
Hints: Tack the material in both directions in groups of 3 stitches as explained in Hint No. 12 in Par. 1.3. Find the centre of the material and work this design from the circle in the centre towards the border.

See Plate 4.7 and Plate 4.9

Key: A. Four-sided stitch.

B. Eyelets.

C. Pulled lines. D. Detached squares. See Fig. 4.26

Use No. 8 cotton. This stitch is worked from right to left like four-sided stitch.

(i) Bind one complete square a b c d, and pass the needle through to e, 3 threads to the left of c.

(ii) Bind a second square e f g h, and repeat.

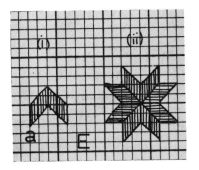

Figure 4.27

PLATE 4.7
Part of design D 4.5

Figure 4.25

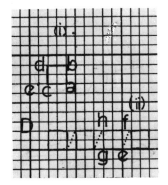

Figure 4.26

E. The larger satin stitch star. See Fig. 4.27
Use No. 5 cotton.

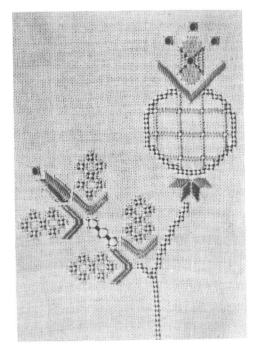

(i) Bring the needle out at a and work 7 satin stitches over 6 threads, each one thread higher than the previous one. Work 6 similar stitches more, each one thread lower than the previous one.

(ii) Work 3 more similar sections so that the stitches meet in the same holes and the 4 centre stitches meet in one hole.

F. Smaller satin stitch star. See Fig. 4.28
Use No. 5 cotton. This is worked exactly like the large one, except that the stitches lie over

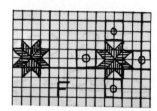

Figure 4.28

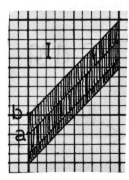

Figure 4.29

3 instead of over 6 threads, and each section consists of 7 instead of 13 stitches. Using No. 12 cotton work the 4 eyelets where required on the design.

G. Pulled square.

H. Diamond-shaped leaves in satin stitch.

I. Diagonal rows of Satin stitch. See Fig. 4.29 Use No. 5 cotton. Bring the needle out at a and insert at b, 6 threads higher up. Bring the needle out next to a but one thread higher and

Figure 4.30

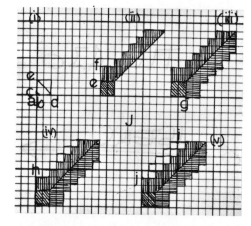

insert next to b, but one thread higher. See hint no. 8 in Par. 1.3. Work another row next to the first one and a third row over 3 threads instead of over 6, as shown on the diagram and design. It is more effective to pull a narrower row with No. 12 cotton when placed next to a wide satin stitch row.

J. The rose-leaf. See Fig. 4.30

(i) Use No. 8 cotton. Find position a on the material according to the design and bring the needle out at b, one thread to the right of a. Insert at c, one thread above a, which means that the first stitch lies diagonally over one thread. Bring the needle out next to b and insert one thread above c. This stitch lies diagonally over 2 threads. Now work diagonal stitches over 3, 4, 5 and 6 threads. This is position d e on the diagram. Bring the needle out one thread above d and insert one thread to the right of and level with e so that the stitch lies diagonally over 5 threads. Work stitches nos. 8, 9, 10 and 11 in the same way. The last one again lies diagonally over one thread. Finish off.

(ii) Use No. 5 cotton. Bring the needle out at e and insert at f, 6 threads higher up and work 6 satin stitches over 6 threads. The next stitch is level at the bottom but stretches over 9 threads. The following stitches all commence one thread higher than the previous one, but remain level at the top in groups of 3 and lie over 9, 8 and 7 threads. Repeat until 5 steps have been completed and then work over 6, 5, 4, 3, 2 and one thread.

(iii) Pass the needle through the back of the satin stitches up to g and work the second half of the leaf in the same way.

(iv) Now use No. 12 cotton and work a row of double faggot, commencing at h as shown on the diagram.

(v) A second row of double faggot is pulled next to the first row, commencing at i and ending at j.

Repeat (iv) and (v) on the other side.

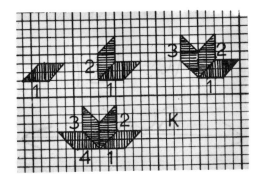

Figure 4.31

K. Four diamond-shaped leaves in satin stitch. See Fig. 4.31
Use No. 5 cotton.

(i) See Par. 1.10, design D 1.3 No. 6E and Fig. 1.43 and work leaf No. 1 exactly as described.

(ii) Pass the needle through the back of the satin stitches and emerge at the top of the first leaf (i.e. on the diagonal side) The second leaf is a mirror-image of the first one and lies perpendicularly on the stitches of the first leaf so that the first 6 stitches meet in the same holes.

PLATE 4.8
Small tea-cloth and cosy in drawn fabric work. Material: Old gold evenweave linen. D: Author, M: Mrs. C. B. Steyl

(iii) Pass the needle through the back of the satin stitches and emerge at the top of the first stitch of the second leaf. Work the third leaf like the first one.

(iv) Pass the needle through the back of the satin stitches and emerge at the top of the first stitch of the third leaf, and work the fourth as a mirror-image of

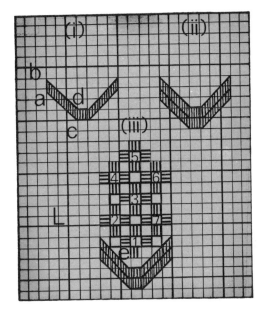

Figure 4.32

the third. Note that the stitches of the second and third leaves lie in the same direction and perpendicularly on those of the first and fourth leaves. Two threads in the centre remain open.

L. The mimosa sprigs. See Fig. 4.32.

(i) Using No. 5 cotton, bring the needle out at a and insert 3 threads higher at b. Emerge next to a but one thread below a and insert next to b but one thread below b. Repeat until 10 stitches have been worked. This is position c d. Work 3 more stitches on the same level as c d. (The 4 stitches will be level at the bottom). Now work 9 stitches each one thread higher than the previous

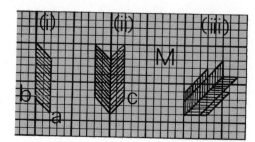

Figure 4.29

one. The last stitch is again level with a b.

(ii) Work a second identical row above the first one.

(iii) Now, using No. 12 cotton, bring the needle out at e, and work mosaic stitch in the sequence indicated on the diagram. Be very careful when pro-

PLATE 4.9
Section of border of design D 4.5

ceeding from one mosaic stitch to the next that the thread does not lie across an open space, as that will give an untidy appearance. In such a case pass the needle through the back of the stitches to avoid a long thread.

M. The small leaves of the large pomegranate in the corner. See Fig. 4.33
Use No. 5 cotton.
The 2 side-leaves.

(i) Bring the needle out at a, insert diagonally over 6 threads from a at b and emerge one thread above a. Insert the needle one thread higher than b and repeat 20 times until 22 stitches have been completed.

(ii) Pass the needle through the back of the satin stitches and emerge again at a. Insert needle at c diagonally over 6 threads from a and work another 22 stitches to form the second half of the leaf.

The centre leaf.

(iii) The method here is exactly the same as for the satin stitch bands described in I. Pull the 2 shorter rows over 3 threads, using No. 12 cotton. The second half is a mirror-image of the first.

N. The largest pomegranate in the corner. See Fig. 4.34

(i) Use No. 12 cotton and work the outline in four-sided stitch.

(ii) Pull 11 upright stitches over 3 threads, work a four-sided stitch and repeat rows of this, 12 threads apart. Identical vertical rows cross the horizontal rows at the four-sided stitches. Work the filling right up to the outline.

(iii) See Fig. 4.35

Complete the pomegranate by using No. 5 cotton and working the top row of satin stitch as follows: Find position a on the material and bring the needle out one thread to the right of a. Keeping all the stitches level at the bottom, work one upright satin stitch over one thread, then one over 2, 3, 4, 5 and over 6 threads. This will be position b c. Now work another 42 stitches over 6 threads level with b c (43

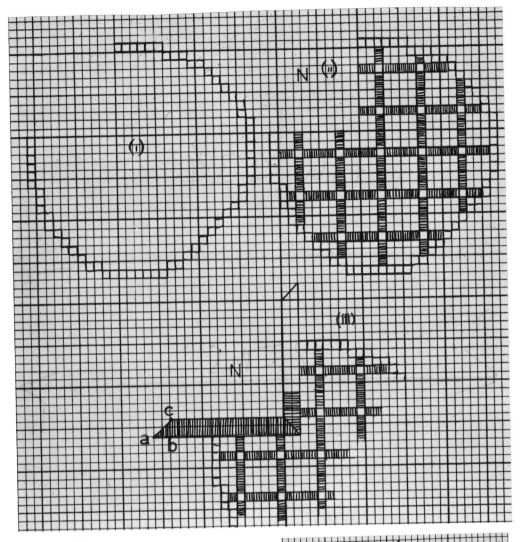

Figure 4.34

stitches in all). Keep the next 5 stitches level at the bottom, but each one thread shorther at the top, and work one stitch over 5, one over 4, 3, 2 and one thread of the material. The last stitch is d e. Bring the needle out next to and one thread above d and insert at e. Work the second half exactly like the first. Also work pulled squares and eyelets.

O. The smaller pomegrantes.

These are worked in the same way as descri-

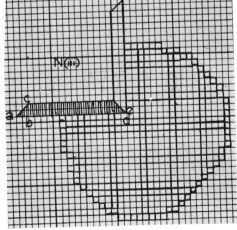

Figure 4.35

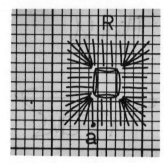

Figure 4.36

bed from (i) — (ii) for the large pomegrante.

    (iii) Using No. 5 cotton. Work the V-shaped satin stitch bands over 6 threads as in I. Work 43 stitches with the 22nd one in the centre below.

P. Double faggot over 6 threads.

Q. Blanket stitch star in the diamond-shaped spaces between the satin stitch stars in the border.

R. Closed mosaic stitch. See Fig. 4.36
Scale: One line equals one thread. Using No. 12 cotton commence at a and pull 4 upright stitches over 3 threads. Work a corner, similar to the corner of an eyelet, by placing 7 stitches together in the same hole on the inside, as shown on the diagram. Then work 3 more upright stitches over 3 threads. Make another corner, etc. Work four-sided stitch over 3 threads in the centre.

S. Greek cross filling. See Fig. 4.37
Use No. 12 cotton. Work this stitch always diagonally from the top left to the right below.

    (i) Bring the needle out at a and insert at b, diagonally over 3 threads from a. Bring the needle out in the centre at c, 3 threads to the right of b and pull through keeping the thread under the needle. Work 2 more blanket stitches d c and e c.

Figure 4.37

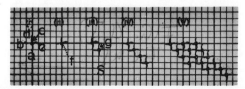

    (ii) Insert needle at c and bring it out at f, diagonally over 3 threads from a.

    (iii) Now work the second cross like the first, commencing at f at the bottom, as at a. Insert needle at a and bring it out in the centre at g, keeping the thread under the needle etc. Note that each cross is started at the bottom.

    (iv) Work the required number according to the diagram (in this case 3).

    (v) Turn the work so that the next row of stitches can be worked diagonally down from left to right. Complete the third row also.

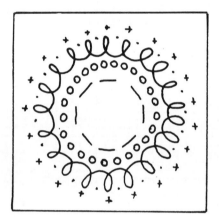

Figure 4.38

Further uses for this design
1. See Fig. 4.38
Use this design 4 times with a as centre for a cushion cover.
2. See Fig. 4.39
This part can be used in many ways:

    (i) It can be placed in the corner of a table- or tea-cloth.

    (ii) Using b as centre, work this part 4 times omitting the 2 small pomegrannets at the bottom, for a beautiful centre panel on a tablecloth. A filling can be worked in the diamond-shape formed in the centre.

3. See Fig. 4.40 and Fig. 4.41
Use this little sprig on luncheon-mats or on a

2 (ii)

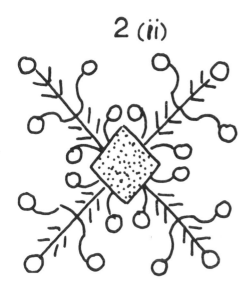

Figure 4.39

4

Figure 4.42

5

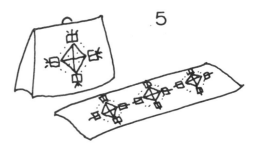

Figure 4.43

3

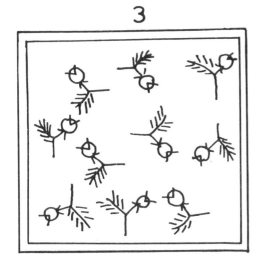

Figure 4.40

Figure 4.41

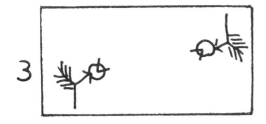

small tea cloth as an allover pattern. Finish off with an effective border at the hem.

4. See Fig. 4.42

Repeat this pomegranate in a border and connect with a line stitch e.g. four-sided stitch. Place it alternately to the top and to the bottom.

5. See Fig. 4.43 and Plate 4.9

Work this design 4 times on a tea cosy or a table-runner, using c as the centre.

4.4 A tablecloth in drawn fabric work
D 4.6 and D 4.7

Schematic diagram: See Fig. 4.44

Size: 225 cm by 127 cm or wider.

Scale of diagram: 25 mm equals 41 cm .

Scale of design: One square equals 3 threads.

Scale of Figures: One square equals 3 threads unless otherwise specified.

This design can also be used in many other ways and on many other articles, as will be indicated at the end of the paragraph.

Hints: Tack the linen in both directions in groups of 3 threads and make sure that the

PLATE 4.10
Section of a table-cloth in drawn fabric embroidery worked in light blue on ecru linen. Size: 127 cm x 127 cm. D: Author, M: Mrs. C. Tidmarsh

Figure 4.44

PLATE 4.11
Design D 4.7. Part of the border worked on linen with approximately 20 threads to 2½ cm

design is not too large for the material. See hint No. 12 in Par. 1.3. Find the centre of the material and work the centre panel first, then the border and lastly the hem. Allow 28 times 3 (84) threads between the star H at the end of the centre panel and the top Algerian eyelet B in the border for the latter to fit the material exactly.

Key to D 4.6
Scale: One square equals 3 threads unless otherwise specified.
A. Four-sided stitch. B. Algerian eyelets. C. Pulled lines. D. Double faggot over 6 threads. Work only one row as shown on the design. E. Now work one row of double faggot over 3 threads next to D as shown on the design. F. Diagonal raised band. G. Detached buttonhole bars. H. Star stitch, outlined. I. Satin stitch diamond. See Fig. 4.45.

(i) Using No. 5 cotton, bring the needle out at a. Keep all the stitches level at the top and work 3 satin stitches over 3 threads 3 over 6, then 7 over 9, 3 over 6 and 3 over 3.

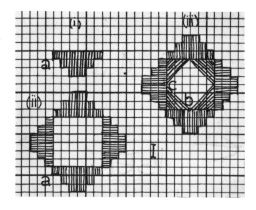

Figure 4.45

(ii) Complete the diamond-shape by working 3 more similar sections so that they meet in the same holes on the corners. In the centre will be 18 by 18 threads.

(iii) Now using No. 8 cotton, bring the needle out at b, at the centre stitch of the side and insert at c, the centre stitch of the adjoining side. (This stitch lies diagonally over 9 threads). Proceed towards the corner by working one

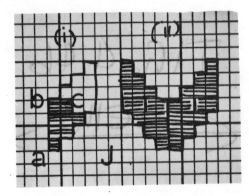

Figure 4.46

stitch diagonally over 8 threads, one over 7, 6, 5, 4, 3, 2 and one thread. Repeat in the other 3 corners. Now use No. 12 cotton to make a star in the centre and for the 2 rows of double faggot to surround it as shown on the design.

J. Satin stitch motif. See Fig. 4.46
Use No. 5 cotton.

(i) Bring the needle out at a, keep all the stitches level at the bottom and work 3 stitches over 3 threads, 3 over 6, 3 over 9 and 4 over 6. This will be position bc. The following 3 stitches are shorter at the bottom by 3 threads and longer at the top by 6 threads so that they lie over 9 threads. Keeping the stitches level at the top, work 3 over 6 and 3 over 3 and finally 4 over 6 right up against the previous group of 4 over 6 threads.

(ii) Work the second section as a mirror-image next to the first one.

K. Eyelet stitch filling. See Fig. 4.47
Scale: One line equals one thread, except in No. (vii) where one square equals 3 threads.
Use No. 12 cotton.

(i) — (v) Commence in the middle at a. Bind a b twice, b being 6 threads lower than and 2 threads to the right of a. Bind on the straight over 4 threads from b to c and then a c twice. Bind diagonally over 4 threads from b to c and then a c twice. Bind diagonally over 4 threads from d to c, twice. a d, which should now be bound is in the same position as a b. Repeat thus clockwise according to the letters on the diagram.

Figure 4.47

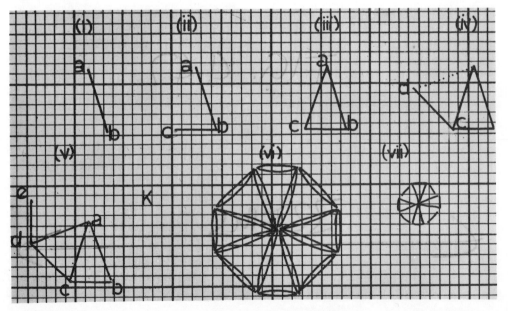

106

(vi) The completed stitch.

(vii) This shows how the stitch appears on the designs. Note that the stitches are each bound twice over 4 threads alternately on the straight and on the diagonal round the edge of little circles.

L. Pulled lines worked diagonally and on the straight of the material. See Fig. 4.48

Use No. 12 cotton and remember that there will be one more stitch than the number of threads that have to be covered. Work every stitch one thread to the right or to the left so as to bring the lines together, e.g. as from a to b. At the end the last 2 stitches of every row are worked over 2 and one thread.

M. Satin stitch around the square in the centre. See Fig. 4.49

Use No. 5 cotton and proceed as follows: Keeping all the stitches level at the bottom, work 3 stitches over 3 threads (3 stitches over 6, 9 over 9, 3 over 6 and 6 over 3) four times. There will however be 7 stitches over 3 threads in the centre instead of 6 and the last stitches will be only 3 over 3 instead of 6 over 3.

N. Basket stitch filling.

O. Satin stitch. See Fig. 4.50

Use No. 5 cotton and work groups of 3 stitches over 6 threads, each 3 threads higher than the previous group. Work 7 stitches in the centre at the top.

P. Window eyelets. See Fig. 4.51

Figure 4.48

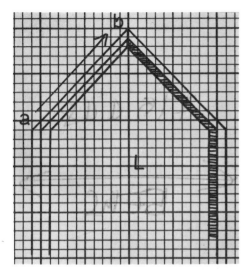

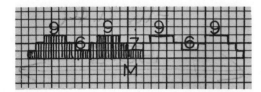

Figure 4.49

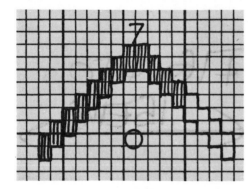

Figure 4.50

Scale: One line equals one thread.

1. (i) Using No. 12 cotton, commence at a and work a corner as for an eyelet, over 2 threads with b as centre, up to f.

(ii) Now bring the needle out at g, 2 threads from f, and work g h, an upright stitch over 2 threads just like a b. Work a second corner so that 2 threads in the centre of this side are isolated.

(iii) Work a third corner and side so that 2 threads are isolated again and

(iv) after completion of the fourth side, 2 threads will form a cross in the middle of the eyelet.

2. (i) — (iii) The larger window eyelet is similar to the first one except that a b lies over 3 threads and the whole eyelet covers 7 by 7 threads instead of 6 by 6. The stitch g h is worked only one thread away from f b so that only a single cross is formed in the centre of the eyelet.

Use the smaller window eyelet for this design.
Fillings for the squares in the centre:

Figure 4.51

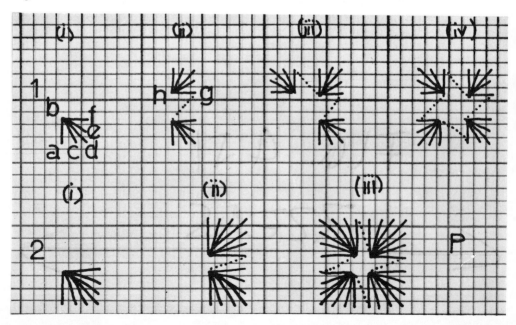

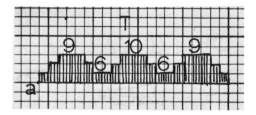

Figure 4.52

Q. Brick stitch. R. Eight-sided stitch. S. Tile stitch.

D 4.7

See Plate 4.11
Key to D 4.7:
A. Four-sided stitch. B. Algerian eyelets. C. Pulled lines. D. Double faggot over 6 threads. E. Double faggot over 3 threads. F. Diagonal raised band. G. Detached buttonhole bars. H. Outlined star stitch. I. Satin stitch diamond. (See D 4.6 I). J. Satin stitch motif. (See D 4.6 J). K. Eyelet stitch filling. L. Pulled lines on the straight and on the diagonal. (See D 4.6 L). T. Satin stitch in the border section. See Fig. 4.52

Use No. 5 cotton and keep all the stitches level at the bottom. Bring the needle out at a and work 3 upright satin stitches over 3 threads. Then work (3 stitches over 6 threads,

Figure 4.53

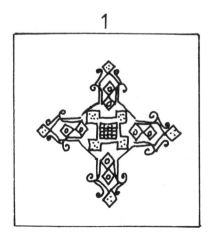

9 over 9, 3 over 6, 6 over 3) three times, except that in the centre 10 stitches are worked instead of 9 over 9 threads, and the last stitches are over 3 threads instead of over 6.

U. Eyelets

Further uses for this design
1. See Fig. 4.53
Flace this part four times around R for a very beautiful motif in the centre of a tea cloth.

Figure 4.54

2. See Fig. 4.54
This is most appropriate for a tea cosy or a chair back. Place motif I on either side for balance.

3. See Fig. 4.55
Repeat this part for a border on a tea cloth and work different fillings in each square.

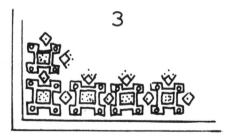

Figure 4.55

4. See Fig. 4.56
Repeat this part for a border on a tray cloth or luncheon-set.

Figure 4.56

5. See Fig. 4.57
Extend the double faggot over 6 threads and
the diagonal raised band so that the 2 sides
meet in a point at the bottom and repeat the
design four times around that point for a cushion cover.

4.5 A table-cloth in drawn fabric work

D 4.8, D 4.9 and D 4.10
Schematic diagram: See Fig. 4.58
Size: 225 cm by 127 cm or wider.
Scale of diagram: 25 mm equals 30 cm .
Scale of design: One square equals 3 threads.
Scale of figures: One square equals 3 threads

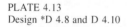

Figure 4.57

unless otherwise specified.

This design has many possibilities as indicated at the end of the paragraph. With a little
imagination it can inspire an enterprising embroideress to use it in many other ways.
See Plate 4.13 and Plate 4.14

PLATE 4.13
Design *D 4.8 and D 4.10

Figure 4.58

Key:

A. Four-sided stitch. B. Algerian eyelets. C. Eyelets.

D. Star with blanket stitch centre.

E. Star with blanket stitch centre, outlined with double faggot.

F. Snowdrops. See Fig. 4.59

   (i) Use No. 5 cotton and work 14 satin stitches over 6 threads in a V-shape so that each stitch is one thread higher or lower than the previous one. Stitches 7 and 8 lie over 9 threads and are worked into the same holes. Note that some of the snowdrops are worked without this long double stitch.

   (ii) Use No. 12 cotton and work the remainder of the motif in double faggot as indicated in (ii), (iii) and (iv).

   (v) This is the completed snowdrop.

G. Diagonal raised Band.

H. Diamond-shaped satin stitch leaves. See also Par. 4.3K.

I. Satin stitch blossoms. See Fig. 4.60

Use No. 5 cotton.

   (i) Commencing at a, work a satin stitch over 3, over 5, 7 and over 9 threads so

PLATE 4.14
Design D 4.9

Figure 4.59

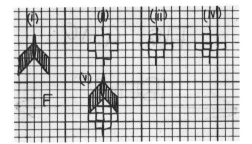

111

D 4.10

that each one is one thread longer at the top and bottom.

(ii) Keep the following 5 stitches level with the last one at the bottom but work them only over 4 threads. This is position b. Pass the needle through the back of these 5 stitches, bring it on the right side again and work another 5 stitches threads one thread away from the previous 5.

(iii) Complete the leaf with another stitch over 9 threads, one over 7, over 5 and over 3 threads.

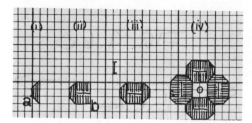

Figure 4.60

(iv) Complete the other 3 sections of the blossom in the same way so that they meet in the same holes on the sides.

PLATE 4.15
A tea-cloth in drawn fabric embroidery, with ecru cotton on cream linen. The free design is very suitable for the fillings. D: Author, M: Mrs. Runa Goldblatt

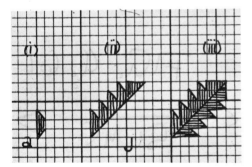

Figure 4.61

Using No. 12 cotton, work an eyelet over 6 threads in the centre.
J. Satin stitch oak leaves on the diagonal. See Fig. 4.61
Use No. 5 cotton.
(i) Commence at a and work 3 satin stitches: One over 9, one over 7 and one over 5 threads so that each is one thread shorter than the previous one at the top and bottom.
(ii) The following stitches again lie over 9,7 and over 5 threads. Work 4 similar points. The following 6 stitches are all level at the top and lie over 6, 5, 4, 3, 2 and one thread.

(iii) Pass the needle through the back of these stitches up to a, and there bring it to the right side of the work. Repeat the whole process in the opposite direction as shown on the diagram. The stitches meet in the same holes in the centre of the leaf.
K. Satin stitch oak leaves worked on the straight. See Fig. 4.62.
Use No. 5 cotton.
(i) Bring the needle out one thread to the

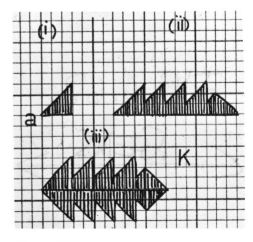

Figure 4.62

113

PLATE 4.16
A table-cloth in drawn fabric embroidery. Material: evenly woven linen with approximately 20 threads to 2½ cm. D: Author, M: Mrs. R. Pienaar

right of position a on the material and, keeping all the stitches level at the bottom, work from over one thread to over 9 threads to make a point.

(ii) The following 6 stitches lie from over 4 to over 9 threads. Make 4 similar points. Work the next point only up to the stitch which lies over 6 threads and then shorten the stitches till the last one is over one thread.

(iii) Pass the needle through the back of the satin stitches and bring it out in the same hole as the first stitch. Work the opposite side in the same way, but reversed. The leaf is one thread shorter on both sides than is indicated on the diagram.

L. The sunflower. See Fig. 4.63
Use No. 5 cotton.

(i) Commencing at a, keep all the stitches level at the top and work from over 9 to over one thread.

(ii) Skip 2 threads and work a mirror-image of the preceding stitches.

(iii) Work the other 3 sides in the same way so that the stitches over 9 threads meet

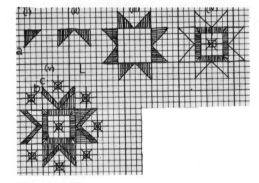

Figure 4.63

in the same hole on the corners. There will be a square of 18 by 18 threads in the sentre.

(iv) Using No. 12 cotton, work a pulled line around the centre square and fill in with a star with a blanket stitch centre.

(v) Again using No. 12 cotton, bring the needle out at b and insert 3 threads higher at c. Now pull 10 stitches over 3 threads along the edge of the satin stitch to the centre below and work another 9 stitches to the top, on all 4 sides. Work another 8 stars with blan-

1

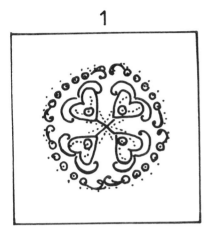

Figure 4.64

2

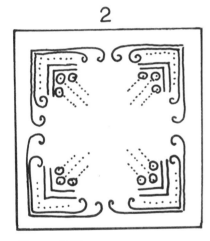

Figure 4.65

5

Figure 4.66

6

Figure 4.67

Figure 4.68

ket stitchcentres in the positions indi-
cated on the design.
M. Detached buttonhole bars. N. See filling
No. 58 in Par. 3.3

Further uses for this design
1. See Fig. 4.64
Use this part on a cushion-cover with a as
centre, or 1 and 4 twice with b as centre.
2. See Fig. 4.65 and Plate 4.14
This makes a most effective corner on a tea
cloth.
3. Place this little sprig at random on a tea
cloth or a tablecloth.

4. See 1
5. See Fig. 4.66
Repetition of this motif will result in a very
rich border for a tea cloth. Or what about only
one motif on a coffee cosy?
6. See Fig. 4.67
Suitable for chair-backs with the wide side at
the bottom.
7. This will be a pretty sprig to place at random on a cloth or on a serviette when a few
extra small flowers are added.
8. See Fig. 4.68
Use this small sprig on the serviettes or on
serviette-bags.

115

Many kinds of embroidery can be classified under whitework some differing entirely in technique and character, others are closely related. Beautiful museum pieces date as far back as the 15th century. When examined closely most examples of white work will be found typical of certain countries at certain times. Enterprising embroideresses through the ages, however, have left their own individual imprint on their work and in this way the character of whitework has changed and has even become more interesting. Especially beautiful work results when the different techniques are used together on one article.

Whitework

Classification

The following kinds of embroidery can be classified under whitework:

1. Swiss embroidery.
2. Irish Mountmellick work.
3. Broderie anglaise
4. Cutwork (1) Simple cutwork.
   (2) Renaissance cutwork.
   (3) Richelieu embroidery.
   (4) Venetian cutwork.
   (5) Reticella lace.
   (6) Hedebo work (Danish)
5. Hand-made lace.
6. Bullion work.
7. Shadow work.
8. Old Hedebo work.

5.1 Swiss embroidery

In spite of the name, this type of embroidery is not confined to Switzerland, but is also done in Italy and other countries, and developed out of broderie anglais. It consists mainly of raised satin stitch, blanket stitch, snail's trail, eyelets-holes, a little cut work filled with lacy rosettes, a little shadow work and also a few fillings like seed stitch and punching. A few drawn thread fillings also, were often used. The material used, is a fine, pure and almost transparent linen cambric, Swiss organdie or muslin.

Broder Spécial in Nos. 25 and 30 is the correct thread to use, but as it is unavailable, use No. 8 and No. 12 pearl cotton and one thread of stranded cotton. Use No. 9 and No. 10 crewel needles. As this type of work is very fine and dainty, the designs are usually very delicate and often taken from Nature. However, any subject may be used, e.g. figures, animals or even abstract ideas. Special carbon-paper, obtainable from most large shops, is used to transfer the design on to textiles in the following way: Lay the carbon-paper between the material and the design and use a knitting-needle to trace carefully over all the lines of the design.

Plate 5.1 shows the corner of a handkerchief in Swiss embroidery.

Plate 6.1 shows a variation with a more modern application.

The different stitches used
1. Raised satin stitch.
This is a technique that requires much skill and practice to perfect. The success of raised satin stitch depends very much on whether the basic layer or padding has been worked correctly. Various methods may be used and the worker should try them out and choose the one she finds easiest. It is always worked on a frame; 2 strands of stranded cotton are used. Commence by tacking along the outline in small stitches or in backstitch and then fill in the area with longer running stitches so that the maximum part of each stitch lies on the surface.

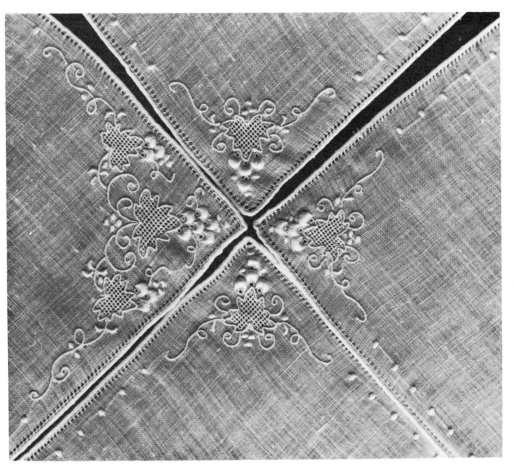

PLATE 5.1
A typical example of Swiss embroidery. Mainly padded eyelet holes, raised satin stitch, snails' trail and punching were used. Origin: Switzerland.

Work a few extra layers in the centre for extra padding.

These padding stitches must be worked just inside the outline and in the opposite direction to the satin stitches. Another method is to use Roumanian stitch (See Fig. 5.1) for the padding.

Bring the needle out at a, 1/3 of the distance from the top of the leaf. Work a small stitch at the top and one on either side of a. Insert the needle just below the top stitch to the right on the outline and bring it out on the left on the outline. Work another little stitch just below a. Repeat until the whole shape has been filled

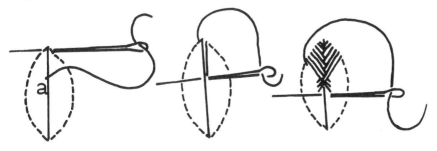

Figure 5.1

117

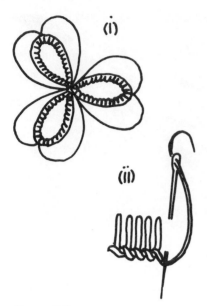

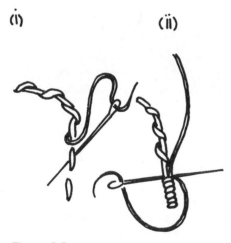

Figure 5.2

Figure 5.3

2. Buttonhole stitch. See Fig. 5.2

Use No. 8 or 12 pearl cotton. This stitch is sometimes worked over the padding instead of satin stitch. Often a narrow row of buttonhole stitches is worked just on the inside of the satin stitches as in Fig. 5.2 (i). Proceed as follows when a small space like the inside of a flower has to be cut open: Tack along the outline of the area and then work a narrow row of buttonhole stitches over the tacking, with the loops towards the side that has to be cut. Fig. 5.2 (ii) shows clearly how this stitch is worked:

PLATE 5.2
A beautiful linen cambric handkerchief, richly embroidered, mainly in shadow work. Seed stitch and punching used as fillings. Origin: Italy

in. The leaf will automatically be padded higher in the centre. Using No. 8 pearl cotton, work the satin stitches right up against the outside of the outline-stitches and perpendicular to the outline. Only when worked without padding, is it allowed that the satin stitches lie diagonally across a shape. A very straight outline and even tension of all the stitches will give the work a professional look, and this is attained only by practice.

3. Snail's trail. See Fig. 5.3

Use one thread of stranded cotton and work without a frame. This stitch is very characteristic of fine white work and is mostly found in Swiss work and broderie anglaise. Use it for slender stems and other lines in a design.

(i) Work a row of small running stitches on the line by picking up as little as possible of the material. Return to the starting point by overcasting every running stitch. The thread is not cut off, but laid on the line as a guiding thread and it will remain loose underneath the stitches to be worked over it.

(ii) Commence with a new thread by tacking the end for a short distance along the same line, and work small upright satin stitches over this base and pick up as little of the material as possible. This is to ensure a raised result. The guiding thread must be lifted and pulled every now and then to get the tension even and to pull the stitches right up against one another. Be careful, however, not to pull too tightly. Cut the guiding thread off short after the last stitch has been made and finish off on the wrong side.

4. Eyelet-holes. See Fig. 5.4

Eyelet-holes appear in almost all examples of white work, and can be made in all sizes, some very small, according to the material. Use No. 12 or one thread of stranded cotton and a stiletto, which is a sharp instrument used to make holes in the material and which is obtainable at all large shops. Work without a frame.

(i) Work a row of very small running stitches on the outline of the eyelet-hole and then pierce the hole with the stiletto from the right side of the work. The stiletto will open up the hole as far as the tacking threads. Place a short guiding thread on the running stitches and overcast these stitches and guiding thread with small firm stitches, completing nearly the whole circle. It will be necessary to open the hole now and then with the stiletto. The last 3 stitches are not pulled tight until the needle has been passed through these 3 loops and through the hole to the wrong side of the work. Then the stitches are pulled tight — first the middle one, so that the first is tight, then the last loop and finally the working threads, so that the last stitch is secure. Cut both treads off short.

(ii) This shows the completed eyelet-hole. Now pierce the hole with the stiletto from the wrong side so that the eyelet is finally opened and rounded.

5. Seed stitch.

Some areas, e.g. half a leaf, are often filled in with seed stitch. It consists of tiny backstitches worked in all directions so that the stitches seem to have been strewn at random.

6. Punching as a filling. See Fig. 5.5

Use D.M.C. Brillanté D'Alsace No. 30 and a tapestry needle, No. 26. Work this stitch diagonally as follows:

(i) Commencing at a, insert the needle a little higher up at b and emerge at c. Pull tightly, a b and c a are the same length and form 2 sides of a square.

(ii) Insert again at a and emerge at d. d c and c a are the same length. Pull tight.

(iii) Insert at c and emerge at e, pull tight, etc.

Figure 5.4

(I)

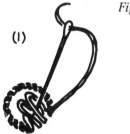

(ii)

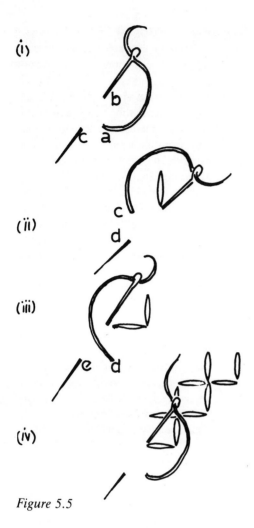

(i)

b

c a

(ii)

c

d

(iii)

e d

(iv)

Figure 5.5

Figure 5.6

(iv) The rows lie in juxtaposition in the same holes and this form squares with holes on the corners.

7. Round cutwork holes. See Fig. 5.6
The open spaces are mostly filled with lacy spider webs and are used very widely in Swiss embroidery.

Use No. 12 pearl cotton and work a row of running stitches around the opening. This is covered with a row of small, firm buttonhole stitches with the loops on the inside. Cut out the centre right up against these buttonhole stitches. Using a very fine thread, work loose buttonhole stitches in about every 4th stitch. Insert the needle into the first loop and over-

cast every loop. Pull fairly tight so that a firm circle is formed. Carry a single thread across the centre of the open space and overcast once over this thread. Then another stitch from the centre and overcast again once. Repeat until 8 bars have been made and weave around the centre a few times to secure them firmly. Overcast over the single bar, pass the needle through one of the loose buttonhole stitches to the wrong side and finish off into the outline. These spider webs are usually worked in the centre of raised satin stitch as they form a striking contrast.

Naturally there are many other fillings for these open spaces and an enterprising embroideress will experiment and design her own fillings. Notice the variety found on Swiss handkerchiefs!

Many exotic examples of white work embroidery are to be found in museums and private collections. Often so many fillings are worked in the open spaces between the satin stitchery that it really resembles lace.

5.2 Mountmellick work

The origin is Irish and it is not as fine as most white work. It does not include any openwork, it does not take long to work and it launders well and is durable. Therefore the work is practical for household articles like table-and bed-linen, childrens clothes blouses etc. A variety of surface stitches is used and

120

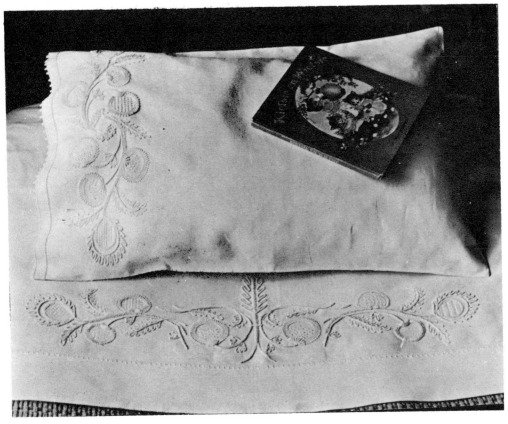

PLATE 5.3
Design D 5.1 and *D 5.2. Mountmellick work on a sheet and pillowcase set in pale blue

the original work was always done in white on white material. It can be done on any closely woven and reasonably smooth material of heavy quality. Irish linen is always a good choice. Use Pearl Cotton No. 8 and No. 5. The old designs were often composed of berries, fruit and flowers, but today one finds a great variety of designs, even abstract ones.

Use carbon paper to transfer the design on to the material. (See Par. 5.1).

Stitches that can be used
Although a multitude of stitches exist, some very old and very popular and some less well-known but just as beautiful, only a few handy and pretty ones will be dealt with here.

Figure 5.7

1. Narrow line stitches.
    (a) Coral stitch. See Fig. 5.7
The diagram shows clearly how this stitch is

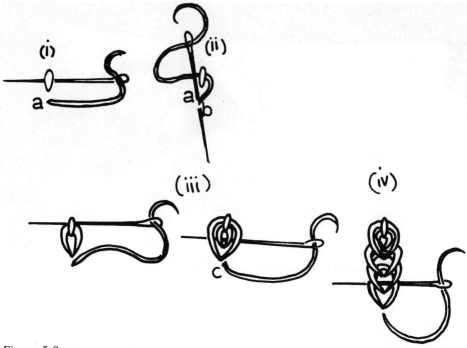

Figure 5.8

worked. Work a small diagonal stitch underneath the line of the design. Then twist the thread over and under the needle and pull it through to form a little picot. These picots can be spaced far apart or very close together, depending on the effect desired.

    (b) Chain stitch.
    (c) Heavy chain stitch. See Fig. 5.8
  (i) Commencing with a small straight stitch, bring the needle out a little lower down at a. Pass the needle underneath this stitch and
 (ii) in again at a and out at b, a little lower down.
(iii) Pass the needle underneath the first stitch for the second time, in at b again and out a little lower down at c.
(iv) Now pass the needle underneath the 2 chain stitches only, in at c again and out a little lower down, again underneath the last two chain stitches and repeat.
    (d) Portuguese stem stitch.
    (e) Double knot stitch.

    (f) Whipped chain stitch. Work a row of ordinary chain stitch and then overcast over each one without going through the material.

2.   Wider line stitches.
    (g) Zigzag coral stitch. See Fig. 5.9
Bring the needle out at a, insert at b and emerge about 3 mm lower down at c. Twist the thread over and under the needle as shown on the diagram and pull it through. Now insert

Figure 5.9

122

to the right at d so that d and c lie in a line and emerge 3 mm lower at e. Twist thread over and under the needle and pull it through. Repeat this once to the right and once to the left, etc.

(h) Double blanket stitch. See Fig. 5.10 Two rows of blanket stitch overlapping make

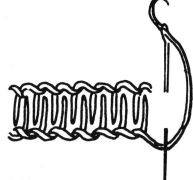

Figure 5.10

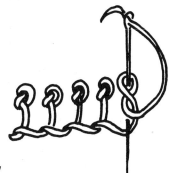

Figure 5.11

a beautiful corded edge for a wide outline. This is notably found in Hungarian embroidery.

(i) Blanket stitch with picots. See Fig. 5.11
This consists of ordinary blanket stitch but the thread is twisted around the needle once, as shown on the diagram, before it is inserted in the material.

(j) Raised chain band. See Fig. 5.12
(i) This stitch is worked in 2 stages. First work horizontal stitches of the same size parallel to each other and about 3 mm apart.

(i)   (ii)

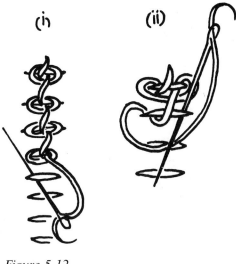

Figure 5.12

(ii) Now work twice over each bar as shown on the diagram.

(k) Feather stitch. See Fig. 5.13
(i) Work an even row of feather stitch as on the diagram.

(i)   (ii)

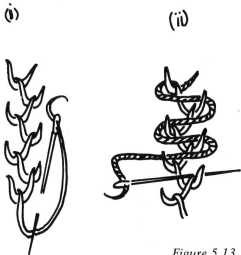

Figure 5.13

123

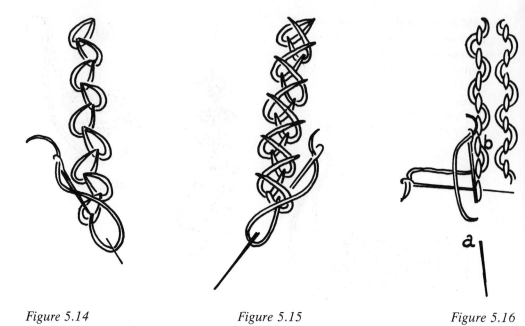

Figure 5.14   *Figure 5.15*   *Figure 5.16*

(ii) Then a thread of the same or contrasting colour can be used to interlace the
  feather stitch. See diagram.

(l) Zigzag chain stitch. See Fig. 5.14
The method for working this stitch is clearly
shown on the diagram.

(m) Plaited chain stitch. See Fig. 5.15
The diagram clearly illustrates the method of
working this stitch. It is similar to ordinary
zigzag chain except that the needle is inserted
on the outside of the loop instead of the inside.

(n) Pekinese stitch. See Fig. 5.16
Work small backstitches as the needle indicates at a. Interlace to and fro underneath the
stitches as on the diagram at b.

(o) Cretan stitch. See Fig. 5.17
Here the stitch is used on a leaf shape, but it
can also be used just as well as a line stitch.
(i) Work one ordinary chain stitch at the
  top end of the leaf.
(ii) Insert needle a little lower down and to
  the right on the outline and emerge in
  the centre of the leaf just below the

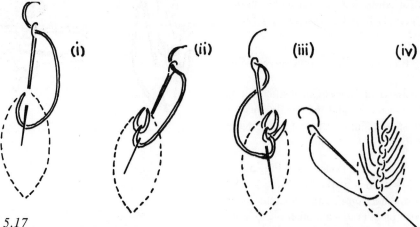

Figure 5.17

chain stitch, with the thread under the needle.

(iii) Repeat on the left side and proceed in this way once to the left and then to the right until the leaf has been filled and a plaited vein formed down the centre.

Figure 5.19

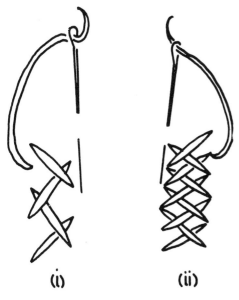

(i)   (ii)

Figure 5.18

(p) Roumanian stitch.
(q) Herringbone stitch. See Fig. 5.18 and Fig. 5.23

The method for this stitch can easily be followed on the diagram.

(i) Note that the one stitch begins at the bottom in a line with the top of the previous stitch and that the spaces between the stitches are just as large as the section of material picked up. Interlace with another thread to decorate it further if desired. See Fig. 5.13

(ii) Here the stitches are worked in juxtaposition to acquire a more solid effect. See Par. 5.7 on shadow work.

(r) Raised stem band. See Fig. 5.19

This stitch is worked in 2 stages. Parallel stitches are first worked about an 3 mm apart. The size of the stitches depends on the desired width of the band, e.g. 6 mm . Then work rows of ordinary stem stitch over the bars only until the latter has been covered completely.

Figure 5.20

(i)

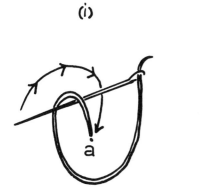

a

(ii)

(iii)

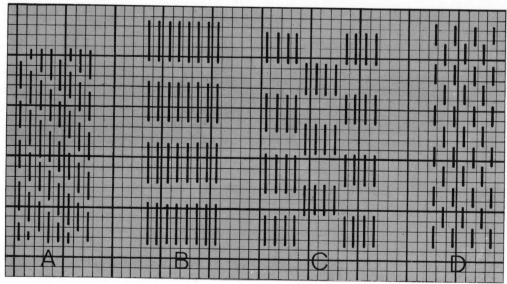

Figure 5.21

3. Effective fillings for open areas.
   (1) Seed stitch. See Par. 5.1 No. 5
   (2) Picots, or Frencn knots. See Fig. 5.20.
   (i) Bring the needle out at a. Keep the thread taut with the left hand and perpendicular to the material. Twist the needle around the thread and bring the point round to a.
   (ii) Insert into the material just a fraction away from a. First pull the thread taut around the needle before taking it to the wrong side.
   (iii) The completed picot.
   Scatter these picots all over for a filling.

   (3) Detached chain stitch.
   Work individual little chain stitches scattered evenly in all directions to form an allover pattern.
   (4) Surface darning.
   Weave according to the thread of the material to a definite plan so that different woven patterns develop. The following are a few examples: See Fig. 5.21
   A. Darn straight over 3 and under one thread of the material. The succeeding rows are clearly indicated on the diagram.

Figure 5.22

Figure 5.23

B. Darn over 4 and under 2 threads throughout.

C. Darn over 3 and under 3 threads and then 4 rows over the alternate threads to form squares.

D. Darn alternate rows over 2 and under 2 threads. An imaginative embroideress will experiment with many different patterns and design innumerable other fillings.

4. Convenient fillings for small motifs like leaflets.
   (1) Cretan stitch.
   (2) Roumanian stitch.
   (3) Buttonhole stitch with picots. See Fig. 5.22

126

Work these close together from the centre vein so that they radiate towards the outer edge.

(4) Herringbone stitch. See Fig. 5.23 The diagram shows clearly how to fit the stitch into the design.

5. Handy stitches with which to secure a hem.

Fold the hems of the material e.g. luncheon-mats to the right side and secure with one of the following stitches.

(1) Zigzag coral stitch.
(2) Double blanket stitch — work one

A sheet and pillow-case in Mountmellick work.
D 5.1 and D 5.2

See Plate 5.3 for the completed articles and Par. 1.3 No. 15 for the method of transfering the design onto the material. The key to the stitches is indicated on the design. Other stitches used here are buttonhole stitch and backstitch wheels.

5.3 Broderie anglaise

This is a very old and well-known type of embroidery. Our ancestors used it to adorn their underclothing, table- and bed-linen and

PLATE 5.4
Mountmellick work in bright colours on luncheon-mats. D: Author, M: Mrs. Cupie Wessels

row on the hem and one just below the hem.

(3) Blanket stitch with picots. Work the picots on the hem and the loops below the hem.

(4) Raised chain band. Work the horizontal stitches of the first stage on and just over the side of the hem.

(5) Feather stitch.

children's clothes richly. Today we find machine-made variations on strips of material sold by the yard and on ready-made dresses and blouses. The machine- made product is so successful and working it by hand so time-consuming, that it is now seldom done.

Any fine white Irish linen, cotton or cambric is suitable. Broder Spécial in Nos. 25 and 30 is the correct thread to use, but as it is unavaila-

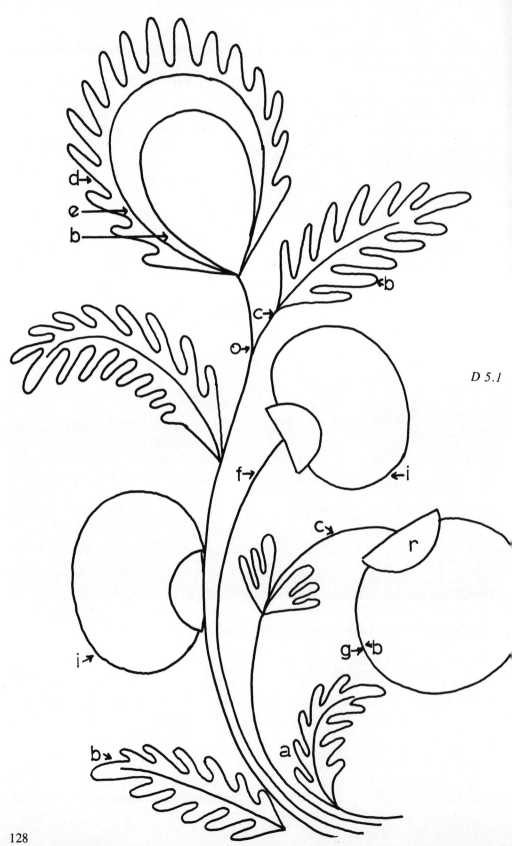

D 5.1

ble, use No. 8 and No. 12 pearl cotton and one thread of stranded cotton, and Crewel needles Nos. 9 and 10.

The designs consist almost entirely of eyelet-holes of different shapes and sizes and arranged in rows or groups to form flowers, sprigs, flowing lines, etc. Carbon-paper is used to transfer the design onto the material. See Par. 5.1.

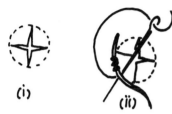

(i)

(ii)

Figure 5.24

Stitches
1. Eyelet-holes.
   (1) Ordinary eyelet-holes made by using a stiletto. See Par. 5.1 No. 4.
   (2) Larger round eyelet-holes. See Fig. 5.24

When the eyelet-holes are too large for the stiletto, they are cut out as follows:
   (i) First work running stitch once round the outline, and then cut from the centre to the running stitches on the straight of the fabric. Turn the 4 sections of the material thus formed to the back with a needle.
   (ii) Use a guiding-thread and with small stitches overcast firmly over the guiding-thread, running stitch and the double material. See Par. 5.1 No. 4 for the method of finishing off. Finally cut away the extra material on the wrong side.

Figure 5.25

(3) Shaded oval eyelets-holes. See Fig. 5.25

The method is exactly the same as described in (2).

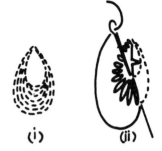

Figure 5.26   (i)   (ii)

(4) Padded eyelet-holes. See Fig. 5.26 To obtain a richer effect, padded satin stitch is often used round part of the eyelet, in which case the stitches will be longer and thus change from overcasting to satin stitch.
   (i) Work a row of running stitch on the inside and the outside of the eyelet and fill the space between the rows with small running stitches which will form the padding.
   (ii) Cut open and overcast over a guiding-thread at the narrow edge and work satin stitches over the wider edge. The tension of the stitches will naturally be less taut when working the satin stitches.

These are the most commonly used eyelet-holes but a great variety of others can be found in old specimens.

2. Padded satin stitch. See Par. 5.1 No. 1. Spots of padded satin stitch are frequently used. Outline with running stitches, pad with satin stitch worked in one direction and then a final layer of satin stitch in the other direction so that the padding stitches are completely covered.

3. Snail's trail. See Par. 5.1 No. 3. This is used for all the fine lines in the design, e.g. for stems.

4. Buttonhole stitch. See Par. 5.1 No. 2. This is used for the scalloped edges with which the

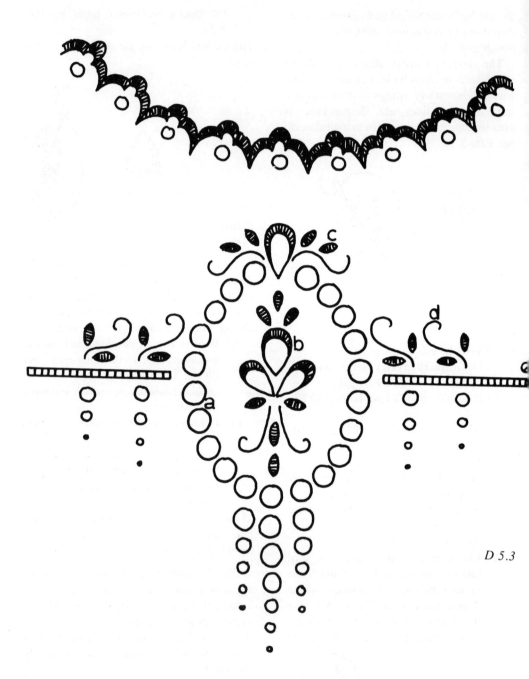

D 5.3

PLATE 5.5
Design D 5.3. Broderie Anglaise on a blouse

work is traditionally finished off. See Fig. 5.27.

Work 2 rows of running stitch just on the inside of the 2 lines of the scallops first and then pad the space in between with running stitches or chain stitch. This is covered with buttonhole stitch with the loops to the outside. Cut away the surplus material close to the loops.

Small amounts of drawn thread work can be added successfully as in the case of the blouse on Plate 5.5.

Broderie anglaise around the neck of a blouse.
D 5.3
See Plate 5.5
Key: a. Eyelet-holes. b. Padded shaded oval eyelet-holes. c. Padded satin stitch. d. Snail's trail. e. Hemstitching. f. Scalloped edge in buttonhole stitch.

Figure 5.27

5.4 Cutwork

(1) Simple cutwork

Although this type of embroidery was very popular in the past, it is seldom done today. A possible explanation is that the designs with so many large open spaces are not hardwearing enough for a washing-machine or the sharp point of an iron.

The work consists of shapes outlined with running stitches over which flat buttonhole stitches of very even size and tension are worked. The design is planned so that small spaces remain open between these shapes where the material is then cut away. An unsatisfactory design will appear unbalanced after these spaces have been cut away and if these spaces are too large, it will be unpractical. The design is usually transferred onto the material in double lines and by means of carbon-paper specially made for textiles and obtainable from most large shops. Use Irish linen. Broder Spécial in Nos. 25 and 30 is the correct thread to use, but as it is unavailable, use No. 8 and No. 12 pearl cotton and one thread of stranded cotton and Crewel needles Nos. 9 and 10 for all kinds of cutwork.

(2) Renaissance cutwork

This is a continuation of simple cutwork, but here bars are worked across the cut space to strengthen and embellish the work. See Fig. 5.28.

These bars are buttonholed or overcast. In the case of buttonhole stitch it is very important that the loops should all lie in the same direction. All bars are carried across and covered with buttonhole stitching simultane-

Figure 5.28

ously with the execution of the running stitch on all the outlines. Take care that a bar is not attached to the material only, but also to a row of running stitch already worked, for extra firmness. Carry a thread 3 times across a space and overcast or cover with buttonhole stitch back to the starting point.

(3) Richelieu work

This type of embroidery is also closely related to the 2 kinds previously described, but the bars are further enriched by the addition of different kinds of picots and bullions. It strikes one how much more beautiful and lacy a piece of work with these enriched bars, appears. There are especially 3 kinds of bullions that can be used.

(a) Picots. This first and smallest one is exactly like the one described in Par. 5.2. Naturally here the needle is not inserted into the material, but into the loop of the last buttonhole stitch.

(b) Bullion picots. See Fig. 5.29. These are slightly larger than picots and are made as follows:

   (i) Insert the needle in the loop of the last buttonhole stitch, put the thread under the needle and pull it through the loop but not too tightly.

  (ii) Hold the loop between the thumb and forefinger of the left hand. Place the needle under the loop and twist the right half of the loop twice around the needle. Pull the needle through but nog tight.

 (iii) Now it is very important that the loop should be pulled tighter very slowly and must often be straightened and opened with the left forefinger and thumb. Only when the picot is about 3 mm away from the bar, may it be pulled very tight.

 (iv) Now pass the needle from below back into the loop of the last stitch of the bar and

  (v) complete the latter in the usual way. More than one picot can be worked on a long bar.

(c) Ring bullion picots. See Fig. 5.30. This is the largest of the 3 and is worked as follows:

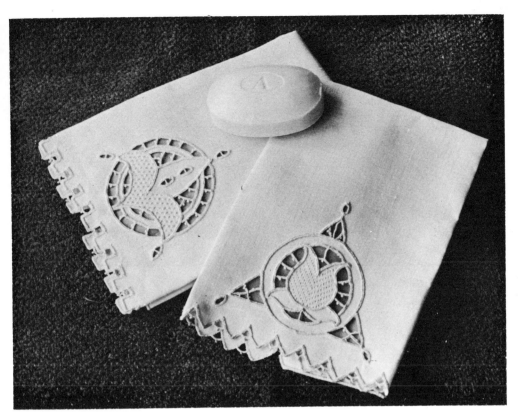

PLATE 5.6
Designs *D 5.4, and *D 5.5. Two guest towels in Venetian cutwork

Note that a needle with a small eye must be used for making these bullions.

(i) Insert the needle into the loop of the last stitch but do not pull it through. Twist the thread from 16 to 18 times round the needle from right to left. Put the left thumb on the needle and pull the latter through carefully.

(ii) Pull very tight so that the picot forms a little closed ring.

(iii) Pass the needle from below back into the loop of the last stitch on the bar, which completes the ring bullion picot.

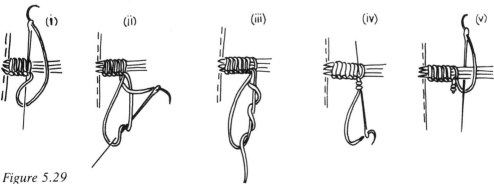

Figure 5.29

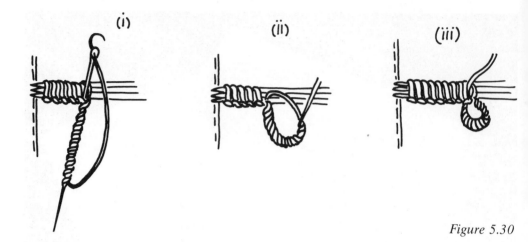

Figure 5.30

(4) *Venetian cutwork*

This is a combination of the 3 previous kinds of cutwork, but it is further enriched by adorning the material shapes lying against the cut background, beautifully with satin stitch, seed stitch, punching or French knots.

Two guest towels in Venetian cutwork
D 5.4 and D 5.5
See Plate 5.6.
Follow the instructions given in (1), (2), (3) and (4).

PLATE 5.7
Section of a tea-cloth richly embroidered in Reticella lace. M: Mrs. Hetta Stegmann

(5) *Reticella lace*

Much of this kind of work is still being done today especially in the south of Italy. Some pieces are very richly decorated, but even the simpler examples are striking and also durable. The simplest form of Reticella lace consists of a cut out square of linen about 3½ cm or 5 cm . The edges are closely overcast to prevent fraying and in this process bars are carried from the middle of each side to the opposite side and also from corner to corner. On this network of bars a few pyramids and/or loops are worked in buttonhole stitch to fill it further. These loose squares were later joined and so larger cut areas developed, still geometrical in shape, but the earlier division between the squares is now replaced by woven bars.

Few people today have time to make lace, but on a small scale squares of Reticella lace can be used on table-linen with great success because it is not particularly time-consuming. Even only a few squares on an article combined with some lines of double hemstitching will give an elegant effect. See Plate 5.8. Beautiful tea cloths, tea cosies, serviette-bags, tablecloths, serviettes, traycloths etc, can all be decorated in this way.

Use a good quality closely woven Irish linen in white, ecru, or ivory and No. 12 Pearl cotton as near to the colour of the material as possible. Originally only a linen thread was used. A piece of drafting linen on which to draw the design will also be needed. If unobtainable, use a piece of firm drawing paper. A clever embroideress could even fill in the squares without the lines of a design. Use No. 9 Crewel and No. 26 tapestry needles.

There are actually 3 methods for making the squares. One method is similar to the one for Venetian lace and will not be discussed here. The other 2 methods are as follows:

PLATE 5.8
Squares of Reticella lace joined by lines of double hemstitching on a tray-cloth. Origin: Italy

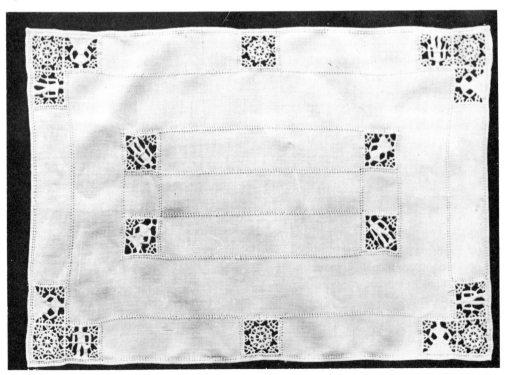

here. The other 2 methods are as follows: Method no. 1.

If the linen is very fine and does not fray easily, proceed as follows: Mark the 4 corners of the proposed square very lightly with a pencil on the linen. Use a Crewel needle and tack from corner to corner on the straight thread of the material. Now cut from the centre of the square to each corner and fold back the 4 pieces of material on the line of the tacking thread. Keep these 4 loose pieces in position by tacking them down. Commence in one corner and work small buttonhole stitches over the folded edge from left to right and so that the loops lie towards the open space. The corners must be worked very neatly with a diagonal stitch exactly on the corner. Now tack the open square onto the drafting linen or hard paper along the inside of the buttonhole stitches. Use very small tacking stitches so that the square will retain its shape when working the filling. Work the basis for the filling next. This consists mostly of woven or overcast bars, which lie from side to side or from corner to corner. An even number of threads (usually 4) are carried across for woven bars. For the method of weaving see Par. 7.2 No. IV. The threads forming the bars, are hooked into the loops of the buttonhole stitches and they must pass underneath the previously worked bars. When they are covered the working thread must pass over the top of the previously worked bars so that they are all joined together. Finally the filling is worked according to the design.

Method no. 2.

See Fig. 5.31.

If the linen is a bit coarse and will possibly fray easily, proceed as follows: Work a row of running stitches around the square first, then an outline of buttonhole stitch over these and finally a row of four-sided stitch to the outside of the buttonhole stitches before cutting the material on the inside close to the loops of the buttonhole stitches. Leave enough threads of the material in the middel of each side to form the 2 cross-bars, which will be strengthened by overcasting or by weaving.

Joining the working-thread in Reticella work:
See Fig. 5.32.

There is only one method of joining, as follows: Leave the old thread hanging after the last stitch. Insert the needle with the new thread from the back through the loop of the last stitch, and pull through to about the last inch. Now work about 6 or 7 buttonhole stitches over the 2 loose ends and cut off the remaining ends.

A Reticella square
D 5.6

The method of working the following square will explain the technique of Reticella work. See Plate 5.9.

(i) Commencing at a, outline the square

Figure 5.31

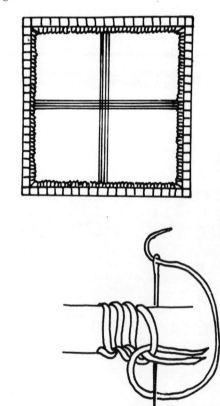

Figure 5.32

with running stitch and let the thread hang at a.

(ii) Cut from the centre towards each corner, fold the material back and buttonhole stitch from left to right around the square up to a again.

(iii) Now tack the square on to drafting linen as previously explained.

(iv) Using the thread hanging at a, carry it to and fro three times from a to b and overcast the little bar firmly back to a.

(v) Overcast into every loop of the outline up to c and carry a bar across to d. Pass the needle through the completed bar ab, back to c and again to d. Bring the needle out in the outline one stitch to the right of d and buttonhole stitch over the 3 threads back to c. The working thread goes through a b as well. Remember to work 2 bullion picots. Insert the needle into the outline just above c, overcast into the outline up to e, carry a thread three times from e to f and buttonhole stitch back to e. Overcast into the ouline up to g. Carry the thread to and fro 4 times from g to h underneath a b. Weave through this bar back to h. Overcast into the outline up to i. Now carry the bar-loop i j across and buttonhole stitch back to i. Overcast in the outline up to k. Carry a bar 3 times from k to l (pass the needle through the centre of the woven and overcast bars). Overcast the bar back to k and then up to m. Carry the bar-loop m n across and work with 2 bullion picots, up to m . Overcast to o, and work the bar-loop o p. Overcast up to q. Carry a thread to and fro 4 times from q to r and keep the threads underneath all the bars in the centre. Weave q r up to s. Now work a circle around 3 times by inserting the needle into every bar. Work buttonhole stitch over the circle from s with the loops towards the outside. Weave up to t. Now work a row of loose buttonhole stitches on the first circle as follows: See Fig. 5.33

PLATE 5.9
Design D 5.6. Reticella lace (slightly enlarged)

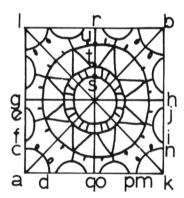

D 5.6

Figure 5.33

137

Work an ordinary buttonhole stitch fairly loosely and insert the needle again into the loop from the back. Take care to keep the tension even and the stitches regular — 2 stitches in each 1/8th section of the circle. When the circle has been completed, overcast into every loose loop thus formed, up to t. Now work a *pyramid* on every 1/8th of the loose row as follows: Work 7 firm buttonhole stitches from t. Bring the thread back and insert from the back into the first loop (between the 1st and 2nd stitches). Buttonhole 5 stitches over this loose thread into the loops of the first row. Again insert the needle from the back into the first loop of the last row, work 4 buttonhole stitches, then 3, 2 and finally only one. Insert through the last loop and leave the thread hanging.

The following method can also be used for working the pyramids. Work the rows of buttonhole stitch to and fro without bringing the thread back after every row. This method, however, does not always give as smooth and even a result as the first one.

Take a new thread and commence on the edge at a. Leave a short piece hanging to finish off into the outline later. Work the 7 remaining bar-loops on the edge. Thread the needle with the piece of thread hanging at the end of the pyramid and insert into the centre of the opposite bar-loop on the edge.

Overcast once or twice over the thread and then 5 times along the left side to the base of the pyramid. Pass the needle through the bar, make the second and all the other pyramids and join them to the bar-loop, which will bring the needle back to t. Weave the bar up to u. Carry the thread 3 times along the apexes of the pyramids to form a circle and buttonhole over these threads with a bullion picot in every 16th section. This brings the needle to u. Weave up to r. Remove the work from the drafting-linen. All the remaining loose threads must now be worked into the buttonhole stitches on the wrong side. Cut the material that was folded back, off.

Additional work to give the squares a softer appearance can now be done, e.g. a row of

Figure 5.34

double hemstitch around the square. Pull one thread of the material out as a guide to keep the stitches even. In addition bullions can be worked in groups as follows: See Fig. 5.34 and Fig. 5.35.

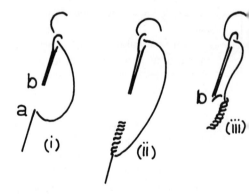

Figure 5.35

Use a needle with a small eye.
 (i) Bring the needle out at a, insert at b and bring it out at a again, but do not pull it through.
 (ii) Twist the thread around the needle from right to left to the length of a — b. Place the left thumb on the needle and pull it through carefully.
 (iii) Pull tight and insert needle at b. These bullions can be grouped in many interesting ways.

138

D 5.7

As mentioned these squares represent the most elementary form of Reticella work, and a clever embroideress can experiment with much larger areas. In this case bars will be carried across an open space and woven to represent the squares and each square can be filled differently. See Plate 5.7.

Fillings for Reticella squares
D 5.7
The accompanying design shows 18 different fillings for Reticella squares. The bars may be woven or overcast as desired. When making Reticella lace, it sometimes occurs that two pyramids have to be worked one on either side of an overcast bar, then the method is as follows: Work the first row of buttonhole stitches for the first pyramid over the overcast bar and complete the pyramid. For the second pyramid, place the stitches of the first row between the basic stitches of the first pyramid.

D 5.7

A simple border in Reticella work
D 5.8

Pretty borders can be done in Reticella work. See Plate 5.10. Here a coarser type of Reticella has been done on linen with approximately 30 threads to 2½ cm. The satin stitch and the outline have been done with Pearl Cotton No. 8 and the rest with No. 12.

Scale: One square equals 2 threads.

Method:

    (i) Using No. 8 cotton, work 2 horizontal rows of running stitch, 20 threads apart.

  (ii) Buttonhole over 4 threads over these running stitches so that the loops are 18 threads apart.

 (iii) Now work vertical rows of buttonhole stitch over 4 threads, also over running stitches, between the 2 rows of buttonhole stitch so that the loops are also 18 threads apart. Repeat 18 threads further on. There are now alternating

140

PLATE 5.10
Design D 5.8. A border in Reticella lace.

squares with looped edges on all 4 sides. These squares are later cut open. Using No. 12 cotton, work a row of double hemstitch over 3 threads on the inside of the other squares and right up against the buttonhole stitches. Now use No. 8 cotton and work 4 triangles on the diagonal in satin stitch, in the open square in the centre. Work each square from the centre diagonally over one, over 2, 3, 4, 5 and 6 threads. Two rows of satin stitch over 4 threads lie 3 threads away from and parallel with the horizontal rows of buttonhole stitches. Using No. 12 cotton work a row of double hemstitching in the open space between the rows. Cut the material in the squares with the buttonhole loops, away on the wrong side of the work, and tack it on to a piece of drafting linen. Use No. 12 cotton and carry 3 threads across from corner to corner. Overcast firmly back to the starting position. Take the needle through the

buttonhole stitches on the wrong side of the work to the next corner. Again carry 3 threads across and overcast to the middle. Attach to the first bar with a little stitch and make a ring bullion picot in each corner at this cross in the centre. Overcast the rest of the incomplete bar to the edge. Pass the needle through the back of the buttonhole stitches to the next square and proceed.

(6) *Hedebo embroidery*
This kind of embroidery is very closely related to Reticella lace. In both the material is cut away and strengthened with lacy fillings. They differ, however, in the following ways:

Reticella work
(1) Design: This is usually composed of squares.

(2) Stitch: The basic stitch is always buttonhole stitch worked from left to right over a thread carried back after each row is worked.

(3) Woven bars are mostly encountered.

141

(4) Flat satin stitch in geometrical designs is often used.

(5) Buttonhole stitch is worked firmly and the stitches right up against one another.

Hedebo work

(1) Design: This is seldom geometrical and usually composed of heart-shapes, crescent moons, circles, cones etc.

(2) Stitch: A special Hedebo buttonhole stitch always worked only from left to right, the return journey being made by overcasting into the loops of the previous row.

(3) Woven bars are never found in Hedebo work.

(4) Raised satin stitch is used here.

(5) Buttonhole stitch is not worked so tightly because the knots push the stitches slightly apart

Hedebo embroidery originated in Denmark. There are 3 kinds: The old kind which will be discussed separately, the intermediate kind, which was not used much and is really only a stepping-stone to the last kind, which came into use in 1850. The first kind suits our hurried way of life better because it is less time-consuming and consequently it is treated fully in Par. 5.8.

The last kind can be used very successfully on table-linen. It must be worked on a good quality and firm Irish linen in cream or white. Although a linen thread was used originally, No. 12 Pearl Cotton is recommended for the open work. For the satin stitch which often appears on the work, No. 8 pearl cotton and for the eyeletholes No. 12 pearl cotton should be used. Further a piece of drafting linen, or firm paper, sharp needles No. 9 and No. 10 and tapestry needles No. 26 will be needed. The design consists mostly of open circles, heart-shapes, leaf-shapes, small diamond-shapes, half-circles etc. The grouping of these shapes is very important. See, for instance, the tea cosy in Plate 5.12 — 8 cone-shapes forming a circle. The technique is actually very simple as it is based on buttonhole stitch and by way of illustration the next design will be dealt with in detail.

A tea cloth in Hedebo embroidery
D 5.9
Schematic diagram: See Fig. 5.36. Size: 64 cm by 64 cm ...

D 5.8

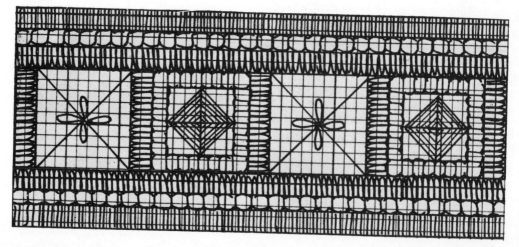

Scale of diagram: 19 mm equals 127 mm .

This design will also be very lovely on a serviette bag, a tea cosy, chair-back, luncheon-set, repeated on a large tablecloth etc.

Key:

A. Needleweaving. See chapter 6

B. Simple drawn thread work. See chapter 6. Transfer the outlines, without the fillings, by means of carbon paper suitable for textiles on to the material.

C. The leaf-shape. See Fig. 5.37

Using No. 12 Pearl Cotton, commence at a and work small running stitches on the outline up to a again. Leave the thread hanging. Cut into this shape a few times from the centre towards the running stitch taking care not to cut the latter. Fold the pieces of material back to the wrong side on the line of the running stitches. Use the thread left hanging at a and work Hedebo buttonhole stitch from a from left to right up to a again as follows:

Insert the needle into the material from the wrong side, pull it through until only a small loop remains, bring the needle through the loop from the back and pull tight. These stitches must be very small (about 3 mm) but regular and of the same size. It is also important to leave a little space between the stitches, otherwise they will be too crowded and the loops not distinct enough to build the second row.

The thread is joined by the same method as for Reticella work. See Fig. 5.32. When the outline has been completed, the surface material is cut away on the wrong side. Now draw the outlines as well as the fillings on the dull side of the drafting linen, using an ordinary pen and ink. Cut it out about 25 mm bigger than the motif and tack it under the open space in the material close to the buttonhole stitch outline. The dull side of the design lies away from the material and the smooth side up. The thread is still at a and from here the lacy fillings are worked. See Fig. 5.39.

Using a No. 26 tapestry needle, overcast

PLATE 5.11
A beautiful example of Hedebo work as it is still made today in Denmark. Origin: Copenhagen

into a few of the following loops in the outline from a to b. Work one loose buttonhole stitch in the corner at a, take the thread through the outline at c and overcast into 2 loops back to b. Then overcast once or twice into the outline to d. Work a buttonhole stitch loosely in each space of the first loose row, i.e. 2 stitches. Catch the thread into the outline and overcast back. The following two rows are the same but note that each row increases by one stitch. The thread is now at e.

To make a pyramid: Work a row of firm (but not too tight) buttonhole stitches over the last loose row, placing 2 or 3 stitches in each space as required. Return by overcasting into every loop. Now work another row of buttonhole stitches in the spaces between each stitch of the previous row and work into the first space but not in the last one. There will now

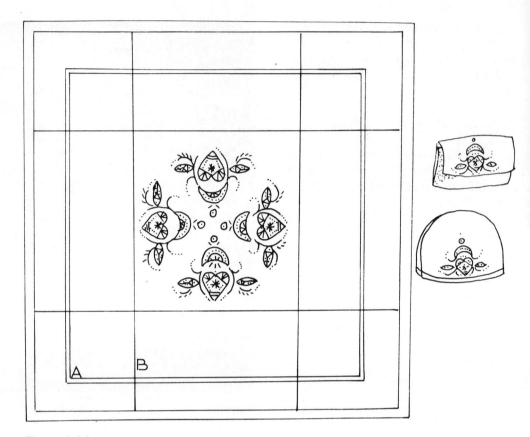

Figure 5.36

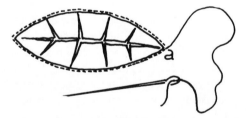

Figure 5.37

Figure 5.38

be one stitch less than in the first row. Overcast back and repeat until only one stitch remains. The overcasting stitches will be the same number as the buttonhole stitches of the previous row. Now carry a long thread to f in the outline, overcast this thread a few times (about 4 times) and catch it in the apex of the pyramid. Overcast along the right side of the

pyramid to g and in the outline to h. Count the outline stitches from h to f and divide by 5. Supposing that there are still 25 stitches, then build 4 little pyramids as described on a base of 5 stitches each. Overcast along the outline to the other side and build 4 other pyramids oposite the first 4. They are joined at the apexes with a thread that is carried across and overcast a few times back. Overcast down the right side of the pyramid to the outline and build the next pyramids, until all have been completed and joined to the opposite side.

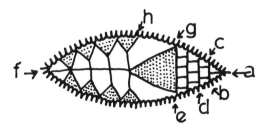

Figure 5.39

D. The crescent moon. See Fig. 5.40.
Commence at a and follow the instructions given for the leafshape, viz. the method for outlining with running stitch, cutting away the material, outlining with buttonhole stitch and tacking it on the drafting linen.

Method of working the loose rings: Twist the thread 3 times round a knitting needle, secure these threads with one buttonhole stitch remove carefully from the knitting needle and cover completely with buttonhole stitches. Pull the needle through the loop of the first stitch and let the thread hang. Make a sample ring first and take a thicker or thinner knitting needle if necessary. The rings must be of the same size with the same number of stitches on each. When the second ring has been completed it is joined to the first. Overcast along about a 1/4 of the circumference of the second ring and leave the thread hanging. Join nos. 3 to 9 in the same way so that there is a row of 9 rings. Place them in position on the drafting linen, tack down and take the loose threads to the outline of the shape, where they will later be finished off. In the meantime they are left hanging on the wrong side. Take the thread hanging at a and overcast to b. Join each ring with an overcasting stitch up to c. Overcast the thread b c a few times, return to b and

again to c. Buttonhole stitch the 3 threads carried from c to b, the loops lying away from the rings. Overcast back to c, also 2 stitches in the outline to d. Now work a row of loose buttonhole stitches from d to e by inserting between the second or third stitches of the previous row. Overcast back to d and cover with a row of buttonhole stitches. This will be position e. Overcast in the outline up to f. Build a pyramid on a base of 4 stitches and join the apex to the top row. Overcast down the right side, build the centre pyramid on 5 stitches and the third on 4 stitches. This completes the crescent moon. After removing the drafting linen, finish off the loose threads neatly on the wrong side.

E. The small circle.
Prepare as described above and work a row of loose stitches round the circle. Note that the stitches of a loose row are always placed farther apart than in a firm row. Now work an ordinary row, then overcast right around and in this process carry threads across the circle 4 times and overcast twice so that there are 8 bars at regular intervals round the circle. While making the last 2 bars, weave around the centre to keep the bars in position and overcast the last one to complete it.

F. The heart-shaped motif. See Fig. 5.41
Commencing at a, do all the preparatory work

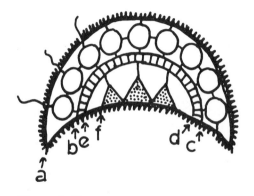

Figure 5.40

and tack on drafting linen. Work one loose row and one ordinary row of buttonhole stitch right around. This is position b. Leave the thread hanging. Now make the star in the centre. See Fig. 5.42.

Make a ring around a knitting needle as described for the crescent moon. The stitches must be divisible by 6 — try to fit in 24 or 30 stitches on which 6 pyramids will be built. When the ring has been completed, build the first pyramid on a base of 4 or 5 stitches. Overcast down the right side back to the ring but not into it and start on the second pyramid straight away. When the second row of the second pyramid has been completed and the needle is back on the lefthand side, 3 threads must first be carried to and from the middle of the righthand side of the first pyramid. Buttonhole over these 3 threads and then proceed to complete the pyramid. Complete the 6 pyramids in this way with the bar-loops joining them. End at the top of the last pyramid and leave the thread hanging. Tack the star in position on the drafting linen. See that the pyramid with the loose thread at the top is near

a, and take the thread through the loose stitches to the material. Leave hanging to finish off later.

Now take the thread at b, carry it to c and back to b. Cover with buttonhole stitches from b to c, overcast back and then work a row of loose buttonhole stitches, overcast and again a row of buttonhole and overcasting to d.

To make a bar-loop: Make a small loop by taking the thread to and fro from d to e twice to form a small arc. Cover with buttonhole stitches to e. Take 2 threads to and fro again and repeat from e to f. Buttonhole only to the middle of the second loop and take 3 threads to and from there to the middle of the first loop. Buttonhole half of this loop. Now join the middle of the loop to the star, overcast this thread a few times and complete the third loop. Now complete the second half of the second bar-loop. Join the point of the star from this position f. Overcast this thread a few times and then make the last bar-loop. This will be position g. Overcast a few times around the corner and make a small bar-loop

PLATE 5.12
A tea-cosy and tray-cloth in Hedebo work. D: Author, M: Mrs. Ria Wessels and Miss Rita Grobbelaar.

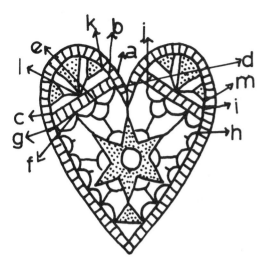

Figure 5.41

with a picot in the middle by twisting the thread around the needle once as described in Par. 7.2 IV No. 3. The next bar-loop has no picot, and is joined to a bar-loop of the star. The next bar-loop again has a picot. Now first join the star to a pyramid as shown in the diagram before the next loop is made and repeat in this way up to h.

Note that a small pyramid is built on a base of 3 stitches over a bar-loop right at the bottom corner. Overcast from h to i and repeat on this side as from b. The needle is now at j. Overcast round the corner up to k, build a pyramid on a base of 5 stitches which is joined at 1. Overcast back to the base and build another pyramid on a base of 3 stitches and join at 1 as well. Overcast back and pass needle through the loose row to the material where the thread is later finished off on the wrong

Figure 5.42

side. Take a new thread and build 3 pyramids from m exactly as described for the other half. This completes all the Hedebo embroidery.

The lines are done in snail's trail, the oval shapes are worked in raised satin stitch and the eyelet-holes further complete the design.

5.5 Handmade lace — Venetian point

The making of lace with a needle evolved naturally out of Reticella work. The stitches are almost similar but there is quite a difference in technique. The pieces of lace are made separately and are only later affixed to the material. The technique will not be discussed here. Although this type of embroidery seems very unpractical in this age of space travel and television etc, it has not really become a lost art and it is still attempted by many embroideresses. See Plate 5.13 and the frontis piece for examples.

In the first instance Venetian lace and Filet lace are used on the same article and made by somebody for whom embroidery and lace making is only a hobby and a pleasant pastime.

5.6 Bullion work

This is a very striking form of embroidery which may be done in white or ecru. Use Irish linen or any fine and smooth linen, and No. 12 pearl cotton. The work consists of outlines in buttonhole stitch with a ring bullion picot in about every 6th stitch. See Par. 5.4, No. 3. There is, however, the difference that the ring bullion picot after completion, is joined to the buttonhole stitch from the top instead of from the back. Against the smooth side of the buttonhole stitches (i.e. not the side with the loops) snail's trail is usually worked and small ringlets in the same technique are massed through the work and are often placed in rows between two lines of snail's trail.

Here and there a shape is cut out, overcast and decorated with a bar. Ring bullion picots are often worked over the edge of these open spaces. In plates 5.15, 5.16 the general appearance can be seen clearly.

It is very effective on luncheon-sets, tea cosies, tray cloths etc.

A border in a variation of bullion work D 5.10
Scale: One square equals 3 threads.
This is a very pretty border to use just inside the hem of small articles. See Plate 5.17
Key: A. One row of double hemstitching on both sides of the panel.
B. Eyelets.
C. Satin stitch.
D. Four-sided stitch.
E. Bullions (24 around an eyelet and 3 above and below the four-sided stitch. See Fig. 5.35
F. Double faggot.
Omit the four corner stitches of the eyelets in the centre of the circle of bullions, so that they appear round. Use designs D 5.4 and D 5.5 also and change them slightly for bullion

work as follows: Do not cut out the spaces intended for open-work, but fill them with rows of snail's trail, ringlets in bullion work and small cutwork motifs. The more elaborate, the richer and more effective the appearance of the work will be. Use this design on luncheon-mats for example, as shown in Fig. 5.43.

5.7. Shadow work

This is a form of white work easily managed by anyone, as the technique is very simple. If the correct material and design are chosen, articles can be decorated very successfully in this way. It is suitable for napery, bedspreads, pillow-cases (especially for babies) decorative pillows, bridal veils, blouses, christening robes, children's clothes etc. In Italy especially, napery is beautifully decorated with shadow work and even at the present time, it

PLATE 5.13
Section of a cloth with a composite design of Venetian point and filet lace and drawn fabric work. Note how the design of the lace is repeated in the embroidery. D: Author, M: Mrs. Elize Stockenström

PLATE 5.14
A runner richly decorated with Venetian point and filet lace and bullion embroidery. DM: Author.

is employed by everyone who loves to embroider.

Shadow work is done on transparent material and from Italy an especially fine linen is obtainable for this purpose. It can also be worked on real silk organza or on a good quality Swiss organdie. Synthetic materials are not recommended. Use one or two threads of stranded cotton and Nos. 8 and 9 needles.

It is especially effective to combine shadow work and drawn fabric work fillings, eyeletholes, small areas of Reticella lace and satin stitch on one article. See Plate 5.2 and Plate 10.8. Used alone, however, shadow work can be just as beautiful. See Plate 5.19

The technique
Trace the design very lightly on the wrong side of the material, using special carbon-

paper and a knitting needle with a very fine point. It is advisable to work on a frame to keep the tension even and to prevent the work from puckering. Shadow work is worked mainly in close herringbone stitch. See Fig. 5.18. The stitches are worked on the wrong side and close together. See Fig. 5.18 (ii). Backstitches will appear on the right side of the work on the outline of the design. Always begin at the bottom end of the shape, the point of the needle towards the worker so that the work progresses away from her. If the shape has a very sharp point it will be necessary to work one or two backstitches on the right side first before starting the herringbone stitch on the wrong side as the outlines widen. The stitches on the inside of a curved shape must be small and those on the outside longer but never so long that the work appears sparse. If

PLATE 5.15
Section of the runner in Plate 5.14

PLATE 5.16
A typical example of bullion embroidery Origin:
Copenhagen

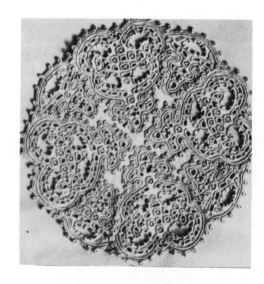

the shape turns very sharply 2 stitches can be
worked now and then on the outside for every
one stitch on the inside. If the shape is very
wide it can be divided down the middle and
the two halves worked separately. Another
method is to work backstitches down the middle on the right side over the herringbone
stitches. This will produce the effect of a vein
and will secure the herringbone stitches.

To finish off: The best way of finishing off
is to take the needle to and fro through the
stitches as near as possible to the outline.

To work a circle: See Fig. 5.44

  (i) First work 3 or 4 backstitches on the
     right side and then

 (ii) Herringbone stitch on the wrong side

(iii) until the circle has been filled as on the
diagram.

(iv) Finally work 3 or 4 backstitches on the
     outline at the top on the right side to
     complete the outline.

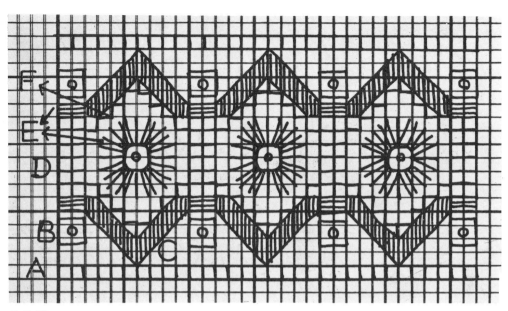

D 5.10

PLATE 5.17
Design D 5.10. A border in bullion work.

When designing for shadow work do not choose shapes that are too wide as the material might pucker and the threads might not re-main in position and appear untidy. The Ita-lian designs mostly consist of beautifully flowing lines and scrolls with little flowers

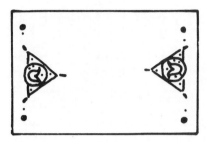

Figure 5.43

and leaves which is most suitable for this delicate type of embroidery.

A luncheon-set in shadow work for a round table
D 5.11 and D 5.12
Schematic diagram: See Fig. 5.45
Size: 29 cm by 47 cm .

Scale of diagram: 25 mm equals 11 cm .
The shape of the mat is slightly curved to fit the round table.
Key: The arrows indicate the middle of the design. Trace the design lightly on transparent paper and then onto the wrong side of the material using carbon paper and a knitting needle. Work herringbone stitch on the wrong side in all the areas filled in on the design. Work stemstitch on the remaining single lines so that these also resemble backstitches on the right side.

Finishing the edges: Work a row of small running stitches around the edge, then small firm buttonhole stitches over these and over a guiding thread of No. 5 Pearl Cotton. Cut away the extra material right up against the loops of the buttonhole stitches. Make the serviettes on the same principle.

Plate 5.20 shows this design executed on a

PLATE 5.18
Small organdie d'oylie with shadow work. Origin: Switzerland.

PLATE 5.19
A very fine piece of shadow work. Origin Switzerland

silk-organza handkerchief sachet. This will also be lovely on a tea-shower. Use this design in groups of 3 in the corners or in the centre of a tea cloth of thin linen material. It is also suitable in the centre of a tea cosy as in Fig. 5.46.

Fold the hem of the tea cosy to the wrong side and work buttonhole stitch through both layers and over a guiding thread of No. 5 Pearl Cotton, shown on the line. Cut away the unneccessary material of the hem on the wrong side. Work the seam of the tea cosy through both layers, just as in the case of the luncheon-mats and cut the material away right

up against the buttonholing.

Shadow work can be worked in white or in coloured threads, the latter giving an opalescent effect through transparent white material. It is advisable to use pastel colours.

5.8 Old hedebo embroidery

As previously explained, there are 3 kinds of Danish Hedebo embroidery. The oldest kind which will now be discussed, is in reality a type of drawn thread work and really very striking and hard-wearing. It can be used very successfully on a variety of household articles. Work in white on white or in cream on

153

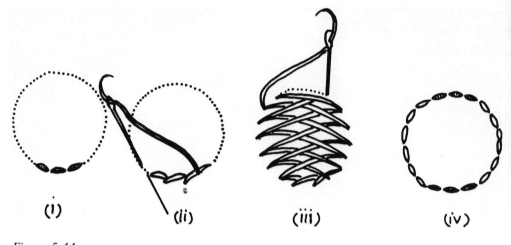

(i)   (ii)   (iii)   (iv)

Figure 5.44

cream. If it is done on pastel coloured material the thread must preferably be in the same shade, especially for the lacy fillings.

The designs are mostly based on simple abstract shapes, often resembling flowers and leaves and are seldom geometrical. These shapes are outlined with 2 close rows of chain stitch, then some of the threads are removed in both directions in the motif. Finally these threads are strengthened and decorated. Around these shapes stems are worked, usu-ally also in chain stitch, and on these stems a variety of leaves, flowers and buds grow, which remind one of Mountmellick work. Almost any type of material is suitable if it is not too coarse or loosely woven in which case it will fray too easily when cut away. Evenly woven linen with approximately 30 or even 20 threads to 2½ cm is very suitable.

Pearl Cotton, nos 5, 8 and 12 is recom-mended, crewel needles No. 7 for the surface embroidery and tapestry needles No. 24 for

Figure 5.45

the fillings.

The technique for old Hedebo embroidery is explained in the following design.

A tablecloth in old Hedebo work
D 5.13
Schematic diagram: See Fig. 5.47
Size: 127 cm by 228 cm .

Scale of diagram: 13 mm equals 25 cm .
This design can also be used for drawn fabric work or blackwork. Use linen 140 cm wide or more. Duplicate the design 8 times by tracing with a pencil on transparent paper. Pin 4 of these around the centre of the material to form a circle. Care must be taken that the lines meet exactly and that the 4 imaginary radia fall on

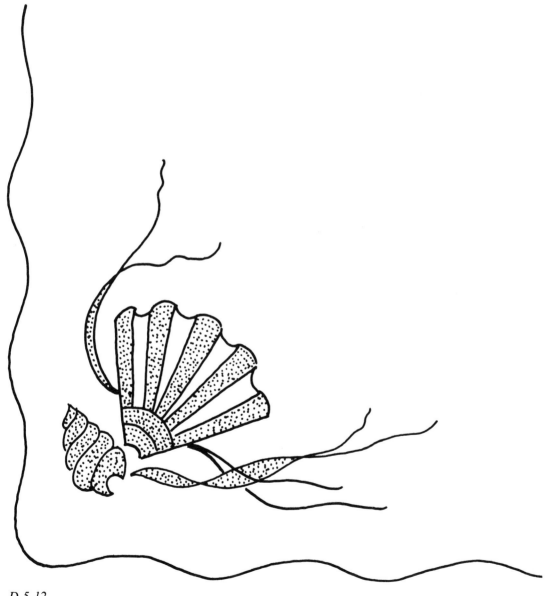

D 5.12

PLATE 5.20
Design D 5.11. A handkerchief sachet in pure silk organza

the straight of the material. Pin the 4 corner motifs in position allowing for the hem.

Now tack the design on the material as described in Par. 1.3 No. 15.

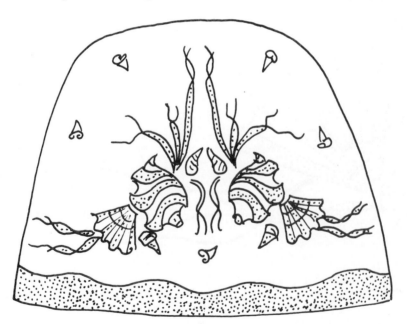

Figure 5.46

156

PLATE 5.21
A lovely tea-cosy in Old Hedebo work. D: Author, M: Mrs. Ria Wessels

PLATE 5.22
Old Hedebo work on a tea-cloth. Note the formal border in drawn fabric work. Size: 137 cm x 137 cm . D: Author, M: Mrs. R. Pienaar.

The technique

(i) Using a sharp needle and No. 12 cotton work 2 rows of small running stitches around the motifs A, which are filled in on the design. These 2 rows serve as a strengthening measure for the drawn thread work which follows.

(ii) Using No. 5 cotton work 2 rows of small chain stitches over the 2 rows of running stitches.

(iii) Where the lines meet the motifs as in B, the outside row of chain stitch is lengthened along this line.

(iv) Work the 3 scrolls C, which branch out of some of the lines, in Portuguese stem stitch, using No. 8 cotton.

(v) Using No. 5 cotton, work the bars D and the 3 shorter crosslines in whipped chain stitch over the lines B.

Figure 5.47

(vi) The line E consists of 3 close rows of chain stitch with No. 5 cotton. Take care not to pucker the work.

(vii) The line F consists of 2 rows of chain stitch in No. 5 cotton.

(viii) The diagonal lines between E and F also consist of 2 close rows of chain stitch with No. 5 cotton.

(ix) Use No. 5 cotton and work the lines G, H and I in double knot stitch.

ing the cross bars in ordinary chain stitch. Use No. 8 cotton again and work all the small leaves in Cretan stitch.

(xi) Now work the drawn fabric work fillings in the motifs A on the design.

Cut and strengthen the mesh as follows: Work on the wrong side. Use small sharp-pointed scissors and carefully lift out and cut 2 threads right up against the chain stitch at both ends

PLATE 5.23
Corner of the cloth in Plate 5.22

(x) The branches with leaves J: Use No. 8 cotton for all the stems in Portuguese Stem stitch and No. 5 cotton for work-

and remove them. Now leave 2 threads and again remove 2. Repeat in both directions until the whole motif is a mesh of pairs of

PLATE 5.24
Detail of cloth in Plate 5.22

threads with open spaces in between. Put the work carefully over a frame with the wrong side up. Using No. 12 cotton and a tapestry needle overcast twice over each bar as is clearly shown in Fig. 5.48.

Always work from left to right and first complete it horizontally and then vertically. All the open-work fillings in old Hedebo work are based on this. In other words, all the loose threads of the mesh are first reinforced before the fillings can be worked, with a few exceptions.

Fillings on the bare mesh
There are a few exceptions, which are worked directly on the bare mesh. The most popular are the following:
1. See Fig. 5.49 and Fig. 5.50
Put the work on a frame with the right side up. Using No. 12 cotton and a tapestry needle, work the stitch diagonally as shown at (i).

Pass the needle under every intersection of the mesh and pull fairly tight.
(ii) Work from side to side and cross these same stitches on the return to the start-

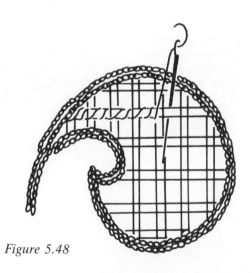

Figure 5.48

160

ing position. Skip one diagonal row of the intersections of the mesh, and repeat until the whole area has been filled.

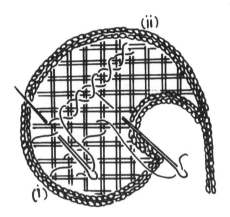

Figure 5.49

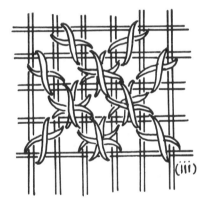

Figure 5.50

(iii) Repeat in the opposite direction as in Fig. 5.50. The thread is pulled fairly tight throughout so that diagonal raised bands that intersect are formed. See Plate 6.5

2. See Fig. 5.51
Put the material on a frame with the right side up. Use No. 8 cotton.
(i) Pass the needle underneath 2 sets of vertical threads, bring out and do the same one square lower but overlapping the first stitch as on the diagram. Then make another similar stitch on a level with the first, then one next to no. 2 etc.
(ii) This same process is now repeated in the opposite direction as shown in Fig. 5.52

Fillings to use on the reinforced mesh
After the mesh has been reinforced by overcasting, it is usually enriched as follows: These fillings mainly comprise 5 methods, which used separately or combined, produce a great number of beautiful fillings.

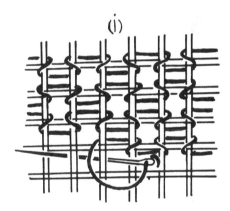

Figure 5.51

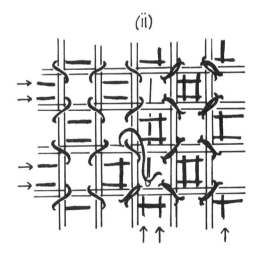

Figure 5.52

1. See Fig. 5.53

The first method is to weave to and fro, using either No. 8 or No. 12 cotton, as preferred, and depending on the texture of the linen. See Fig. 7.9 for this process of weaving as in the Hardanger bars. The same principle is fol-

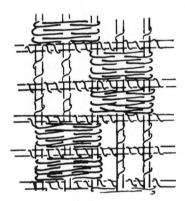

Figure 5.53

lowed in old Hedebo work, but over more bars if necessary according to the design. Fig. 5.53 is an example of 4 adjoining squares filled in and 4 left unworked to form a check pattern. Fig. 5.57 illustrates a number of woven patterns. One square on the diagram equals one open space and each line equals one bar of the mesh.

2. See Fig. 7.19 and Plate 6.6

The second method is exactly the same as described in Par. 7.2 IV No. 12 and closely related to the well-known flower in Hardanger work. This stitch is indicated in Fig. 5.57 by means of a cross. One of these florets fills one open space in the mesh.

3. See Fig. 5.54

The third method covers 4 open spaces in the mesh and is executed as follows: Carry a bar from one corner to the other across the specified open spaces and overcast twice, finishing at the starting point. Four similar bars meet in the centre as shown in Fig. 5.54

Weave around the centre a few times to form a small web before finishing off along the last bar. Plate 5.21 clearly shows this stitch especially in the lower border. In Fig. 5.57 this stitch is indicated by means of a large cross

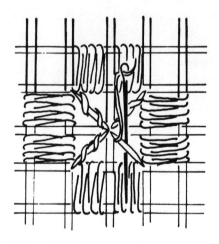

Figure 5.54

over 4 squares. If a web should be woven around the centre, it will be indicated by a small circle on the diagram.

Besides these 3 general methods other stitches are also sometimes used to enrich the work, e.g.

4. See Fig. 5.55

Weave through the open spaces twice and in both directions to make the existing mesh still

Figure 5.55

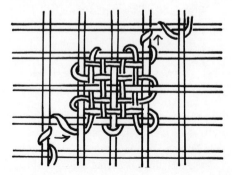

finer. Always use No. 12 cotton. The method
is clearly shown in Fig. 5.55.

5. See Fig. 5.56
This stitch consists of groups of threads
woven to and fro around the 4 corners of a
square. Use No. 12 cotton and weave each
corner until the adjacent sides have been covered halfway.
The fillings
See Fig. 5.57
Scale: One square equals one open space in
the mesh.
Key:
1 — 39: These are all woven to and fro in the
usual way until the squares have been filled.
The direction is indicated. When proceeding
from one part of the design to another across
an open square, the thread must be taken
through the overcasting stitches of the mesh
on the wrong side of the work.
40 — 48: Method nos. 1 and 3
49: Method nos. 1 and 5
50: Method nos. 1 and 3
51: Method nos. 1 and 4
52: Method nos. 1 and 2

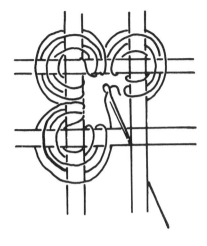

Figure 5.56

53: Method nos. 1, 2 and 3 and a backstitch
wheel (Par. 7.2 II No. 13) around the 4 bars
crossing in the centre.
54 — 57: Method nos. 1 and 2
58: Method nos. 2 and 4
59: Method nos. 1, 2 and 5
60: Groups of backstitch wheels.
61: Method No. 3 which is further enriched
by weaving through the 8 bars to form a web.

PLATE 5.25
How elegant to dine on a beautiful table-cloth like this! Old Hedebo work on white linen. Size: 127 cm x 228 cm. D: Author, M:
Mrs. E. Stockenström

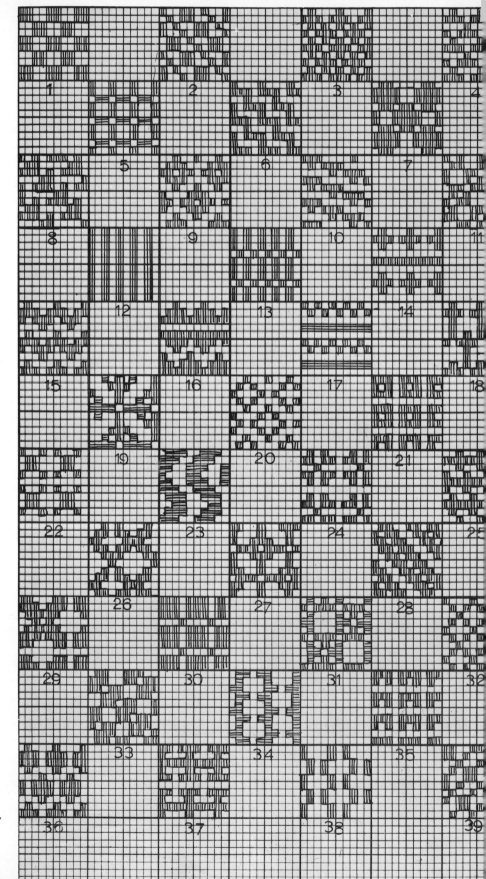

Figure 5.57

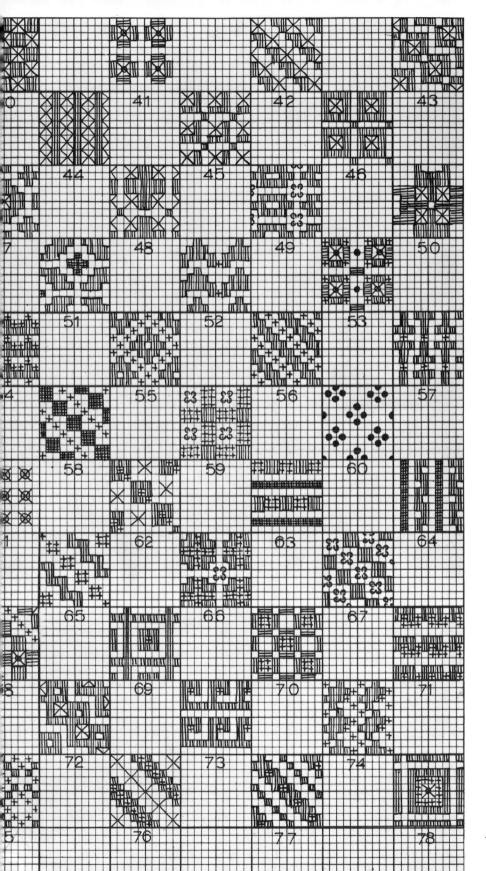

Figure 5.57

Because of the even number of bars, the needle must pass underneath 2 consecutive bars, once in every round.

62: Methods nos. 1, 2 and 3
63: Methods nos. 1, 2 and 4
64: Methods nos. 1 and 4
65: Methods nos. 1 and 2
66: Methods nos. 1, 2 and 5
67: Methods nos. 1 and 5
68: Methods nos. 1, 2 and 3
69 — 71: Methods nos. 1 and 2
72: Methods nos. 1 and 3
73 — 75: Methods nos. 1 and 2
76: Methods nos. 1, 2 and 3
77: Methods nos. 1 and 2
78: Methods nos. 1, 2 and 3

A border in old Hedebo embroidery `
D 5.14

Schematic diagram: See Fig. 5.58. Width: 20 cm .

Scale of diagram: 25 mm equal 20 cm .

Although geometrical designs are not characteristic of old Hedebo there is no reason why we may not deviate a little from the original. This design, definitely more modern and geometrical in character, is just as suitable for the technique of old Hedebo as any original design. It can also be used for drawn fabric work, blackwork or a combination of white and blackwork. In the latter case the instruc-

PLATE 5.26
Detail of cloth in Plate 5.25

Figure 5.58

166

tions are followed exactly except that black-word fillings are substituted for the drawn thread fillings in the motifs.

Key: Make enough duplicates of the design on transparent paper for the whole border. Tack the design on to the material according to Hint 15 in Par. 1.3. Work old Hedebo fillings in all the parts of the design that are filled in. Take great care to keep the circles round and note that all the straight lines lie on the straight of the material. Follow the instructions already given. Work the same filling in the identical shapes but the fillings for the sunflowers A, may all differ.

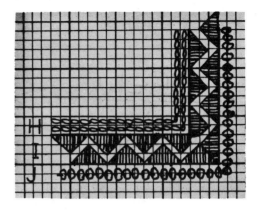

Figure 5.60

Figure 5.59

A. The sunflower. See Fig. 5.59.
Use drawn thread work in the middle circle, outlined with 2 rows of chain stitch as described previously. Use No. 8 cotton and work the leaves a in Cretan stitch. Now use No. 5 cotton for working line b in double knot stitch and line c in chain stitch.

B. Use No. 5 cotton to work all the lines B in double knot stitch.

C. All the lines C are worked in chain stitch, using No. 5 cotton.

D. Use No. 5 cotton and work the stem D over line C in raised chain band.

E. Again using No. 5 cotton, the roots are worked in Portuguese stem stitch.

F. Use No. 5 cotton to work the leaves in

Figure 5.61

Cretan stitch.

G. Use No. 5 cotton to outline the 2 circles with double knot stitch and work 2 close rows of chain stitch on the inside. Using No. 12 cotton, fill the spaces between the 2 outlines completely with rows of double faggot.

H. Two rows of chain stitch in No. 5 cotton.

I. The geometrical satin stitch band. See Fig. 5.60.

Commencing at a, keep all the stitches level at the bottom and work satin stitch from over one to over 6 threads. Skip one thread of the material and repeat. Now skip 3 threads and repeat the whole process so that the corners of the triangles fit in.

J. Work a row of raised chain band on the outside, using No. 5 cotton.

Figure 5.62

Application of design D 5.1 for old Hedebo work

Use this motif for old Hedebo work and decorate with any of the fillings already described. Use the same surface stitches given in the key for this design, or use only chain stitch throughout. The large open areas are always outlined with 2 rows of chain stitch.

Work this motif in an allover pattern on a tea cloth or table-cloth, on a tea cosy or a luncheon-set as shown in Fig. 5.61.

It will also be very effective on a table-runner or a tray cloth. The design can be repeated in a border or arranged in a circle in the middle of a cloth with all the stems towards the centre, as shown in Fig. 5.62.

The name is deduced from the fact that some of the threads of the material are cut and removed in groups in one direction or in alternate groups in both directions. The remaining threads are then strengthened and decorated. Hardanger work and old Hedebo embroidery also belong to this group, but are discussed in separate sections.

The hems of small articles like tray cloths, luncheon-mats and serviettes, however narrow, can be decorated with a border of drawn thread work, with very striking results. An ordinary hem can become an elegant frame for a beautifully embroidered table-cloth or tea cloth by removing a few threads and adding decorative stitchery to the remaining ones. Because drawn thread work must inevitably be done on the straight of the fabric, it will naturally be geometric and angular in character and therefore used alone it is seldom as attractive as when combined with e.g. drawn fabric work, old Hedebo or cross stitch.

Drawn thread work shows up most beautifully when used as lacy fillings in the open spaces in other kinds of embroidery. These fillings are described in Par. 6.2.

6.1 Narrow borders of which the threads have been removed in one direction only

The simplest form of drawn thread work is the one in which a group of threads is removed in one direction and the remaining ones are grouped together with a thicker thread to form a narrow border. This can be done on any kind of material consisting of strong and reasonably evenly woven threads, which can easily be removed. From the finest Irish linen to the coarsest evenly woven linen will be suitable. Use tapestry needles and a frame. The thread will depend mainly on the material. Generally the thread used is nearly the same colour and thickness as the thread of the material. Some kinds of drawn thread work require a thicker thread for decorative purposes.

Drawn Thread work

Preparation

Before the threads of the material are removed the sides of the proposed panel must be strengthened with a thinner cotton. Remove a single thread on either side of the panel to indicate the width. Strengthen the sides in any of the following ways before removing any more threads:

1. By means of double hemstitching. This is an excellent method especially as it divides the threads into groups simultaneously.

2. By using hemstitching. Place a thicker thread underneath the hemstitching to ensure a neater result.

3. By using satin stitch. Work a row of satin stitch perpendicular to the drawn thread. This is a satisfactory way of reinforcing the sides, it forms a striking edge, but it does not group the threads.

4. By using plait stitch.

5. By means of ordinary buttonhole stitch with the loops towards the inside where the threads are to be removed.

6. By using herringbone stitch.

Thus the necessary framework is completed on both sides of the threads that have to be removed.

There are 5 general methods used to reinforce the two ends of the panel where the threads will be cut.

1. See Fig. 6.1

If the hem forms the one side of the border,

PLATE 6.1
A modern version of Ayrshire work, which was so popular in Ireland at the beginning of the 19th Century. It was mainly padded white work countrasted with many lacy drawn thread fillings. Beautiful examples can be found in museums in England and Europe. DM: Author

the threads are cut a few inches away from the corner, pulled out up to the hem and folded in underneath it. In this case hemstitching is usually used to reinforce the edge and to secure the hem.

2. The following method is commonly considered the most satisfactory when the panel is in the middle of an article. See Fig. 6.2.

Cut the threads about 5 cm away from the end. Draw the threads out as far as necessary, use a tapestry needle to darn them back into the material over 5 or 6 threads and cut off on the wrong side. For convenience' sake the stitches for reinforcing the ends have not been indicated on the diagram.

3. Another method is to work a row of buttonhole stitch exactly where the band ends with the loops facing the edge to be cut. This method must never be used on coarse linen or on material that frays easily.

4. Follow the instructions given in 3, but use satin stitch instead of buttonhole stitch.

5. Fold the threads to the wrong side, secure with a few running stitches and cover with satin or buttonhole stitch. Cut off the extra ends of the threads.

Figure 6.1

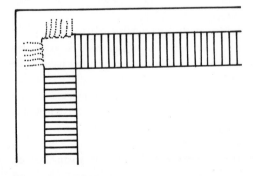

170

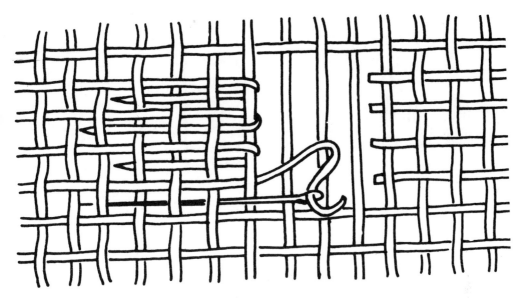

Figure 6.2

The panel has now been reinforced on all sides, the threads have been cut and removed and the remaining threads can now be strengthened, grouped and decorated.

Strengthening and decorating the threads
There is a great variety of methods and the clever embroideress can experiment by working different stitches over the threads. The following are a few suggestions:

Figure 6.3

A. See Fig. 6.3
If the panel is narrow the groups or bars can be left unworked.

Figure 6.4

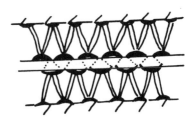

Figure 6.5

B. See Fig. 6.4
Group 4 threads together by means of hemstitching along the one side. Repeat on the other side so that the first groups of threads are divided in two.

C. See Fig. 6.5
Remove 4 threads, leave 3 and again remove 4. Hemstitch at the top and again at the bottom to halve the top groups. Use a thicker thread and work wave stitch over the 3 horizontal threads in the middle dividing the groups further as indicated on the diagram. This panel can be widened by leaving another 3 threads and removing 4, and this can even be repeated again, grouping the 3 threads with wave stitch each time.

D. See Fig. 6.5 and C for the method of

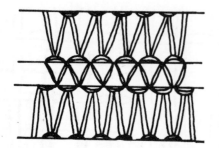

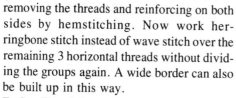

Figure 6.6

Figure 6.7

removing the threads and reinforcing on both sides by hemstitching. Now work herringbone stitch instead of wave stitch over the remaining 3 horizontal threads without dividing the groups again. A wide border can also be built up in this way.

E. See Fig. 6.6

Remove 4 threads, leave 4 and remove 4. Use any of the above methods to group the threads so that each is halved at the top and bottom. Now work three-sided stitch over the centre group of 4 threads as described in Par. 2.6 No.

9, but note that there the stitch is described over 6 threads. By repetition a wide panel can be build up.

F. See Fig. 6.7

Use any of the above methods to reinforce the band on both sides and use a firm crochet cotton to work coral stitch over the groups to bind them still further. By removing more threads, wider panels can be built up and two or more rows of coral stitch can be worked

PLATE 6.2

Examples of drawn thread work. The runner left: Blue linen, different blue cottons used in the needleweaving. Tea-cosy: White linen, white-cotton; Old Hedebo motif and Russian drawn thread border.
Runner right: White linen, white cotton; composite work. Border in drawn thread.
D: Author, M: Mrs. E. Geldenhuys, Mrs. R. Wessels, Mrs. C. Wessels

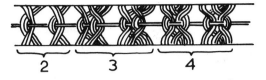

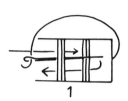

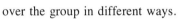

Figure 6.8

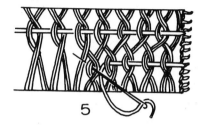

over the group in different ways.
G. See Fig. 6.8
Very interesting results can be achieved by twisting the groups around one another. The diagrams 1, 2, 3, 4 and 5 show the method clearly. Crochet cotton is recommended for this method.
H. See Fig. 6.9
Remove a few threads, e.g. 6, hemstitch on both sides and using No. 5 Pearl cotton, work

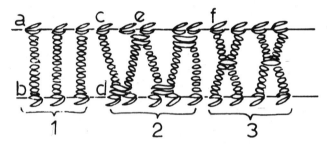

Figure 6.11

Figure 6.9   Figure 6.10

chevron stitch over the groups as shown on the diagram.
I. See Fig. 6.10
Use No. 5 cotton and work feather stitch over the groups as on the diagram.
J. See Fig. 6.11
There are also other methods by which the groups of threads or bars can be strengthened, e.g. by overcasting with a thread of the same thickness as one thread of the linen.

A pretty drawn thread edge instead of a hem.
Strengthen the border where the threads have been removed near the raw edge of the material, using satin stitch on both sides.

Work a row of buttonhole stitch right up against the outside of the satin stitch. Commencing at a, overcast the group up to b as shown in Fig. 6.11 No. 1. Take the needle through the back of the work to the next bar

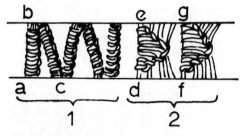

Figure 6.12

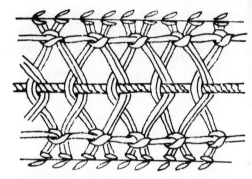

Figure 6.13

and repeat. Cut the material off along the buttonhole stitch edge.

The following are a few variations of this method.

1. Commence at c and overcast each bar almost to its end, where 2 stitches are worked over 2 groups, drawing them together. Overcast the next bar up to e, draw the 2 groups together, etc.

2. Commence at f, and overcast the group completely. Take the needle to the next group along the back of the work, overcast to the middle, work one or two stitches over both groups, drawing them close together, complete the second group and repeat.

K. See Fig. 6.12

Two variations using buttonhole stitch.

1. Buttonhole from a to b and from b to c, etc. The bars will automatically pull together at the sides.

2. Commencing at d, work one buttonhole stitch over one group, then one over 2 groups, over 3, over 4, then again over 3, over 2 and over one. Finish off on the wrong side at e, pass the needle through the back of the buttonhole stitches to d, then to f and repeat on the right side to g. Use a thread of the same thickness as one thread of the material.

L. See Fig. 6.13

Very striking effects can be achieved when all the methods described above are used together to build up wider panels.

Use for instance Glenshee linen and remove 24 threads. Hemstitch at the top and bottom with No. 8 cotton. Use No. 5 cotton and twist the groups of threads over one another in pairs. Now bind these groups, again in pairs, on both sides with coral stitch

using No. 8 or crochet cotton.

The following are two examples of drawn fabric fillings, which can however be used in borders where the threads are removed in one direction only.

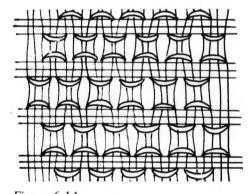

Figure 6.14

PLATE 6.3
Drawn fabric filling. See Fig. 6.14

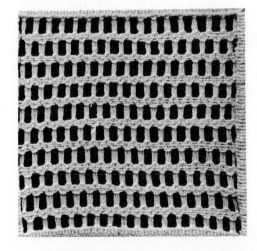

1. See Fig. 6.14 and Plate 6.3

Cut 4 threads and leave 3 alternately in one direction only. Use No. 12 cotton and work wave stitch over the horizontal groups of 3 threads. The diagram clearly shows each succeeding row.

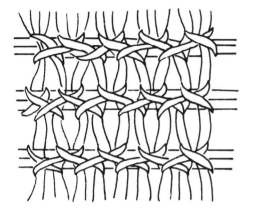

Figure 6.15

PLATE 6.4
Drawn fabric filling. See Fig. 6.15

2. See Fig. 6.15 and Plate 6.4

Cut 4 threads and leave 3 alternately and in one direction only. Use No. 8 cotton and work herringbone stitch over 3 threads. Note that the stitches of the next row will halve the groups of the first row.

Experiments made on a separate piece of material should yield many new ideas as the possibilities are numerous. The above examples are only a few elementary ideas on which to build. Wide borders in this kind of drawn thread work are no longer popular because they are not durable.

Fillings for the corners where the bands of drawn thread work meet

It is obvious that open squares will be formed in the corners where the 2 sides of the border meet and these open spaces will have to be strengthened, decorated and filled up. The embroideress should choose a filling that will match the border pattern.

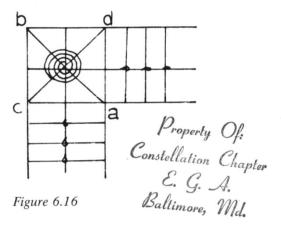

Figure 6.16

A. See Fig. 6.16

Where a thicker thread was used to twist the groups of threads over one another, or to bind them with coral stitch, a cross resulted in the open corner, and these 2 threads were joined by means of a coral knot. Carry 2 more threads from the corner a to b and from c to the centre. The result will be a wheel with 7 bars. Weave under and over the bars around the centre to form a rosette and end where the missing bar should be. Finish off at this position on the wrong side and carry the missing bar from the centre to d.

B. See Fig. 6.17

Carry threads across the corners and from the middle of each side to the opposite side. Work a rosette in the centre as described in A. Now

175

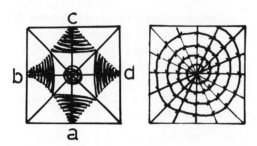

Figure 6.17   *Figure 6.18*

carry 4 threads from the middle of each side to the middle of the adjacent side from a to b, b to c, c to d and d to a, and make a coral knot where these threads cross the others. Now weave over and under the 3 bars starting at the same point up to the spokes coming from the corners.

C. See Fig. 6.18
Carry threads across to form bars as shown, commence at the centre and work a spiral by tying each spoke with coral stitch as shown on the diagram.

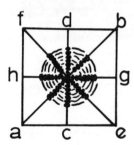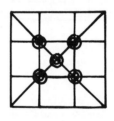

Figure 6.19   *Figure 6.20*

D. See Fig. 6.19
Carry a thread from a to b and overcast 3 times back to a, then from c to d and again 3 times back to c. Similarly from e to f and back to f, from g to h and back to the centre in 2 stitches. Now work a backstitch wheel over these bars and finish the incomplete spoke by overcasting twice back to g.

E. See Fig. 6.20
Bars must be made as shown on the diagram on the same principle as described in D. Secure the threads with coral stitch at the 5 points

where they cross and weave small rosettes as described in A, at these points.

6.2 Drawn thread work with groups of threads removed in both directions

This type of drawn thread work is suitable for fillings or borders. The two methods commonly used to strengthen the edges of this type of drawn thread work are:
1. by means of satin stitch, and
2. by means of buttonhole stitch.
This is drawn thread work at its prettiest as the embroideress can achieve a delicate lacy effect without much trouble, e.g. place 2 panels 5 — 6 cm wide along the short sides of luncheon-mats, as shown in Fig. 6.21.

Figure 6.21

One idea gives birth to the next and the following fillings do not pretend to be a complete collection. They are, however, representative of the different types and again offer scope for the enterprising embroideress to devise her own variations or compositions.

Combined with blackwork, white work and even drawn fabric work, wonderful effects can be achieved. See Plate 10.12 and Plate 10.18. A word of warning that care should be taken to strengthen the edges very carefully where the threads have been cut. The edge can be strengthened further by working a row of double hemstitch as well on the outside of the satin or buttonhole stitch.

Further ideas for drawn thread fillings may be found in the chapters on Hardanger work and old Hedebo work.

Figure 6.22

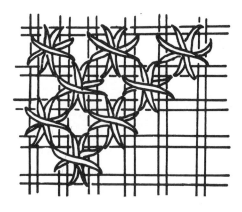

Figure 6.23

PLATE 6.5
Drawn fabric filling No. 1. See Fig. 6.22 and Fig. 6.23

PLATE 6.6
Drawn fabric filling No. 2. See Fig. 7.19

1. See Fig. 6.22 and Fig. 6.23, also Fig. 5.49, Fig. 5.50 and Plate 6.5.

Cut 2 and leave 2 threads alternately in both directions. Use No. 12 cotton. The diagrams show the method of working this filling clearly. Work diagonally in both directions, first from the top left to the right below and back, then from the top right to the left below and back over the intersections of the ground.

See Fig. 7.19 and Plate 6.6

Cut 2 and leave 2 threads alternately in both directions. Use No. 12 cotton. The method is clearly shown on the diagram.

3. See Fig. 6.24 and Plate 6.7

Cut 4 and leave 6 threads alternately in both directions. Use No. 8 cotton and weave 8 times over and under 3 threads around a square of material. After each round the needle is brought behind 2 groups as there is an even number of bars. Secure the thread on the wrong side of the work and proceed to the next square etc.

4. See Fig. 6.25 and Plate 6.8

Cut 6 and leave 8 threads alternately in both directions. Use No. 12 cotton and work geometrical shadow work on the wrong side

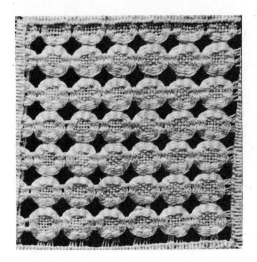

PLATE 6.7
Drawn fabric filling No. 3. See Fig. 6.24

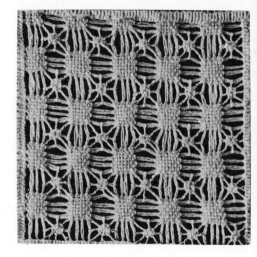

PLATE 6.8
Drawn fabric filling No. 4. See Fig. 6.25

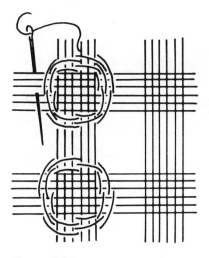

Figure 6.24

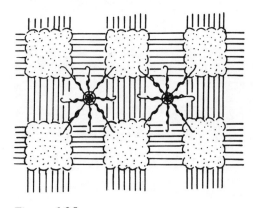

Figure 6.25

of the squares of material. Pass the needle through the back of a group of threads to the next square and repeat till all have been completed. Eight bars will be needed in the open spaces and a wheel is formed by weaving 4 times around the centre, using No. 12 cotton for both the bars and the wheel. Bring the needle through the back of the work to proceed to the next position.

5. See Fig. 6.26 and Plate 6.9

Cut 6 and leave 6 threads alternately in both

directions. Use No. 8 cotton and weave to and fro 4 times around the 2 halves of each square as shown on the diagram. Pass the needle invisibly through the back of the work to the new position. Use No. 12 cotton and proceed as follows where the 4 corners of an open space pull a circle in the mesh: Bring the needle out in one corner of a square of material at a. Work 7 loose buttonhole stitches as shown on the diagram. Overcast from underneath into each loop thus formed and pull tight to form a firm circle. Overcast into the first loop again, overcast to a and finish off at the back of the weaving.

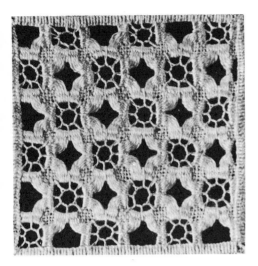

PLATE 6.9
Drawn fabric filling No. 5. See Fig. 6.26

PLATE 6.10
Drawn fabric filling No. 6. See Fig. 6.27

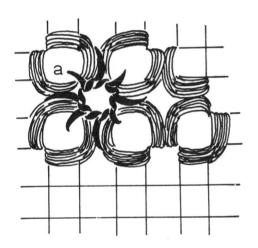

Figure 6.26

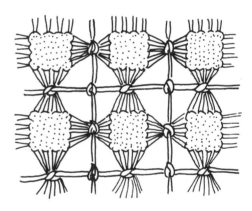

Figure 6.27

6. See Fig. 6.27 and Plate 6.10
Cut 8 and leave 8 threads alternately in both directions. Use No. 12 cotton and work geometrical shadow work on the wrong side over each solid square. Now use No. 8 cotton and work coral stitch to bind all the horizontal groups of 8 threads between the solid squares. Bind the vertical groups in the same way making a coral knot at the intersections.

7. See Fig. 6.28 and Plate 6.11
Cut 2 and leave 6 threads alternately in both directions. Using No. 5 cotton commence at a

and work diagonal rows as shown on the diagram. Three rows lie alternately up and down to fill the whole area.

8. See Fig. 6.29 and Plate 6.12
Cut 4 and leave 8 threads alternately in both directions. Use No. 12 cotton.

(i) Commence at a and weave over the 4 centre threads up to b. Now bind twice diagonally over 2 threads in the corner. Overcast 2 threads up to c, bind twice diagonally over 2 threads in the corner, overcast 2 threads up to d, bind the corner again, overcast up to e, bind the corner and overcast to b. Now weave

179

PLATE 6.11
Drawn fabric filling No. 7. See Fig. 6.28

PLATE 6.12
Drawn fabric filling No. 8. See Fig. 6.29

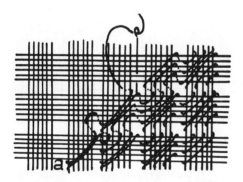

Figure 6.28

from f to g and from h to i. h i is worked
like a b, therefore repeat.

(ii) Commence at k and follow the same
method as in (i). Repeat until the whole
space has been filled.

9. See Fig. 6.30 and Plate 6.13
Cut 4 and leave 8 threads alternately in both
directions. Use No. 8 cotton and twist the
threads of the material over one another in
pairs. See Fig. 6.8 also. Repeat in both directions. Again using No. 8 cotton, the needle is
inserted diagonally over 2 threads of the
corner of a solid square as at a and is brought
out diagonally over 2 threads of the opposite
corner as at b. Take the thread diagonally

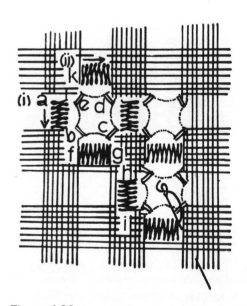

Figure 6.29

across an open space and repeat as at c d.
Repeat at the opposite diagonal and work a
coral knot at the intersections.

10. See Fig. 6.31 and Plate 6.14
Cut 6 and leave 6 threads alternately in both
directions. Commence at a and overcast 3
threads firmly 10 times, pass the needle underneath a solid square and repeat up to b.

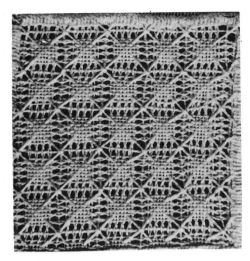

PLATE 6.13
Drawn fabric filling No. 9. See Fig. 6.30

PLATE 6.14
Drawn fabric filling No. 10. See Fig. 6.31

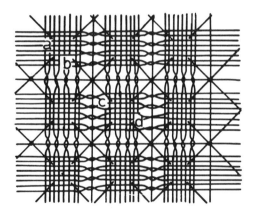

Figure 6.30

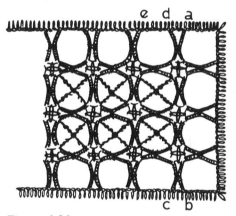

Figure 6.31

Now bring the needle out at c, overcast the other 3 threads of the group 4 times, then twice over all 6 threads and again 4 times over 3 threads. Pass the needle underneath a solid square and repeat up to d. Bring the needle out at e and repeat the whole process until all the vertical bars have been covered. Repeat in the horizontal direction working a cross over the open space and one on the solid square at the same time.

6.3 Needleweaving

This is a very old form of drawn thread work. It consists of the removal of groups of threads,

mostly in one direction only, which are then replaced with embroidery cotton or wool in different shades of colour or in one contrasting shade or in the same shade as the fabric. Although there are various methods of strengthening and decorating the remaining threads as will be shown, the best known is by weaving or darning.

Use any material, preferably evenly woven, with a strong thread that can easily be pulled out. The working thread must be of the same thickness or a little thicker than the thread of the material. No. 8 Pearl cotton will be suitable on evenly woven linen with approx-

PLATE 6.15
Needleweaving in two shades of blue on white Glen'shee linen for a tray-cloth. Note how the additional embroidery further enhances the article

imately 30 threads to 2½ cm or Hardanger linen, No. 5 on linen with approximately 20 threads to 2½ cm etc. Tapestry needles and an embroidery frame are necessities. Although the technique is very simple, the success of the work depends largely on maintaining an even tension throughout, which might not be so easy in the beginning. When coloured cotton or wool is used, the tension of the work must be exactly the same as that of the material. In monochromatic work, e.g. white on white or blue on blue, etc., the tension has to be slightly firmer as the idea is to create spaces between the bars or groups which will give the work a lacy effect. The tension must never be too tight.

Panels in needleweaving on cushion covers or on all kinds of table linen are very pretty, also when combined with other stitches and methods.

Preparation
The preparation for needleweaving is exactly the same as for drawn thread work. See Par. 6.1.

This preparatory work serves 4 purposes:
1. To strengthen the edges.
2. To bind the threads in groups.
3. To decorate.
4. To assist in passing from one group to the next on the wrong side of the work.

It is sensible to remove the threads only in parts as the work progresses, as it is easier to handle. If a wide band is planned, it is recommended that the strip be divided lenthwise by leaving a few threads at intervals over which some decorative stitchery can be worked. See Plate 6.16. It is also advisable to start weaving from the middle of the panel so that the ends will be exactly similar. For strengthening the short sides the second method (See Par. 6.1) should preferably be used.

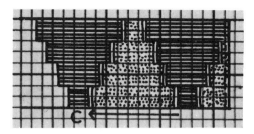

Figure 6.32

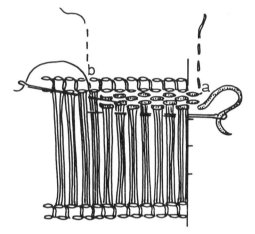

Figure 6.33

The darning or weaving method

1.   Needleweaving in different colours

As stated before the tension of the embroidery must be exactly the same as the tension of the material. The designs for needle-weaving in colour are usually geometric — broken vertical lines, diagonal lines, triangles, squares or zigzag lines, etc. Take care not to make the vertical lines too long as large open spaces are not desirable.

Technique: See Fig. 6.32 and Fig. 6.33
Scale: One vertical line equals one group of threads, or bar.

The design is worked out on graph paper beforehand. See Fig. 6.32. Use, for example, pale blue linen and a deeper shade of blue (No. 799) No. 8 D.M.C. Pearl cotton and also white.

(i)   Remove the 2 boundary lines (threads).

(ii)   Use blue cotton and work a row of double hemstitch over 4 threads on both sides of the drawn threads, so that the groups of threads correspond at either side.

(iii)   Cut the threads in between about 8cm from the right side of the panel, and after unravelling them to the right end of the panel, they must be woven back into the material as described in Par. 6.1.

(iv)   Pull out the threads a little way to the left. Count the number of vertical groups, steps or sections of the design (in this case 4) and using any coloured cotton, mark as many steps on the material along the right end of the panel. See Fig. 6.33. This will be an indication when to proceed to the next part of the design.

(v)   Put the work on a frame.

(vi)   Use blue cotton and tack the thread loosely in the material up to a in Fig. 6.33. The loose end will be finished off into the back of the weaving later on. Now weave to and fro over 7 more groups of threads or bars up to the first mark. The woven threads must be pushed up well so that the material does not show. Weave the same width over 6 bars up to the second mark, again over 4 bars, and finally over only 2 bars which will bring the work to the other side.

(vii)   Pass the needle to and fro through the back of the middle group of woven threads and cut off. Although it will be neater to finish off each colour separately, the thread can be left hanging until it can be brought to the new position via the double hemstitching as at c in Fig. 6.32.

(viii)   Using white cotton, commence in the same way as with the blue and bring the needle out between the next 2 groups at b in Fig. 6.33. The method is the same, but begin over 2 bars and end over 8.

This completes the pattern which is now repeated for the desired length to

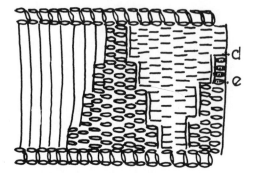

Figure 6.34

This is a very simple design and recommended for beginners. Many more elaborate designs can be devised and a large variety of colours may be used.

Two designs

1. See Fig. 6.35. Width: 3 cm .

Proposed colour-scheme: Material: Pink. Cotton: a is white b is pink like the material and c is a deaper shade of pink.

2. See Fig. 6.36. Width: 6 cm .

Proposed colour-scheme: Material: Ecru. Cotton: A is dark brown, B is rust, C is dark

end as it was begun. If the length of the panel is decided on at the beginning, work must commence from the middle.

(ix) See Fig. 6.34. Using white cotton bring the needle out at d and overcast the edge of the material, up to e, weave over the edge and one bar and then over the edge and 2 bars.

Figure 6.35

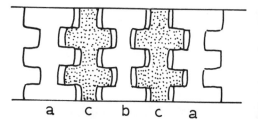

a   c   b   c   a

PLATE 6.16
A cushion cover with needleweaving in wool in shades of blue, grey and rust.

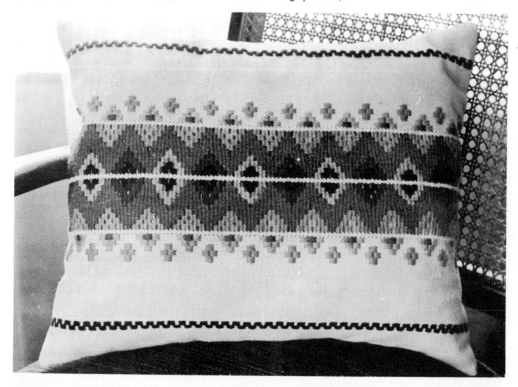

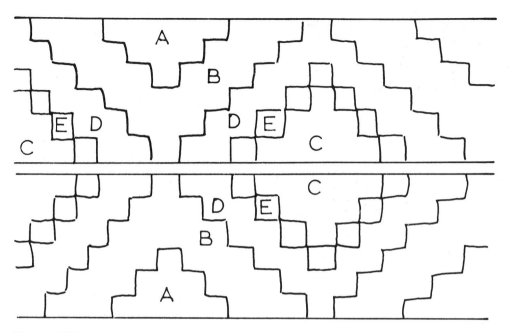

Figure 6.36

green, D is pale green and E is ecru.

    Or

Material: Ivory. Cotton: A is bright blue, B is greyish blue C is navy blue, D is ivory and E is copper.

    Note that threads of the material divided the panel in the middle. Once the technique of needleweaving has been mastered, an embroideress will be able to work from any photo or drawing.

2. *Needleweaving with the material and the cotton in the same colour*
    (1) Weaving only.

In this case the tension must be much tighter than when using colours, so that open spaces result which will give the work a lacy effect. In narrow borders the bars may be woven only in part. See Fig. 6.37

Width of panel: 9 mm .

Commence at a on the wrong side, bring the needle out at b, then weave to and fro over 4

bars and over the thread a b. Take the needle from c through the back of the woven group to d, across to e and emerge at f. Repeat as at b. Fig. 6.38. Width of panel: 31 mm .

This is a wider panel completely woven.

PLATE 6.17
Bands of needleweaving in white or grey linen looks very sophisticated M: Mrs. R. Pienaar

185

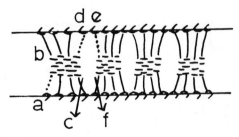

Figure 6.37

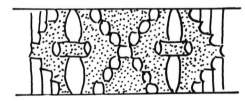

Figure 6.38

(2) Weaving with bars and overcasting.
See Fig. 6.39

Width of panel: 28 mm

(i) First finish the weaving by commencing at a and ending at b.

(ii) Bring the needle out at c and overcast the bar up to d.

(iii) Repeat from e to f.

(iv) Take the needle through b to g. Overcast up to the middle then 3 stitches over all 3 completed bars, pulling these bars together. Complete to h.

(v) Complete i j.

(vi) Bring the needle out at k, complete k l,

but overcast all 3 bars twice as shown on the diagram.

(vii) Complete m n and bind two bars in the centre.

(viii) o p is worked like i j and q r like k l.

(ix) Now weave from s and end at t. Pass the needle to u and complete u v and w x. Repeat from (ii).

(3) Weaving and bullions.
See Fig. 6.40

Width of panel: 13 mm

(i) Strengthen the sides with buttonhole stitch.

(ii) Remove the horizontal threads.

(iii) Cut 6 and leave 8 vertical threads alternately.

(iv) Bring the needle out at a. Make a ring bullion picot in the corner. Pass the needle through the back of the work to b and make another ring bullion picot there.

(v) Weave 8 threads (over 4 and under 4) up to c. Make 2 more ring bullion

Figure 6.39

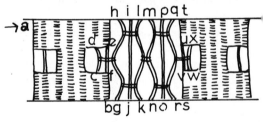

PLATE 6.18
All white needleweaving looks lacy. M: Mrs. Aletta Wessels

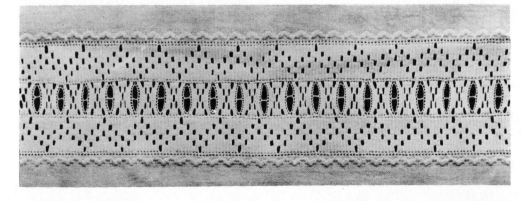

Figure 6.40

picots at c and d.

(vi) Pass the needle through to e and repeat.

(4) Needleweaving and feather stitch.

See Fig. 6.41

Width of panel: 19 mm .

(i) Strengthen the panel on both sides using satin stitch.

(ii) Remove all the horizontal threads.

(iii) Cut 4 and leave 8 vertical threads alternately.

(iv) Commence at a and weave over and under 4 threads up to b.

(v) Bring the needle out at c and weave up to d.

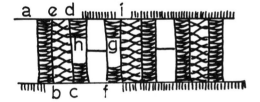

Figure 6.41

(vi) Insert needle on the edge of the weaving on the opposite side at e. Work feather stitch to and fro between the bars, keeping the thread under the needle.

(vii) Pass the needle through on the wrong side to f and weave up to g in die middle of the border. Now insert needle at h in the middle of the previously woven bar and overcast back to g. Complete the bar up to i. Then weave the next bar and repeat.

(5) Needleweaving and twisted bars.

See Fig. 6.42

Width of panel: 9 mm .

(i) Strengthen the border on both sides using hemstitching or double hemstitching.

(ii) Remove all the horizontal threads.

(iii) Commence at a and weave over 6 threads up to b.

(iv) Pass the needle through on the wrong side to c, 6 threads away. Weave over 6 threads up to d and repeat all along.

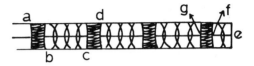

Figure 6.42

(v) Bring the needle out at the side and in the middle of the panel at e. Twist the loose threads over one another in pairs. See Fig. 6.8. Work a small stitch at f at the edge of a woven bar, pass the needle underneath the weaving, work a small stitch at g, twist the 6 loose threads in pairs, etc.

The Scandinavian method

This is a very pretty, light and lacy type of weaving and especially interesting when combined with the ordinary darning method. It should preferably be done in white or cream.

Technique

The method is as follows: See Fig. 6.43

A. The first row: Commence at a and overcast the first bar once.

Figure 6.43

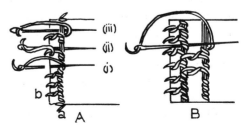

(i) Work the second stitch in the material at b, keeping the thread under and to the right of the needle.

(ii) Pass the needle underneath the bar.

(iii) Overcast the bar again once and repeat from (i). The over-casting keeps the long stitches a little apart.

B. The second row: The long stitches pass over the overcasting of the previous row. The design is built by means of the long stitches and when they are omitted, the overcasting takes their place.

This method can be applied to all kinds of needleweaving and can be combined with overcast bars with success.

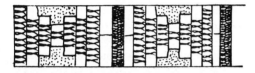

Figure 6.44

Figure 6.45

Two designs

Here ordinary needleweaving is combined with the Scandinavian method. See Fig. 6.44 and Fig. 6.45.

The Roumanïan method

This is a smooth, close and neat kind of weaving. See Fig. 6.46 and Fig. 6.47.

Commence at a and carry the thread across the required number of bars to b and proceed as shown on the diagrams. When the number of completed bars has to be decreased, the needle passes through the back of the work to the right position, e.g. one bar less as shown in Fig. 6.48c.

To increase, pass the needle underneath the

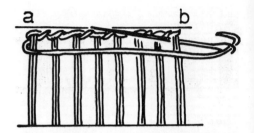

Figure 6.46

Figure 6.47

bars to the desired position and when the next row is worked, this thread is also covered.

This method can be applied to all kinds of needleweaving and can be combined very successfully with the Scandinavian method and with overcast bars.

Additional embroidery

Needleweaving, especially when done in colours, can appear hard and severe and it is often necessary to do a little additional embroidery along the sides of the borders to give the work a softer effect. A great variety of stitches may be tried, but it will be found that counted work will be most satisfactory. Small geometric satin stitch motifs combined with Holbein stitch, narrow borders in cross stitch or even interesting designs in running stitch, will all be suitable. Often the design of the needleweaving could be repeated in the small borders of embroidery.

Figure 6.48

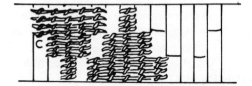

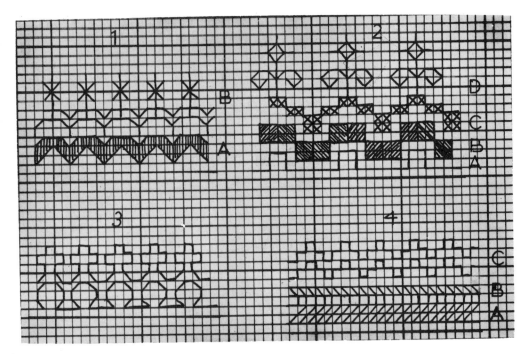

Figure 6.49

The following are a few suggestions:
See Fig. 6.49
Scale: One square equals 3 threads.
1. A. Satin stitch. B. Holbein stitch.
2. A. Holbein stitch. B. Satin stitch squares worked diagonally. C. Cross stitch. D. Holbein stitch.
3. Two rows of Holbein stitch.
4. A. Satin stitch worked diagonally over 6 threads.
B. Satin stitch worked diagonally over 3 threads. Work upright stitches over 3 threads in the space between A and B.
C. Two rows of Holbein stitch.

6.4 Russian drawn thread work
This is another kind of drawn thread work reminiscent of French filet lace because of the fine mesh made in the linen in squares or geometric shapes and on which designs are darned or woven.

Use any strong, fairly evenly woven linen, but even a good quality Irish linen is suitable if it is coarse enough for the threads to be counted. The cotton must be the same, or closely resembling the colour of the material and the work should preferably be done in white or off-white. To outline the mesh, use No. 5 or No. 8 Pearl cotton, depending on the texture of the fabric. To strengthen the mesh a finer thread is used, e.g. No. 12 Pearl Cotton or even a single thread of Stranded cotton. For darning the pattern, use No. 8 or No. 12 cotton.

The work is especially pretty and suitable on table-linen and on chairbacks, cushion covers, etc.

The border around the mesh
This must be worked before the mesh is made. There are several methods:
1. Buttonhole stitch. This is the most common method. Use cotton of the same thickness as the thread of the material. Work over 4 threads and between every thread of the material with the loops where the mesh will be cut. Work only one diagonal stitch in the corner.
2. Satin stitch. Follow the instructions for

buttonhole stitch.

Cutting the mesh

Use a pair of sharp-pointed scissors and cut
and leave 2 threads alternately from side to
side on the wrong side of the work and in both
directions. Commence at the side and see that
the last 2 threads are cut. In the case of a very
fine linen like Irish linen the threads may be
cut and left in groups of 3 instead of 2.

Strengthening the mesh

Choose the design and the method of execution as this will decide the method of
strengthening the mesh. The procedure will
therefor differ in every specific case. The size
of the mesh will depend on the size of the
design. But, if the mesh is intended for a
specific position in the article, it has to be
made first, the number of open spaces
counted and the design worked out accordingly. The design is worked out on squared
paper and one square equals one open space of
the mesh. The design must not fill the mesh
right up to the sides.

PLATE 6.19
A very rich corner of a wide border of Russian drawn
thread on a tea-cloth. The additonal drawn thread embroidery breaks the hard outlines of the Russian drawn
thread work. D: Author, M: Mrs. Anne Brink

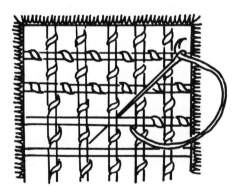

Figure 6.50

1. Overcasting. See Fig. 6.50.
This is generally used and can easily be followed on the diagram. Always work from
right to left and if the linen is coarse, two
stitches must be worked in each open space.
2. Close overcasting. See Fig. 6.51 and Fig.
6.52.
Scale: One square equals one square of the
mesh.

The mesh is overcast completely with close
stitching from right to left and in both directions. This has a more solid effect and usually
the design is already included in the process:
Overcast all the horizontal bars. Then commence on the vertical bars, but keep the design in mind.

   (i) The first row is overcast in the usual
       way from right to left.
  (ii) Turn and work from right to left up to
       the middle of the space that has to be
       filled. Now work a floret as shown in
       Fig. 7.10 and proceed with the over-

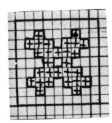

Figure 6.51

casting. In this way the whole design is constructed with florets where indicated.

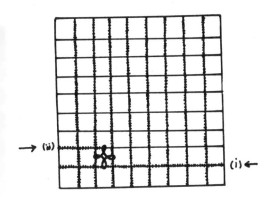

Figure 6.52

3. Four-sided stitch. See Fig. 6.53
Work this on the mesh by binding only once and use it especially in conjunction with the filling No. 1 A, Fig. 6.54. The design is first woven on the bare mesh and the rest is then strengthened by using four-sided stitch. The positions of the 4 needles in Fig. 6.53 (i) — (iv) explain the method.

Figure 6.53

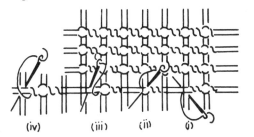

Fillings
1. The method commonly used is ordinary weaving or darning.
A. Weaving in one direction only: See Fig. 6.54

> (i) Strengthen the mesh by overcasting only horizontally. Weave in the design.

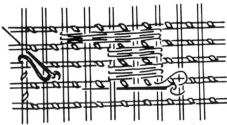

Figure 6.54

> (ii) Strengthen the rest of the mesh in the opposite direction. Note the way in which the needle proceeds to the middle of a new row. This prevents irregularity of the outline.

B. Weaving in both directions: It adds to the interest when parts of the design are woven in the opposite direction as it gives a lighter effect. In this case the whole mesh is first prepared as in Fig. 6.50.
2. The second method includes the filling in of florets in each space that is part of the design. See strengthening of the mesh No. 2.
3. Prepare the mesh by overcasting all the horizontal threads. Darn in the design in a horizontal direction as described in the Roumanian method in Par. 6.3. Strengthen the remaining vertical threads by overcasting. Alternately, the design can first be worked as described above, and the remaining mesh strengthened by using four-sided stitch as shown in Fig. 6.53.
4. For a fourth method, known as filet darning, a reasonably coarse linen (not finer than approximately 20 or 30 threads to 2½ cm in both directions) is recommended. Weave the design on the bare mesh using threads of the material so that it resembles the linen and

191

strengthen the remaining mesh by any method discussed above.

Rules for filet darning:

(1) Weave to and fro over one row of holes before proceeding to the next row. In other words, it is not allowed to change direction in the middle of a row.

(2) Do not begin in the middle of a row.

(3) There is never a choice of direction but only a single route through a design.

(4) Disregard rule (1) when there is only a single open space in the design and proceed as follows: Weave right up to the open space, then to the left of the latter, as far as required and back to the open space. Then weave through the required number of squares up and down back to the open space, then to the right and back and again down to the beginning, completing the first movement.

(5) The embroideress will come to a stage where the work has already been completed in both directions. Pass the needle then through the loop formed by the 2 already existing working threads. The needle may be passed through from the top or from below depending on whether the last stitch passed over or under a thread. The working thread must always preserve the rhythm of over and under strictly. This process gives a pretty scalloped edge, which would otherwise be hard and unfinished. The edge of the design is scalloped in parts in the process of weaving, but other parts remain unfinished, and will be scalloped eventually. This happens automatically if the rules are carefully followed. Having completed the design, the unfinished edge must be scalloped up to the initial starting position.

(6) Scallop around an open space formed by a few squares, before moving away from this open space permanently.

(7) To join the thread: Simply leave the old thread hanging and begin the new thread by also leaving part of it hanging on the wrong side. Later these two threads are twisted around one another once and then separately and invisibly woven into the design.

A simple design for filet darning
See Fig. 6.55, Fig. 6.56 and Plate 6.20.
Scale: One square equals one open space of the mesh.

Commence at a and follow the method clearly indicated in Fig. 6.56.

5. Another method of darning is to strengthen the whole mesh first according to method No. 1, and to add the design afterwards by filet darning with No. 12 or No. 8 Pearl cotton. Treat the 2 combined threads of the mesh as one.

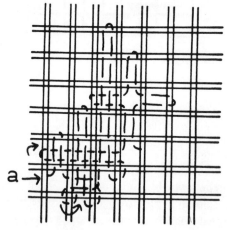

Figure 6.56

A variation of Russian drawn thread work
The following is another method which is regarded as the same kind of drawn thread work.

The design is freehand, i.e. not worked out on counted threads. Use heavy chain stitch or 2 adjacent rows of ordinary chain stitch to outline the design. Then cut and strengthen

Figure 6.55

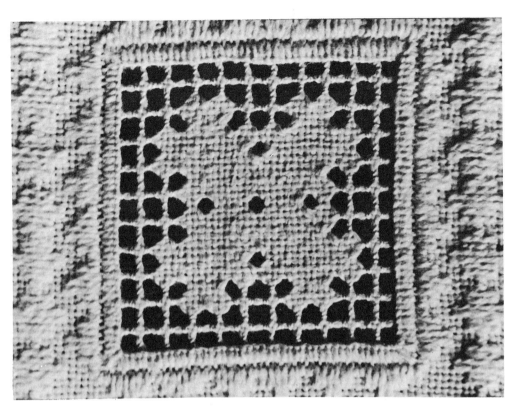

PLATE 6.20
Filet weaving. See Fig. 6.55

the mesh which will form the background.
Finally the design is decorated with geometric
satin stitch fillings. The whole design and the
mesh that surrounds it, lie in a framework of
satin or buttonhole stitch. This can be regarded as the opposite of old Hedebo work.

Additional stitchery
As shown in Plate 6.19 and Plate 6.21, additional stitchery is almost a necessity to finish
off the work. Russian drawn thread work is
often combined with drawn fabric work,
counted work, needleweaving, etc. Although
white or cream is the most effective for this
work, additional colours used in good taste
may be added. See Plate 10.14, 10.15 and
10.16 where blackwork and Holbein stitch are
successfully combined with Russian drawn
thread. A clever embroideress can experiment
and perhaps develop her own individual style.
By repeating the design of the drawn thread

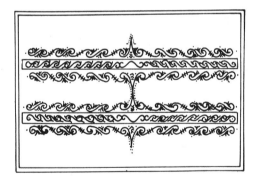

Figure 6.57

work in the additional embroidery, a pretty
effect can be achieved. Long borders of Russian drawn thread work about 6 cm to 8 cm
wide, can be used to divide a tablecloth into
panels and these will give the effect of lace
insertions. Similarly a border 4 cm to 5 cm

193

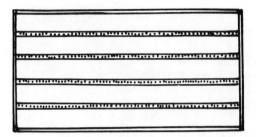

Figure 6.58

wide will be very striking used next to the narrow hem of luncheon-mats.

A tablecloth in Russian drawn thread work D 6.1
Schematic diagram: Fig. 6.57. Size: 127 cm by 230 cm .
Scale of diagram: 6 mm equals 25 cm .
Scale of design: One square equals one space of the mesh, and 3 threads for the drawn fabric work.

Use Glenshee or Evensweave linen preferably. The drawn thread work panel can also be used without the additional drawn fabric

PLATE 6.21
Alternate squares of Russian drawn thread and drawn fabric embroidery make up this beautiful tea-cloth. D: Author, M: Mrs. R. Pienaar

work as in Fig. 6.58.

In this case the long panels are repeated lengthwise on the tablecloth.
Key:
A. Russian drawn thread work. Use buttonhole stitch to strengthen the sides of the panel. Work the design on the panel according to any one of the methods described in this paragraph. It will be interesting if, for example, B is worked in filet darning, the scrolls C, in the Roumanian method and the whole sprig D by darning. Then overcast the mesh as described in Fig. 6.50.
E. Drawn fabric work. F. Four-sided stitch. G. Eyelets. H. Satin stitch, using No. 5 Pearl cotton. I. Satin stitch, using No. 5 cotton. J. First work the four eyelets in the centre, using No. 12 Pearl cotton, and then the satin stitch around them in No. 5 cotton. Complete the floret and the remaining eyelets using No. 12 cotton.

Motifs for Russian drawn thread work D 6.2 and D 6.3
Scale of design: One square equals one open space in the mesh. These little designs may also be used for cross stitch, Sorbello or plait stitch. D 6.3 is the design for one of the squares in the tea cloth in Plate 6.21.

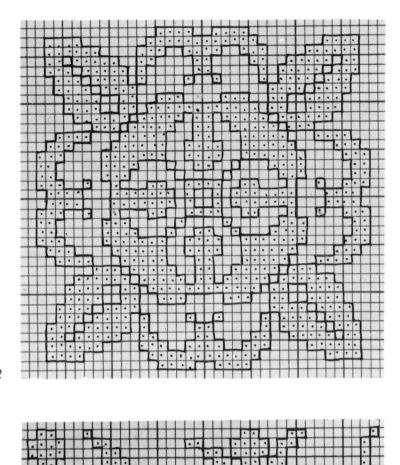

D 6.2

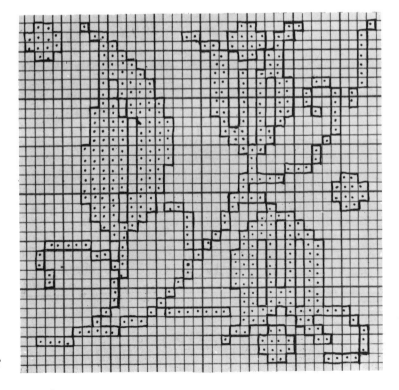

D 6.3

Hardanger work

7.1 Introduction and materials

Hardanger work is very well known and popular because it is reasonably simple to understand and execute. Even a beginner can succeed with her first attempt. At the same time it is most effective and also very durable when done on the correct material. Briefly it can be described as a kind of drawn thread work because threads of the material are removed in both directions to form an open mesh which is then strengthened and decorated. The beautiful and richly-embroidered Hardanger work in museums often have so much drawn thread and cutwork added that they are reminiscent of Hedebo work and Reticella lace. Hardanger work has its own distinctive appearance and character immediately recognised by small satin stitch kloster blocks, which are always worked where the groups of 4 threads have to be cut. These blocks thus serve to strengthen, enrich and adorn the work.

Hardanger work originated in Norway, and takes its name from the Hardanger province along the Hardanger Fjord in Southern Noway, where much of the work is still done. Originally, Hardanger work was usually done in white on a variety of household articles as well as on men's shirts, aprons, bonnets, etc. Many beautiful pieces have been preserved in most of the museums in Europe. In recent times the work has often been done in colour, but care must be taken not to use dark shades as the charm of the work lies in the contrast between the open work and the solid stitches. The lacy effect will be lost if either the material or the cotton is too dark. When using a pale shade of material the working thread may be in the same shade, slightly darker or white. Alternatively a thread in pastel shades may be used on white material. No matter what the choice is, it is advisable to do the open work in a pale shade and finally, Hardanger work in white is always beautiful and successful.

Looking at the very old pieces it strikes one that the work was often done on evenly woven, almost transparent material, but today a special cotton and linen Hardanger fabric is available in different widths up to 170 cm . It has a characteristic flat, double thread, evenly woven, not liable to fray easily and not springy. Work on loosely woven and springy material will not be durable.

The thread used for the satin stitch must be slightly thicker than a thread of the material. Anchor Pearl cotton No. 5, which is slightly thicker than D.M.C. Pearl cotton, is recommended for most kinds of Hardanger material. For strengthening the mesh No. 12 Pearl cotton is suitable although many needlewomen prefer No. 8 because it speeds up the work considerably, but using the latter, the effect will be coarser and not really lacy. Use the same Pearl cotton for the additional embroidery and tapestry needles with blunt points No. 's 22, 24 and 26 depending on the thickness of the thread. A tambour frame is essential as well as a small sharp-pointed pair of scissors for cutting the threads.

The old Hardanger work designs were strictly geometric and formal, consisting of triangles, diamond-shapes or zigzag patterns. Today the imagination is given free scope and many new variations have developed on an old but always beautiful theme. The designs are now mainly of two kinds. Firstly that in which the open work forms the design on a linen background and secondly that in which the linen forms the design on a background of Hardanger work. The first kind is more common and gives greater scope for variety and

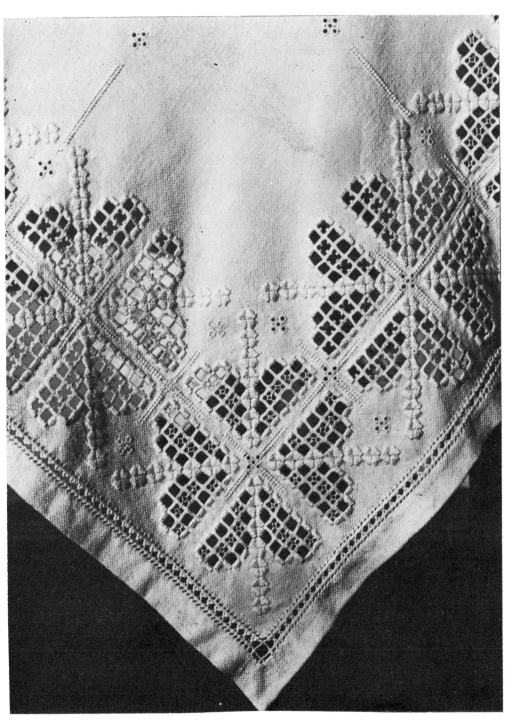

PLATE 7.1
The corner of a tea-cloth in Hardanger work. Size: 152 cm x 152 cm . Open Italian hem. D: Author, M: Mrs. Elize
Stockenström.

additional embroidery. It is absolutely necessary to plan the design on squared paper first
according to which one square equals two
threads. This is to ensure that all the threads
which are to be cut and removed, will be
secured at both ends by means of satin
stitches.

Hardanger work alone often appears hard
and angular because of its geometric character, but it can be combined successfully with
additional stitchery to soften and finish it off.
The stitches used are mostly satin stitch and a
limited number of pulled work stitches.
Panels of needleweaving or drawn thread
work combine well with Hardanger work and
finishes off an article beautifully.

PLATE 7.2
A richly embroidered tea-cosy in a simple Hardanger
pattern. DM: Author

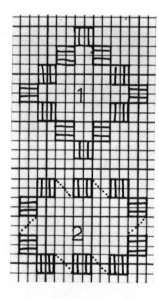

Figure 7.1

7.2 Technique
1. *The kloster blocks*
See Fig. 7.1
Scale throughout: One square equals 2
threads.

Use a frame and work the kloster blocks
first, using No. 5 cotton. The simplest form of
Hardanger work consists of cutting and removing 4 threads, and leaving 4 threads alternately in both directions, inside a framework
of kloster blocks in satin stitch. The cutting of
the threads is left to the very last. A kloster
block consists of 5 satin stitches worked over
4 threads of the material where a group of 4
threads are going to be cut and removed.
These stitches always lie in the same direction
as the threads of the material to be cut. The
direction of the stitches is indicated on the
squared paper by 2 lines as in Fig. 7.1. When
the blocks are worked on the straight of the
material a slanting stitch at the back of the
work will take the thread from one block to
the next as shown in Fig. 7.1, No. 2. But
when the blocks are worked diagonally a
slanting stitch is not allowed at the back of the
work as it will show after the threads have
been cut. To finish off the thread it is advisable to weave to and fro 3 times through the
back of a kloster block catching the first and
last stitches at each turning. This will be firm
enough and will look neater than taking the
thread through the back of a whole row of

blocks. This last method is permissible when the satin stitches have been worked diagonally. When all the kloster blocks have been made the framework is complete and the additional embroidery is then done before cutting the threads.

II. Additional embroidery

1. Satin stitch. This is always worked with No. 5 cotton. Use any satin stitch motif and the length of these stitches may vary from over one to over 10 threads. A star is very popular and is often found on old pieces.

The following are a few variations on the star motif:
See Fig. 7.2. Scale: One square equals 2 threads.

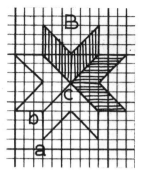

Figure 7.2B

rection. Some of the stitches will meet in the same holes in the corners. Repeat until the star has been completed.

B. Bring the needle out at a and insert 6 threads higher at b. Now work a V-shape consisting of 19 stitches with the 10th stitch at

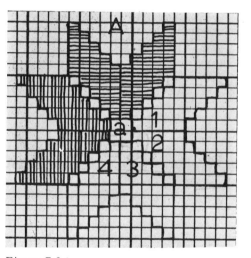

Figure 7.2A

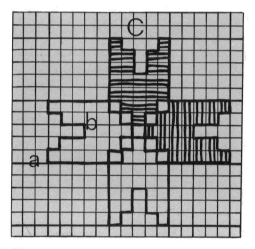

Figure 7.2C

A. (*) Bring the needle out at a and work 2 upright satin stitches over 2 threads, keeping the stitches level below, work 2 more stitches over 4 threads, then 2 over 6, 2 over 8 and 3 over 10 threads. Now keep the stitches level at the top and work 2 stitches over 8, 2 over 6, 2 over 4 and 2 over 2 threads.* This completes section 1. Pass the needle through the back of the work to a and work 2 in the same way and adjoining 1, but reversed. Work 3 and 4 similarly but with the stitches in the opposite di-

the base in the centre. Work the other 3 sides in the same way being careful that each side meets the previous one in the same hole and all 4 stitches in the centre at c.

C. See Plate 7.5. Bring the needle out at a, keep the following 11 stitches level below and work 2 stitches over 2 threads, 4 over 4, and 5 over 10 threads. The following 2 stitches are 2 threads shorter at the top and bottom covering 6 threads and similarly the next 2 will be over

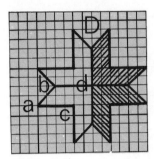

Figure 7.2D

2 threads. Pass the needle through the back of the work to b and work 4 stitches over 4 threads and 2 over 2 to complete one section. Work the other 3 sections in the same way, taking care of the direction of the stitches and seeing that they meet in the same holes on the sides and form an open space of 2 threads by 2 in the centre.

D. Bring the needle out at a and pass it diagonally across 4 threads to b. Work 8 more similar stitches over 4 threads up to the corner c d. Work the following 8 stitches in the same way but emerge below c every time and insert below d. Work the other sections in the same way and see that they meet in the same holes on the sides and all 4 stitches in the centre at d.

E. Bring the needle out at a, keep all the stitches level below and work 2 stitches over 2 threads, 2 over 4 and 7 over 6. Now keep them level at the top and work 2 over 4 and 2 over 2.

Figure 7.2E

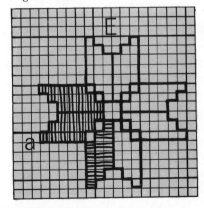

Work a mirror-image of this adjoining the first section and complete the other 3 sections in the same way. Note that the corners meet in the same holes on the sides and that an open square of 4 threads by 4 threads results in the centre.

F. See Plate 7.5. Commence at a, keep the stitches level below and work 2 stitches over 2 threads, then 3 over 4. Work 3 steps of 2 stitches over 4 threads, each 2 threads higher than the previous one and then 2 stitches over 2 threads level with the last step at the top. This is position b. Bring the needle out at c, 4 threads to the right of b and repeat the second half in the same way right up against the first half. Complete the other 7 sections of the star in the same way, taking care that the corners meet and form a square of 4 by 4 threads.

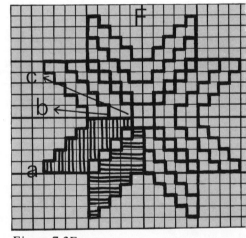

Figure 7.2F

2. Eyelets. Use No. 12 cotton and work the eyelets over a square of 4 by 4 threads with 5 stitches on each side. They are usually worked closely in groups.

3. Hardanger single faggot stitch. See Fig. 7.3
Scale: One line equals one thread.
The method for double faggot stitch has been described in Par. 1.7, where each group of threads is bound twice. Now use No. 8 cotton

bind only once and in such a way that the back of the stitch is on the right side of the material.

(i) Bring the needle out at a, insert at b, 2 threads diagonally across from a and bring it out at c, 2 threads to the right of b.

(ii) Insert at d, 2 threads diagonally across from c and bring it out at b.

(iii) Insert at e, 2 threads diagonally across from b and bring it out at d. b e is worked like a b. Repeat as far as necessary.

(iv) The diagram shows the second row worked right up against the first one resulting in double stitches in the middle.

(v) and (vi) show the method of changing the direction of work.

4. Four-sided stitch. Use No. 8 cotton and bind only once over 2 threads for Hardanger work.

5. Algerian eyelets. Use No. 8 cotton over 2 threads and again bind only once.

6. Diagonal raised band. This is worked in the same way as in drawn fabric work.

7. Rice stitch is worked on the material over 4 threads.

8. Cross stitch.

9. Sorbello stitch

10. Plait stitch.

11. Herringbone stitch.

12. Surface darning. Use a tambour frame and No. 8 cotton. This is a most effective decoration with any kind of embroidery and on any material. It is worked over threads of the same or different lengths radiating from a

Figure 7.3

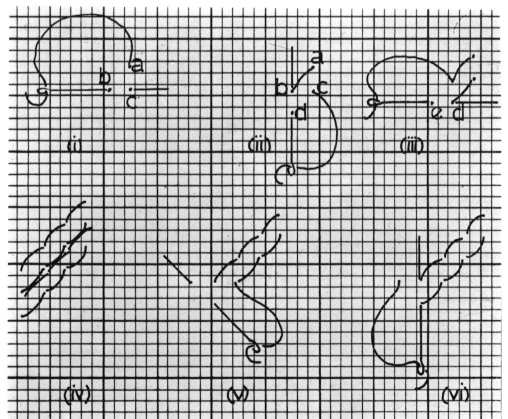

centre. The darning is done over these threads covering them completely or only partially and quite detached from the material. Strengthen the parts of the threads not covered by overcasting. See Fig. 7.6 for a few examples of this type of darning. There are many more similar possibilities, and the shape can be planned according to a given space. Enrich and decorate the ends of these threads with a bullion as follows: See Fig. 7.4.

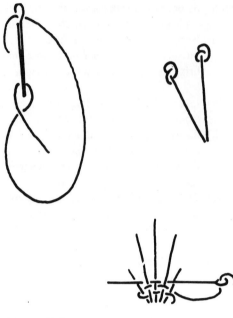

Figure 7.4

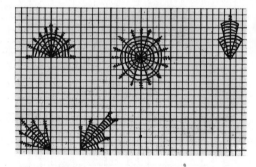

Figure 7.5

Take care that the bullion does not slip through to the wrong side. The method is clearly shown in Fig. 7.5.

13. Backstitch wheels. See Fig. 7.7

Use No. 8 cotton. This also consists of threads radiating in the shape of a wheel over which backstitch is worked. Bring the needle out near the centre of the wheel. Insert it from the top over one and under 2 of the bars and repeat in a circle until the whole wheel has been covered.

14. Drawn thread work of any kind especially needleweaving, is very beautiful with Hardanger work.

When all the additional embroidery has been done, the threads are cut, strengthened and decorated.

III. *Cutting of the threads*

Frayed ends of threads never show on a perfect piece of Hardanger work. Remove the frame temporarily when cutting the threads. Cut 4 threads of the material right up against the 5 stitches of the kloster block, so that no raw ends are visible. It is very difficult to cut

Figure 7.6

off these ends afterwards without damaging the satin stitches. Raw ends will be more noticeable when the satin stitches have been worked in a contrasting colour. Lift the thread of the material a little with the scissors and then cut right up against the satin stitch. Another way in which to eliminate raw ends is as follows: See Fig. 7.8

According to the weave of the material 2 of the 4 threads to be cut pass over the first horizontal thread in front of the kloster block and 2 lie underneath the horizontal thread. Now cut only the 2 top threads on the right side of the work and cut the remaining 2 on the

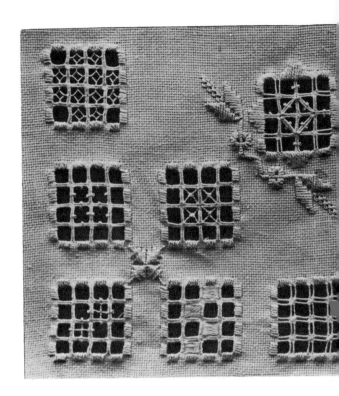

wrong side where they will then lie above the horizontal thread. Remove the groups of 4 threads in both directions.

Figure 7.7

IV. Strengthening and decorating the remaining threads

1. Woven bars. See Fig. 7.9
Use No. 12 or No. 8 cotton. The bars must always be woven diagonally. Cross over to the next bar lying perpendicular to the previous one as shown on the diagram. Make a habit of always passing the needle under the first and over the last 2 threads when the bars are woven. It is especially necessary later when the picots are added. Pull the thread tight so that the bars will be firm and narrow.

2. Woven bars with a Hardanger flower. See

Figure 7.8

Fig. 7.10 and Plate 7.3
This method is typical of Hardanger work. The spaces to be decorated with a flower must be indicated on the design beforehand by means of a cross. Begin the flower from the middle of the 4th side of the space as indicated in (i), (ii) and (iii) of the diagram. Bring the needle out in the middle of the incomplete bar and proceed with the weaving.

PLATE 7.4
Fillings and motifs in Hardanger work. From left to right: nos. 9 and 12; No. 11, 13, 7, 9 and 12.

203

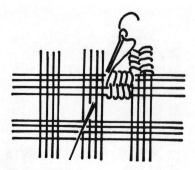

Figure 7.9

3. Woven bars with picots. See Fig. 7.11 and Plate 7.3

Work all the bars of an open space in this way or use the picots intermittently or only on one side of a bar depending on the effect desired. Weave a bar up to the middle. Twist the thread around the needle once as shown on the diagram. Keep the thread taut and pull the needle through while the picot is held in position between the thumb and forefinger. Now make the picot on the opposite side of the bar and complete the weaving of the bar. Twist the thread around the needle twice if a bigger picot is desired.

4. Woven bars with a cross. See Fig. 7.12 and Plate 7.3

Decide beforehand which open spaces are to be filled. Complete the 4th side of an open space and proceed as follows: Bring the needle out at a in the centre of a solid square. Insert at b and overcast the thread twice. Then insert at c, overcast this new thread twice up

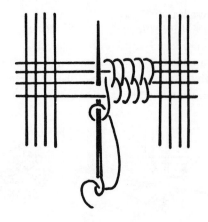

Figure 7.11

to the middle, repeat to d and back. Weave twice around the 4 bars in the centre to join them together and overcast the single thread from a twice. Pass the needle through the back and proceed with the weaving.

5. Woven bars with a flower and picots. See Fig. 7.13 and Plate 7.3

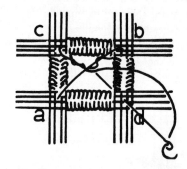

Figure 7.12

Figure 7.10

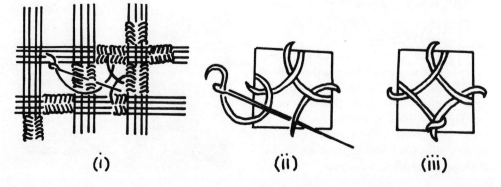

(i)   (ii)   (iii)

204

Always use No. 12 cotton. While weaving, place 4 picots outside of an open space and then make a Hardanger flower inside with an extra stitch of overcasting which gives it a different appearance, as is clearly shown on the diagram.

Figure 7.13

6. Woven squares. See Fig. 7.14 and Plate 7.3

Weave all the horizontal bars in the usual way, using No. 12 cotton. In this case it cannot be done diagonally. Now use No. 8 cotton and weave over the alternate open space as shown on the diagram. Fill the spaces in diagonally.

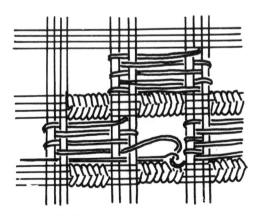

Figure 7.14

7. Single overcast bars. See Plate 7.4 Overcast in firm, close stitches over all 4 threads of a bar. Overcast and woven bars should not be used on the same article as each one gives

quite a different character to the work. They are also not suitable for a loosely woven material. Always use No. 12 cotton.

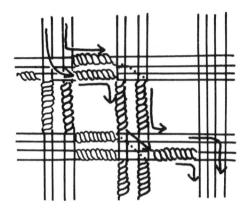

Figure 7.15

8. Double overcast bars. See Fig. 7.15 and Plate 7.3

A very pretty method is to halve the threads of each bar and to overcast each half separately so that small and neat double bars result. First overcast one half of each bar diagonally over the whole area and then the second half.

9. Double overcast bars with a flower. See

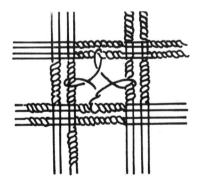

Figure 7.16

Fig. 7.16 and Plate 7.4

Overcast the bars as described in No. 8. Work a Hardanger flower on the inside of an open space as shown on the diagram. See Fig. 7.10 also.

10. Single overcast bars with a flower. Follow the same method as in No. 9 but over single overcast bars.

11. A simple filling. See Fig. 7.17 and Fig. 7.18 and Plate 7.4
A few fillings e.g. No.'s 11, 12 and 13 are worked without strengthening the threads beforehand. This is also a very pretty and quick method, but naturally not as durable as the others. This method is shown clearly on the 2 diagrams and also the way in which the subsequent rows follow the previous ones.

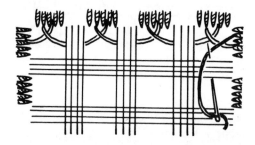

Figure 7.17

12. Filling with a flower. See Fig. 7.19, Plate 7.4 and Plate 6.6
This is worked in the same way as the Hardanger flower in No. 2. The diagram shows the diagonal working method from the top left to the right below as well as the way in which to proceed from one flower to the next. Use

Figure 7.18

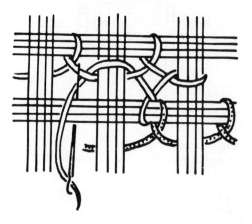

this filling in alternate squares and catch the long thread at the back of the work when making the next flower.

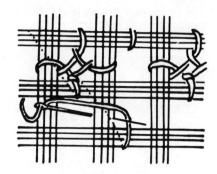

Figure 7.19

13. Blanket stitch filling. See Fig. 7.20 and Plate 7.4
Using No. 8 cotton work this very attractive filling by making 4 loose blanket stitches on the 4 sides of the bare mesh with the loops on the inside. Overcast so that a firm circle is formed in the centre. Always commence in the top lefthand corner of a space and after completion pass the needle through the back of the work to the next open space as shown at a on the diagram. Fill the open spaces alternately.

Figure 7.20

14. Diagonal leaf filling. See Fig. 7.21, Fig. 7.22 and Plate 7.4
This is a beautiful filling for the more experienced needlewoman. A variety of interesting effects may be achieved by arranging these diagonal bars as shown in Fig. 7.21. Decide

206

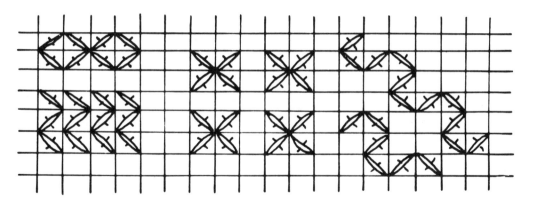

Figure 7.21

beforehand on the squares to be filled and use No. 12 or No. 8 cotton.

While weaving, take a thread 5 times diagonally from corner to corner where indicated. Now weave back (3 threads in one group and 2 in the other) to the initial corner. Keep the tension firm near the corner and slacker in the centre to get the effect of a leaf. Add two picots for further decoration. The mesh may be overcast instead of woven which will allow more space for the small diagonal leaves.

Figure 7.22

15. Combinations. See Fig. 7.23
Very attractive results may be achieved by combining the different fillings. Use, for example, nos. 8, 14, 2 and one together as shown on the diagram.

7.3 Small motifs

There are many small motifs which may be

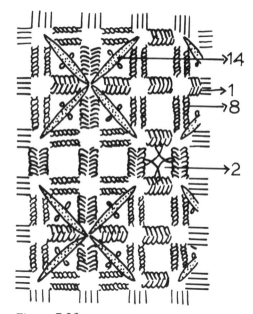

Figure 7.23

used in advanced Hardanger work. They usually consist of an outline in satin stitch around 6, 8 or more threads, which are totally or partially removed.

These open spaces may be filled with a variety of lacy fillings, many of them reminiscent of the corners of drawn thread work panel. Scale throughout: One square equals 2 threads. The following are a few examples: See Plate 7.5.

1. See Fig. 7.24 No. 1
The diagram shows the method of working

207

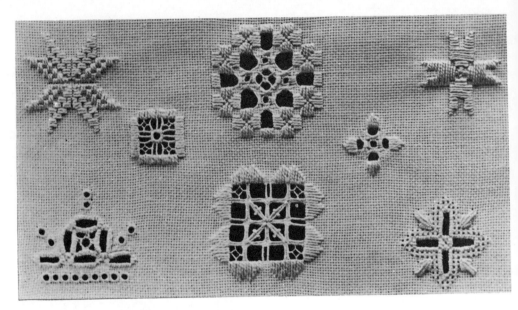

PLATE 7.5
Motifs in Hardanger work. From left to right: Satin stitch star: Fig. 7.2, no F; motif: Fig. 7.26 no 8; Motif: Fig. 7.25 no 4; Motif Fig. 7.24 no 1; Motif: Fig. 7.25 no 6.

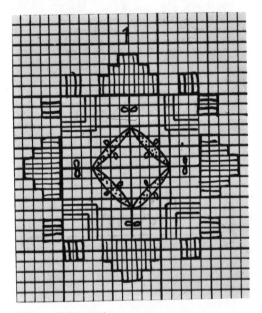

Figure 7.24 no 1

Figure 7.24 no 2

or No. 8 cotton (Fig. 7.15) weave the rest with picots where shown. Work diagonally woven leaves (Fig. 7.21) in the middle.

2. See Fig. 7.24 No. 2 and Plate 7.4
The diagram shows the method of working the satin stitch outline, using No. 5 cotton. Cut 4 and leave 4 threads alternately in both directions. Overcast the 2 bars in the centre, carry 3 threads from corner to corner over the straight bars, and overcast back, passing the needle underneath the straight bars to secure the latter. Overcast the last diagonal bar up to

the satin stitch outline, using No. 5 cotton. Inside this outline the threads are cut right up against the satin stitch. Cut 4 threads and leave 4 alternately in both directions. Double overcast the bars in the corners using No. 12

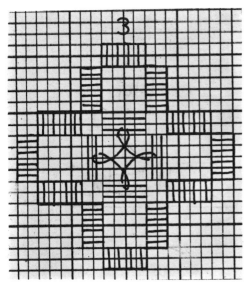

Figure 7.24 no 3

the middle and make a backstitch wheel over the bars as in Fig. 7.7. Complete the last bar.

3. See Fig. 7.24 No. 3 and Plate 7.4
Work double kloster blocks with 9 satin stitches over 4 threads as shown on the diagram. Cut 8 threads in both directions to form a cross. Double overcast the remaining bars and decorate with a Hardanger flower in the centre.

Figure 7.25 no 4

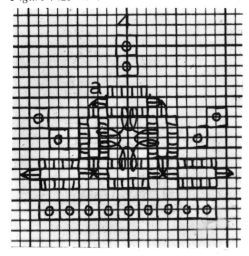

4. See Fig. 7.25 No. 4 and Plate 7.5
These oblong open spaces are often found on old Hardanger work. Use No. 5 cotton* commence at a and work 9 satin stitches over 2 threads, then one over 2, one over 3 and one over 2 threads on the corner. Then again 9 satin stitches over 2 threads and another corner like the previous one up to a *. Now work 4 similar small motifs from * to * in a square of 8 threads by 8 threads in the middle. Work 2 more similar motifs on either side below and eyelets with No. 12 cotton or DMC Brillanté D'Alsace No. 30 over a square of 4 by 4 threads as on the diagram. Now cut out the whole area between the rows of satin stitch

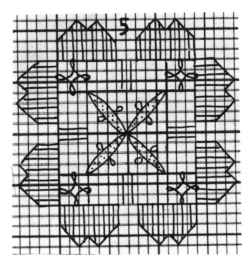

Figure 7.25 no 5

over 2 threads as well as the square in the middle. Work a double Hardanger flower in No. 8 cotton in this square and overcast around the centre of the flower once.

5. See Fig. 7.25 No. 5 and Plate 7.3
Use No. 5 cotton and work the satin stitch outline as shown on the diagram. Cut 4 and leave 4 threads alternately. Overcast the bars in the middle of each side in pairs and weave the rest. Make 4 diagonal woven leaves in the centre and a Hardanger flower in each corner.

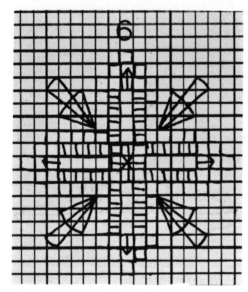

Figure 7.25 no 6

6. See Fig. 7.25 No. 6 and Plate 7.5
Place 4 motifs as described in No. 4 from * to
* with the corners meeting in the centre. Now
work a row of four-sided stitch in No. 8 cotton
around these motifs as shown on the design
and a motif in surface darning in each corner.

7. See Fig. 7.26 No. 7 and Plate 7.5

Figure 7.26 no 7

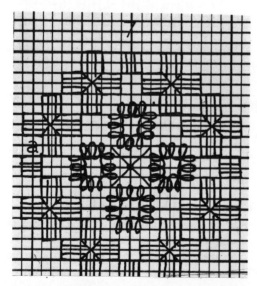

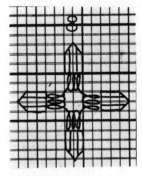

Figure 7.26 no 8

Use No. 5 cotton and work the outline in satin
stitch as shown on the diagram. *Commence
at a and work one stitch over 4, one over 5 and
one over 6, again one over 5 and one over 4*,
and repeat according to the design. Cut 4 and
leave 4 threads alternately in the centre. Work
the buttonhole stitch filling in the 4 open
spaces and a cross in the centre.

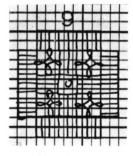

Figure 7.26 no 9

8. See Fig. 7.26 No. 8 and Plate 7.5
Using No. 5 cotton, work 4 satin stitch
squares in position as described in No. 7 from
* to *. Cut the 4 threads between the opposite
squares. Now work buttonhole stitch (see
Fig. 7.20) fairly tightly over the remaining 4
threads of each side and overcast once
through the loops of the stitches.

9. See Fig. 7.36 No. 9 and Plate 7.5
Using No. .5 cotton, work 15 satin stitches
over 4 threads on each side of a square. Cut 4,
leave 6 and cut 4 threads in the middle. Use
No. 12 cotton or DMC Brillanté D'Alsace No.
30 and work an eyelet of 6 threads by 6 in the
centre. Double overcast the remaining 6

210

threads on each side (3 in a group) and work a Hardanger flower in each corner.

7.4 Designs for hardanger borders

The following are a few narrow panels in Hardanger work which are worked diagonally or on the straight. They are very useful for finishing off an article or wider borders can be based on these ideas.

1. See Fig. 7.27 No. 1
A diagonal band. Work the kloster blocks in position as shown and cut the 4 threads between the opposite squares. The remaining groups of 6 threads are overcast in pairs.

2. See Fig. 7.27 No. 2
Use No. 5 cotton and work the zigzag pattern in satin stitch. Commence at a and work 4 satin stitches over 4 threads, the following 5 stitches are 2 threads shorter below and 4 threads longer above (therefor over 6 threads). The next 4 stitches are again in a line with the first 4. Now work the 5 lower stitches over 6 threads. All the motifs meet in the corners. Next the open motifs are worked. Use No. 5 cotton and work a square with 13 satin stitches over 4 threads on each side. Cut 4, leave 4 and cut 4 threads in both directions inside these

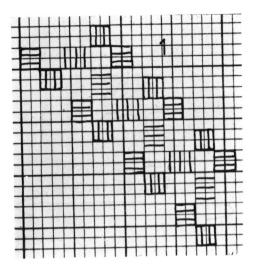

Figure 7.27 no 1

motifs. The open mesh may be strengthened and decorated in various ways as shown on the diagram.

3. See Fig. 7.27 No. 3
This is an easy and pretty border. Using No. 5 cotton, commence at a and work 3 stitches over 4 threads. The following 5 stitches remain level with the first 3 at the top, but are 4 threads longer below and therefore over 8 threads. Then again 3 over 4, 5 over 8 etc. Work the second row a shown on the dia-

Figure 7.27 no 2

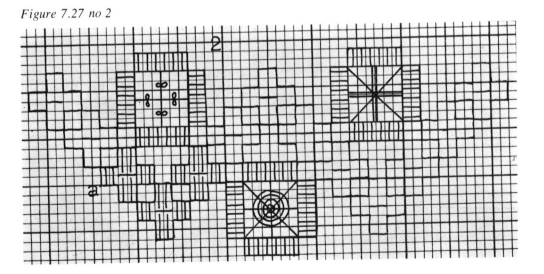

gram. Work the kloster blocks in position and cut the holes on the inside.

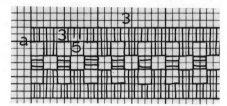

Figure 7.27 no 3

4. See Fig. 7.27 No. 4
An exceptionally pretty diagonal band. Work the kloster blocks in position, cut the necessary threads and overcast the exposed threads in pairs.

Figure 7.27 no 4

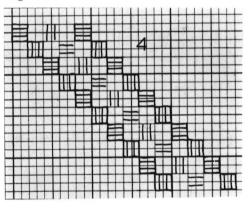

5. See Fig. 7.27 No. 5
Using No. 5 cotton, work 9 satin stitches over 2 threads, and work one satin stitch over 2 threads on the corner perpendicular to the previous ones. Work a second row of 9 satin stitches right up against the first group and again one stitch in the corner. Work a row of double faggot diagonally and a second row right up against the first. Now cut a slit between the 2 groups of 9 stitches. A very effective wide panel can be built up in this way.

7.5 **A Beautiful hem for hardanger work**
See Plate 7.6, Fig. 7.28 and Fig. 7.29

Scale: One square equals 2 threads.

The following is a particularly beautiful way in which to finish off the hem of any article, e.g. a tea cloth, guest towels, etc. Use No. 5 cotton, commence at c, at least 14 threads from the raw edge of the material. Work a row of satin stitches over 2, 3, 4, 5 and 6 threads, then again over 5, 4, 3, 2 and one

Figure 7.27 no 5

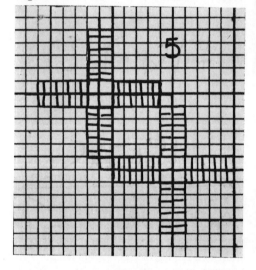

thread, and repeat. Again using No. 5 cotton, work a zigzag row of satin stitches over 4 threads right up against the previous row. Work a similar row in the opposite direction, but over 2 threads except for the top-most stitch which is over 4 threads. Work a pulled

Figure 7.28

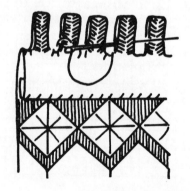

PLATE 7.6
A beautiful hem in Hardanger work. See Fig. 7.28 and Fig. 7.29.

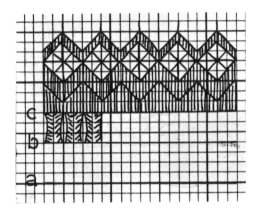

Figure 7.29

work star in the open diamonds using No. 8 cotton. Now remove 6 threads below c up to b. Use No. 8 cotton and weave bars consisting of 4 threads — under and over 2 threads — to and fro. Now fold the material to the wrong side so that these bars are folded double. Use No. 12 cotton and, on the wrong side, overcast in small stitches between each loop to join the 2 parts in this way.

Pass the needle through a loop to overcast between the next 2 loops, (Fig. 7.28) Now fold the 8 threads to the wrong side in a small hem and secure it by slip-stitching into the satin stitches using thin cotton.

7.6 A Cushion cover in hardanger work
D 7.1
See Plate 7.7
Scale of design: One square equals 2 threads.
Size: 45 cm by 33 cm .

The original cushion cover consisted of 2 shades of blue Hardanger material joined in the middle. The position of the design is clearly shown on Plate 7.7. Pale blue cotton is used on the darker half and vice versa. This design can be arranged in many different ways. It can also be used on a variety of articles e.g. for the border on a cloth, on curtains etc.
Key:
A. See Par. 7.2 IV No. 2. B. See Par. 7.2 IV No. 1
C. See Par. 7.2 IV No. 3. D. See Par. 7.2 IV No. 13
E. See Par. 7.2 IV No. 8. F. Satin stitch. G. Eyelets.

7.7 A border in hardanger work
D 7.2
Schematic diagram: See Fig. 7.30
Width: 18 cm . Scale of design: One square equals 2 threads.

Parts of this design may be used for other purposes as explained at the end of the paragraph.

See Par. 2.2 before attempting this design.

D 7.1

PLATE 7.7
Design D7.1. A cushion in Hardanger work.

PLATE 7.8
A typical piece of Hardanger work straight from Norway!

Figure 7.30

Key:

A. First work all the kloster blocks shown on the design — this forms the framework and in this way the position of the design can be planned.

B. The method of working this design is explained in Par. 7.3 No 2.

C. The groups of satin stitch leaves at the base: Using No. 5 cotton, commence at the bottom and work 2 stitches over 2 threads, 2 over 4, 5 over 6, 2 over 4 and 2 over 2. The corners of the 4 leaves meet and the stitches of the 2 in the middle are perpendicular to the 2 leaves on the sides. The leaves along the stem: Work 2 stitches over 2, 2 over 4, 2 over 6, 3 over 8, 2 over 6, 2 over 4 and 2 over 2 threads.

D. Eyelets. E. See Fig. 7.31

Scale: One square equals 2 threads. Use No. 5 cotton and bring the needle out at a, insert at b, 4 threads to the left of a. Work another stitch over 4 threads similar to the first one (a b). Then work 2 stitches over 8 threads (2 threads longer than a b on either side). Now bring the needle out in the middle of and next to the last stitch and work 5 stitches over 6 threads — i.e. c d. Bring the needle out at e, i.e. 4 threads below c and work 2 stitches over 8 threads (2 shorter than d) and then again 2 stitches over 4 threads, 2 threads shorter on either side. Take the needle through to c and

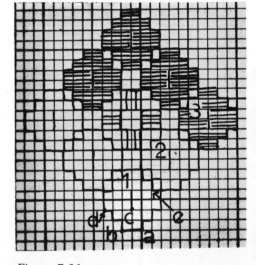

Figure 7.31

work 5 stitches over 6 threads towards e. This completes 1. Work 7 more in the same way and take note of the way in which they are arranged so that all the corners meet and all the stitches lie in the same direction. Work 4 kloster blocks in the centre and cut an open space of 4 by 4 threads.

F. This is described in Par. 7.3 No. 8

G. The stem of the flower is worked in satin stitch over 4 threads and using No.5 cotton.

H. The 2 branches on either side of the main stem are worked in rows of Hardanger double

216

PLATE 7.9
A lovely border in Hardanger work. D: Author, M: Miss Helena van der Merwe.

PLATE 7.10
A scone-cover in Hardanger work. D: Author, M: Miss. R. de Villiers.

faggot. (Par. 7.2 II No. 3.)

I. The filling of the W-shape at the base consists of woven bars with picots. (Par. 7.2 IV No. 3.)

J. The filling of the pyramid-shape consists of woven bars with Hardanger flowers where indicated on the design. (Par. 7.2 IV No. 2.)

Additional use of this design

1. This part used alone will result in a very pretty narrower border.

2. Repeat this motif 4 times with a as centre. Add smaller motifs in the open spaces to form a pretty design for a cushion cover.

3. Place the motif in a straight or zigzag row for a border. See also Chapter 10, Par. 10.1 for more Hardanger work designs.

8.1 Introduction and materials

Blackwork

Blackwork is a very old type of embroidery especially popular in Spain and England during the 16th century, which explains why it is also known as Spanish blackwork or Elizabeth blackwork. The oldest pieces found in museums were mostly worked with a single thin black silk thread on fine white or cream-coloured material. Although the blackwork of today is usually much coarser, even being done in wool, the finer and more delicate examples are still the most beautiful. The charm of blackwork lies in the choice and arrangement of the variety of fillings, which give interesting diversity as well as rhythm and balance to a piece of work. As in photography, interesting contrasts can be achieved by using white and black as well as all the shades of grey. It goes very well with our modern interior decoration and atmosphere and this accounts for the interest lately shown in this lovely type of embroidery.

A very famous piece of blackwork of the 16th century can be seen in the Victoria and Albert Museum in London. The design consists of vine-leaves and grapes. Ever since then there has been a tendency to repeat these motifs in blackwork, but almost any theme is suitable and designs can roughly be classified as follows:

1. Designs with freehand outlines and reasonably large motifs in which fillings are worked, and

2. designs based on counted thread, also with open spaces for fillings.

3. Designs on which the motifs are only outlined while the background is worked in blackwork. See Plate 8.5.

In the designs of the first kind much use is made of surface stitchery on the lines of the design, the most popular being chain stitch, Portuguese stem stitch, double knot stitch and coral stitch. This is done after completion of the fillings. The working thread being black, a great variety of stitches will not show up well and diversity and contrast are more easily achieved by using different thicknesses of thread. The outlines of the second type of

PLATE 8.1
Section of a large tea-cloth (230 cm x 127 cm) in blackwork and Holbein work. D: Author, M: Mrs. Ria Wessels.

219

blackwork are mostly in Holbein stitch, diagonal raised band, pulled lines, four-sided stitch and double faggot, worked before the fillings. Algerian eyelets and eyelets, pulled squares and even geometric satin stitch may be used. There is no limit to the imagination of the needlewomen with a little experience and enterprise, exploring the possibilities of blackwork.

Here and there small motifs can be used to soften the effect of the work.

Use evenly woven white or cream-coloured material with round or flat threads. The material must not be loosely woven as the fine black threads will not remain in position and the result be untidy. Evenly woven linen with approximately 20 threads to 2½ cm is suitable for blackwork if the stitches of the fillings are worked over 2 threads. Fine Hardanger material is also suitable.

Through the years blackwork has changed so much in character that it may even be worked in white on black or in colour, e.g. white on red, white on blue, blue or brown on white, etc. Even further from the original, but technically still related, are different colours used on cream or white in the same article. See Plate 8.11

Use a sharp-pointed needle for the first type, i.e. freehand designs, and always tapestry needles with blunt points for the fillings on the counted thread. Use a tapestry needle through-out for the second type of design. Different kinds of thread should be kept at hand, e.g. stranded cotton in the D.M.C. or Anchor range or pure silk Filoselle in black of which only one thread is used for the fillings and 2 or more for the outlines where necessary. Pearl cotton nos. 8 and 5 may also be used. Some needlewomen prefer to use Pearl cotton for the filling because it is more durable than one thread of the stranded cotton but being a twisted thread it is consequently firmer and less flexible and therefore not very suitable

PLATE 8.2
Section of a tea-cloth in blackwork. DM: Author

for delicate geometric fillings. It cannot be finished off as neatly and firmly on the wrong side as is the case with a softer thread.

Blackwork is suitable for many articles, especially table linen, because it is durable. It is also beautiful worked on a coarser scale on cushion covers, bedspreads, curtains — e.g. a snowflake design in black wool scattered here and there on cream coloured curtains would be very effective in a modern room. It can also be used on wall panels, firescreens in wrought-iron frames, etc.

8.2 Rules

The following rules apply to blackwork:

1. As in photography, the effect depends on the contrasts of light and dark shades, and therefore the position of the fillings is most important.

2. The choice of the fillings is also important

nerve for a leaf-shape. In the same way a filling that imitates the grain of wood could be very effective in the right place, or a filling with a woven effect for a figure, etc.

3. The outline could be very clear and definite or very light or not worked at all. A Greek urn, for example, could have a distinct outline on the one side fading away to nothing on the other.

4. Additional small motifs enrich and fill the work and give the work a softer appearance.

5. Any type of design, free or geometrical or abstract and modern is suitable if it allows for fillings.

6. Blackwork can be as fine as it was originally, or very coarse.

7. Work the fillings first and then the outlines except in the case of a design based on counted thread, when the outlines are worked first of all.

PLATE 8.3
Blackwork on a tray-cloth. D: Author, M: Esthé van Wyk (11 years)

as special effects depend on these. A filling, for example, with a leaf- or flower-motif, will be suitable in related shapes, or use a filling worked diagonally, which changes direction along the centre to give the impression of a

8.3 The fillings

Many traditional blackwork fillings have been taken from Museum-pieces, but there is much scope for an imaginative embroideress to design her own on graph paper. By doing

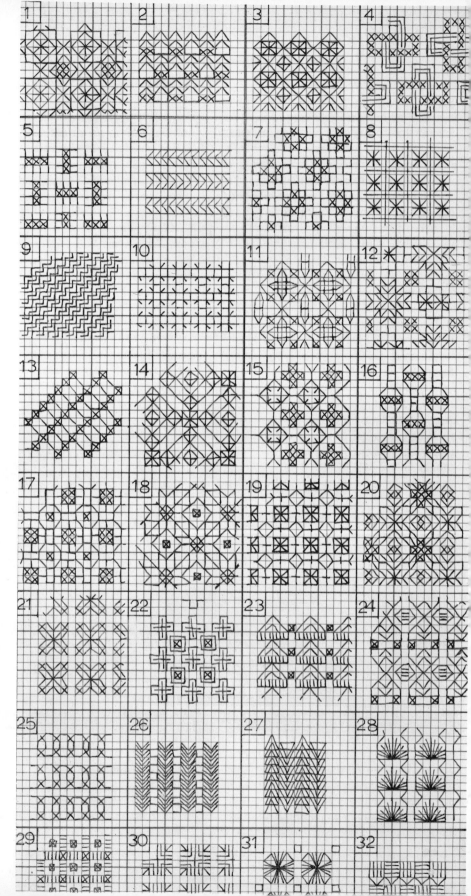

Figure 8.1

222

this her work will reflect the freshness of her own personality. The variety of fillings is therefore unlimited and they are all done on counted thread. Keep squared paper at hand so that new ideas can be jotted down and tried out. Some fillings are dark, others very light and some are medium light or dark.

Rules for working the fillings

1. All fillings consist of small stitches worked over 2 threads of the fabric either diagonally or on the straight. They must be studied beforehand to find a specific working method throughout in order to keep the back of the work as neat as possible. Many of the fillings can be partly worked on the principle of Holbein stitch which is an exceptionally neat method. Some are worked more easily diagonally instead of horizontally or vertically.

2. The wrong side of blackwork will not be exactly the same as the right side as in the case of Holbein work, but it must have a rhythmic appearance which must remain the same throughout the whole filling. (E.g. if one square is worked clockwise, all the squares must be worked in the same way, etc.) It is not necessary to start all the rows from the same side. The pattern formed on the wrong side when working from left to right will differ from the one returning from right to left, but these 2 rows must always be repeated in the same way.

3. The fillings must be worked right up to the outline of the motif. Even if there is only one thread left for a stitch, it must still be worked.

4. Try not to join the thread in the middle of a row, but at the end where it can be finished off into the outline later by overcasting to and fro or using a slip-stitch.

5. Choose small and delicate fillings for small areas.

6. To achieve a certain effect, fillings may be thinned out towards one side by omitting some of the stitches rhythmically. See Plate 8.2.

It is not practicable to prescribe the working methods of the fillings. No two persons will necessarily work a filling in the same way and yet both can be neat and technically correct.

The following are a number of blackwork fillings grouped according to whether they are dark (Fig. 8.1) or light (Fig. 8.2) or medium (Fig. 8.3).

Scale for fillings throughout: One square equals 2 threads, even if the rest of the design is worked over 3 threads.

Just as a guide, fillings No. 25 in Fig. 8.3 and No. 5 in Fig. 8.2 will be explained. Note that this is not the only method of working them.

1 See Fig. 8.3 No. 25 and Fig. 8.4
Scale: One square equals 2 threads.
    (i) Commence at a and work running stitch over and under 2 threads clockwise up to a again.
   (ii) Work running stitch again from a anti-clockwise back to a, covering all the open spaces.
  (iii) Bring the needle out 2 threads above a and
  (iv) Work the centre star and the square around the star.
   (v) Bring the needle out at b and work running stitch clockwise back to b.
  (vi) Again running stitch from b anti-clockwise back to b to cover all the open spaces.
 (vii) Bring the needle out diagonally across one thread from the lower lefthand corner of the square and work the small square of 2 by 2 threads on the same principle.
(viii) Bring the needle out at c in the middle of the square at the top and repeat from a. Work all the rows in this way right up against each other as in Fig. 8.3 No. 25.

2. See Fig. 8.2 No. 5 and Fig. 8.5
Scale: One square equals 2 threads.
    (i) Commence at a and work running stitch over and under 2 threads clockwise back to a.

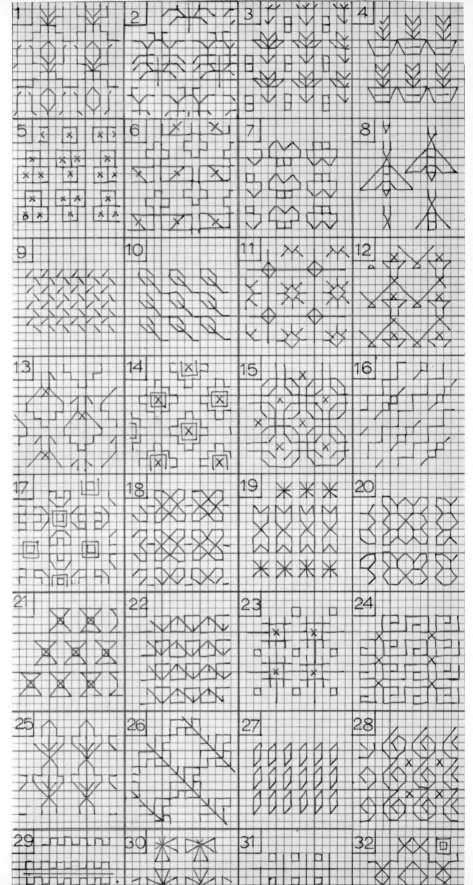

Figure 8.2

224

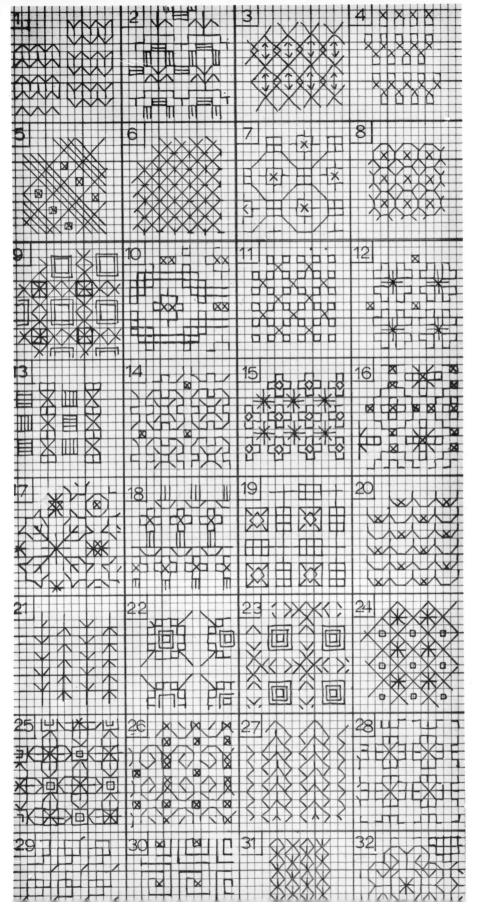

Figure 8.3

225

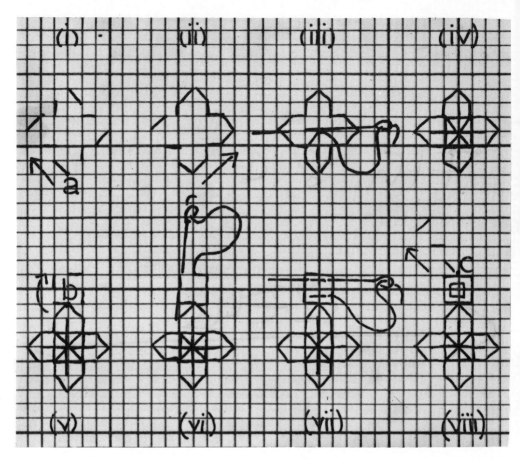

Figure 8.4

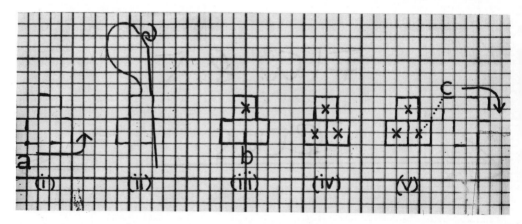

Figure 8.5

(ii) Work anti-clockwise back to a, covering all the open spaces.

(iii) Bring the needle out at b and work the upright stitch and the 2 stitches to

Figure 8.6

227

PLATE 8.4
Tea-cosy: Blackwork in a free design. Sampler: 16 blackwork patterns and 20 drawn thread fillings. D: Author, M: Mrs. S. Tack and Mrs. Cupe Wessels.

PLATE 8.5
A wall panel, using different **blackwork** fillings for the background. D: Author, M: **Mrs. Rita** Gouws.

complete the top square. Work the cross diagonally over 2 threads by 2 threads in the top square.

(iv) Complete the 2 lower squares by working the missing stitch and work the 2 crosses.

(v) Bring the needle out at c and repeat according to the diagram.

8.4. **Motifs**

See Fig. 8.6. Scale: One square equals 2 threads. The following are a few geometric motifs to use with a blackwork design. See Plate 8.1. Beautiful borders can also be planned by using one or more of these motifs in rhythmic repetition.

8.5 **Writing in blackwork**

Blackwork can be used for writing on material. An example can be seen on Plate 10.12 where a part of the 23rd Psalm was written around a cloth and which forms a border on the inside of a wider one which combines drawn thread work and blackwork. This is an example of a combination of 2 or more methods to give a richer and more striking and interesting effect. There are infinite possibilities to be explored by the imaginative and enterprising embroideress.

8.6 A mural decoration in blackwork
D 8.1

Schematic diagram: See Fig. 8.7
Size: 30 cm by 45 cm . Scale of diagram: 5 mm equals 25 mm .

This mural will be popular for a boy's room as it consists of Red Indian motifs. It is also suitable for an entrance hall or a study. Worked on a coarser scale it will be very effective against a stone wall, near hand-woven covers, hangings or cushion covers. This mural can also be worked in 3 shades of

Figure 8.7

brown on cream-coloured material to heighten the atmosphere.
Key: Cut a piece of material 38 cm by 53 cm

to allow for framing. To transfer the design onto the material: See Par. 1.3 No. 15. Tack all the lines except the bands A, N, B and C. Use a blue or green tacking thread in contrast with the black working thread. The bands A and N. See Fig. 8.8.

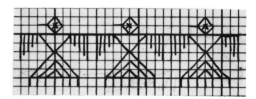

Figure 8.8

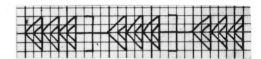

Figure 8.9

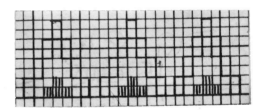

Figure 8.10

Scale: One square equals 3 threads.
Holbein stitch (See Chapter 9).
B. See Fig. 8.9. Holbein stitch.
Scale: One square equals 3 threads.
C. See Fig. 8.10. Holbein stitch.
Scale: One square equals 3 threads.
D. The outline. Couching. See Fig. 8.11
Lay 2 threads of No. 5 Pearl cotton on the line and secure with small stitches using No. 12 cotton.
E. Use No. 5 cotton and work chain stitch.
F. The side of the filling b will therefore have no outline. Use No. 8 cotton for G and for H and work a row of double knot stitch. Use No. 5 cotton for I and No. 8 for J and work chain stitch.
K. Use no. 8 cotton and work Portuguese stem stitch.

L. Use No. 8 cotton and work the 2 parts of the horizontal line in chain stitch. Use one thread stranded cotton and work the steps in the centre in Holbein stitch.

The two short lines crossing E: Holbein stitch using No. 8 cotton. The motifs:

1. The eagle at the top left: The top line and head: Chain stitch using No. 8 cotton. The rest of the outline except the tail: Portuguese stem stitch using No. 8 cotton. The tail: Use No. 8 cotton and work satin stitch zigzag on the counted thread. Outline the 2 squares and motif on the chest in chain stitch using No. 8 cotton. The eye: Outline in chain stitch using No. 8 cotton. Filling for the whole eagle: Fig. 8.3 No. 1.

Figure 8.11

2. The tents at the top right:
   (i) The bottom tent: Use No. 5 cotton and work Portuguese stem stitch on the 2 diagonal sides, the door and flags. Filling for the tent: Fig. 8.3 No. 31.
   (ii) The middle tent: Use No. 8 cotton and work chain stitch on the left side and on the right side as well as the door and flags. Filling for the tent: Fig. 8.1 No. 27.
   (iii) The top tent: No outline except for the door and the flags which are worked in chain stitch, using No. 8 cotton. Filling for the tent: Fig. 8.2 No. 27.

3. The Red Indian motif near the tents: To the left of line E the motif is only outlined in chain stitch, using No. 8 cotton. To the right of the line: Work the diamond-shape in double knot stitch. Filling: Fig. 8.3 No. 15. The rest of the motif: Use No. 5 cotton and work Holbein stitch on the vertical line and on the 2 horizontal lines. Using No. 8 cotton, work the V-line in chain stitch.

4. The centre panel with the horses:
   (i) The rider: Use No. 8 cotton and outline the whole figure in chain stitch. Work the hair in close satin stitches and the feathers on his head in chain stitch using only one of the 6 strands. Fillings: The jacket: Fig. 8.1 No. 9. The trousers: Fig. 8.1 No. 6. The rope in coral stitch, using No. 12 cotton. The foot: Use No. 12 cotton and outline in chain st.
   (ii) The first horse on the left: Use No. 8 cotton and outline the whole horse in Portuguese stem stitch. Use No. 8 cotton and work the manes of all the horses in 2 adjoining rows of chain st. Filling: Fig. 8.1 No. 10.
   (iii) The horse second from the left: Use No. 8 cotton and outline in chain stitch. Filling: Fig. 8.2 No. 9.
   (iv) The horse third from the left: Outline,

PLATE 8.6
A wall panel in black and gold and silver embroidery. Material: Irish linen. Size: 46 cm diam. D: Author, M: Mrs. Aletta Wessels

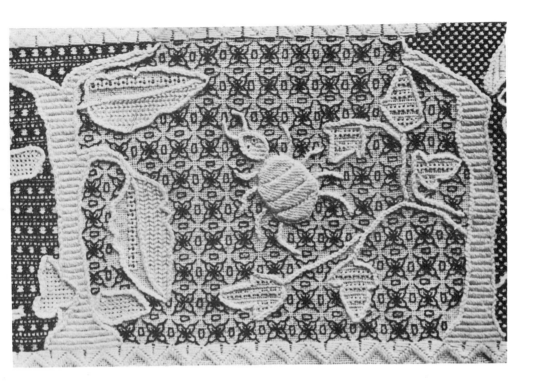

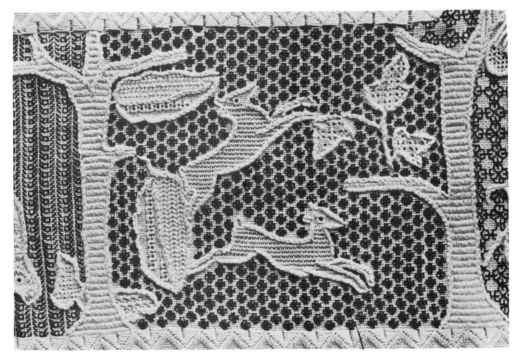

PLATE 8.7 AND PLATE 8.8
Sections of a wide border in black and white embroidery on a tea-cloth of 127 cm square. In 1957 this cloth won the Silver Floating Trophy of the British Embroiderers Guild for South Africa. D: Author, M: Mrs. Louise Geldenhuys.

using a single strand of the skein in coral stitch. Filling: Fig. 8.1 No. 32.

(v) The horse fourth from the left: Outline, using a single strand of the skein, in coral stitch. Filling: Fig. 8.1 No. 22.

5. The feathers on the arrow: Use No. 8 cotton to outline in Portuguese stem stitch and No. 8 cotton to work the quill in chain stitch. The head of the arrow: Use one thread stranded cotton to outline in Portuguese stem stich and fill with vertical pulled lines over 2 threads.

6. The 2 eagles: The one in front: Use No. 8 cotton and outline the whole eagle in chain stitch. Filling: Fig. 8.1 No. 26.

The one at the back: Use No. 5 cotton and outline the head only and the top parts of the wings in chain stitch. Filling: Fig. 8.3. No. 21.

7. The clay vase: The embroideress can give free reign to her imagination as these vases are always very decorative and any Holbein border will be suitable. Work the lines and outlines at the top and on the left side only in chain stitch and use different thicknesses of thread. Filling at the bottom: Fig. 8.3 No. 24. Filling at the top: Fig. 8.1 No. 28.

8. The 2 geometric motifs: Outline using different thicknesses of thread and any stitch.

9. The panel with horses at the bottom right:
 (i) The rider: Use No. 8 cotton and outline the top part of the figure in coral stitch and the rest in chain stitch. Work the hair in 3 adjoining rows of chain stitch. Filling for the top part: Pulled lines over 2 threads. Filling for the bottom part: Fig. 8.1 No. 25.
 (ii) The first horse: Use No. 8 cotton and outline the whole horse in chain stitch. Filling: Fig. 8.1 No. 13.
 (iii) The second horse: Use No. 5 cotton to outline in chain stitch. Filling: Fig. 8.2 No. 16.

(iv) The third horse: Outline in chain stitch, using No. 5 cotton. Filling Fig. 8.3 No. 20.

(v) The fourth horse: Outline in coral stitch, using No. 8 cotton. Filling: Fig. 8.2 No. 7.

(vi) The section of a horse: Filling: Fig. 8.1. No. 8, without any outline.

Fillings for the background:
a. Fig. 8.1 No. 19 b. Fig. 8.3 No. 28. c. Fig. 8.3 No. 6. d. Fig. 8.2 No. 24

This is only a guide and need not be followed strictly. The embroideress may use her own ideas.

8.7 Blackwork combined with white work

Blackwork can be combined most beautifully with white work as is shown on these Plates. A lovely example is a cloth with a 15 cm border divided into sections by means of trees. Figures and animals in white work in each of these sections are most striking on a

PLATE 8.9
Design D 8.2. Motif from a border in black and white embroidery

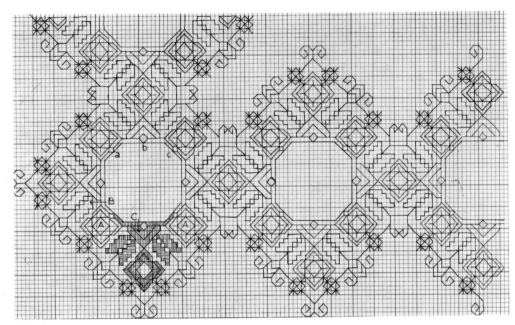

D 8.2

Figure 8.12

background of various blackwork fillings. See Plate 8.7 and 8.8.

Blackwork and drawn fabric work and needleweaving in white as shown on Plate 8.4 and Plate 10.12 on one article give a very rich effect. In old Hedebo work blackwork instead of drawn thread fillings may be used with rich and beautiful results Geometric satin stitch motifs around blackwork fillings are especially striking — see Plate 8.9. Blackwork can even be combined with Hardanger work.

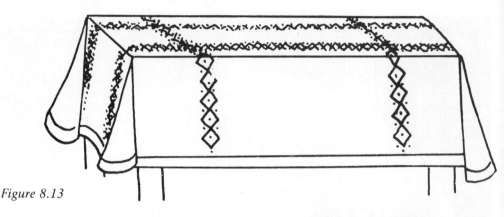

Figure 8.13

A border in geometric satin stitch and blackwork
D 8.2

Schematic diagram: See Fig. 8.12 and Fig. 8.13. Width: 17 cm .
Scale of design: One square equals 3 threads. See Plate 8.9

This design will be beautiful as a border on a tea cloth on a tablecloth (see Fig. 8.13). a table-runner or a tea cosy. Although it is intended for white geometric satin stitch, blackwork fillings and a little black Holbein work, there is no reason why it may not be used for other purposes as well. Use ivory linen for example, work the satin stitch in 2 shades of ecru (D.M.C. No. 644 and 642) and in white, then work black Holbein stitch around the satin stitch and use DMC Brillanté D'Alsace No. 30 in shade 644 to work pulled fillings in the spaces. The combination of black, ecru and white on ivory linen is extremely pretty and can be recommended.

Naturally many other combinations may be used, e.g. white and 2 shades of blue or grey, white and black, or red, white and black. This design lends itself to a variety of possibilities and the results can be unrecognizably different. See Plate 8.9 where the design has been changed into a motif. It is worked on evenly woven linen with approximately 30 threads to 2½ cm, the satin stitch and Holbein work with No. 8 and the filling with one thread of the stranded cotton. On a coarser linen this motif will be very pretty in the centre of a cushion cover.

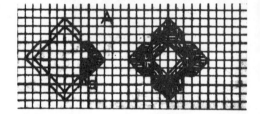

Figure 8.14

Key: Use any evenly and firmly woven line ·,

As a border around a tea cloth:

See Par 1.3 No. 13. Use No. 5 or No. 8 Pearl cotton throughout depending on the choice of the material, unless otherwise advised. Commence at a and work 7 vertical satin stitches over 3 threads each next to and one thread higher than the previous one. Work 12 more similar stitches level at the top and bottom and then one over 2 and one over one thread — the last 2 stitches level with the others at the bottom, but shorter at the top. This is position b. Skip 2 threads and work a mirror-image of the first part up to c, where the first stitch of the next side begins. Repeat all round. The motif A. See Fig. 8.14. Scale: One square equals 3 threads.

Commence at d, keep the following 4 stitches level at the top and work one satin stitch over 6 threads, one over 5, over 4, and one over 3 threads. Then work one over 4,2 threads higher and one thread shorter at the bottom than the previous ones, then one over 2, one thread shorter top and bottom. Bring the needle out at the top of the stitch which lies

PLATE 8.10
A wall panel in black and gold embroidery. DM: Author

over 3 threads and work one stitch over 3 threads here, one over 4, over 5 and one over 6 threads. This last stitch will be level with the very first one. Repeat all round. A square of 12 by 12 threads will result in the centre. Work 13 stitches over 3 threads on each point,

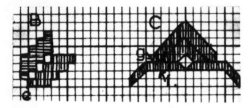

Figure 8.15

the 7th stitch in the middle at the top. Work 6 diagonal stitches in each corner of the square in the centre — diagonally over one, over 2, 3 4, 5 and 6 threads.

The pairs of leaves B. See Fig. 8.15 Scale: One square equals 3 threads.

Commence at e, keep all the stitches level at the bottom and work 3 upright satin stitches over 3 threads, 3 over 6, and 3 over 9 threads. The next 4 stitches are 3 threads shorter at the bottom and 3 longer at the top, i.e. over 9 threads too. Keep all the stitches level at the top and work 3 over 6 and 3 over 3. Pass the needle beneath these stitches on the wrong side of the work to e and work the second leaf as a mirror-image of the first so that they meet in the corners.

C. The small triangle: Find the middle of the side and bring the needle out 8 threads to the left at f, right next to the satin stitch. Keep the following 6 stitches level at the bottom and work one over one thread, one over 2, over 3, 4, 5 and 6. Work the next 3 stitches over 6 threads, each one thread higher. From here a mirror-image is worked of the preceding part. Bring the needle out at g, i.e. 4 threads to the left of f, keep the next 4 stitches level at the bottom and work one over 3, over 4, 5 and over 6. Work the following stitches over 6 threads, each one thread higher up to the centre at the top and repeat the mirror-image. This completes the satin stitch.

Use black No. 8 cotton and work groups of Algerian eyelets joined by Holbein stitch as shown on the design.

Now work the blackwork fillings using one thread of the stranded cotton.

Besides the drawn fabric work (pulled work), Hardanger work and blackwork already dealt with, there are other kinds of counted thread work, i.e. work of which the technique is based on the counted thread of the material. All counted thread work is most satisfactory because the result is always precise and very neat. Always use evenly woven materials and tapestry needles with blunt points. The following are further classified under counted thread work:

1. Geometric satin stitch
2. Cross stitch
3. Sorbello work
4. Plait stitch work

Counted thread work

PLATE 9.1
Mainly geometric satin stitch with a few drawn fabric stitches were used in this attractive luncheon-set. Material: Cream linen embroidered with 3 shades of blue. D: Author, M: Mrs. Erica Potgieter

5. Holbein work
6. Assisi work
7. Canvas embroidery

9.1 Geometric satin stitch
Geometric satin stitch was already dealt with in the previous chapters, much of it in connec-

tion with drawn fabric work. Inevitably it is often found with any kind of open work because it contrasts and accentuates the latter most effectively.

It is not especially time-consuming and when done in colours e.g. red on cream, brown on yellow, blue on white or cream or grey on pink etc, a beautiful and effective

PLATE 9.2
A runner in geometric satin stitch, canvas stitches and drawn fabric embroidery in shades of gold D: Author, M: Mrs. Lulu Heyns

article can be finished in a relatively short time. The thread for geometric satin stitch must be thicker than the thread of the material so that the latter will be covered completely and the work will look rich and embossed. A soft and pliable thread like nos. 5 and 8 Pearl cotton or any other soft cotton thread or wool must preferably be used. Wool is especially suitable for cushion covers and other upholstery. It is important to change the direction of the stitches as this gives a varied effect of light and shade, which enhances the work. See Plate 10.10. The stitches must never be

too long and the tension too slack with laundering in mind. The tension must be the same as that of the ground, easily accomplished when a tambour frame is used. The back of the work must be kept very neat. See Hint No. 7 in Par. 1.3.

Many beautiful designs can be devised with geometric satin stitch, e.g. wide and narrow borders, allover patterns and motifs, etc. suitable for tablecloths, luncheon-mats, cushion covers, chairbacks, serviette bags, tray cloths, tea cosies, runners, etc.

See Hints No. 7, 8 and 9 in Par 1.3 in

PLATE 9.3
Geometric satin stitch plays an important role in this design for a green and cream coloured table cloth. D: Author, M: Mrs. C. Tidmarsh

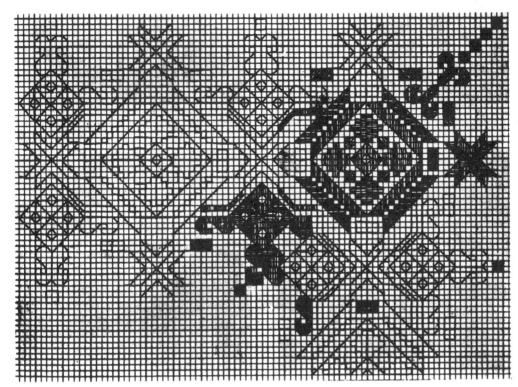

D 9.1

connection with the execution of geometric satin stitch.

Fillings
See Fig. 9.1 and Plates 9.4 to 9.28

There are exceptionally pretty and rich geometric satin stitch fillings for various uses. Use them in a free design or alternately with fillings in drawn fabric work, old Hedebo work, blackwork, etc. They are also applied to a kind of Russian drawn threadwork — See Par. 6.4

Beautiful narrow borders can also be planned with a section of one filling or a composition of several. E.g. work filling No. 1 for a lovely little border. As it will be impractical to describe each filling step by step, plates and diagrams of each are given from which the working method can easily be followed.
Scale: One square equals 3 threads.
A border
D 9.1

Width: 13 cm . Scale: One square equals 3 threads.

This border may be worked without the corner as a panel across a cushion cover, e.g. in wool on a coarse and evenly woven material. It will also be effective on a knitting-bag, curtains or any table linen.
A motif
D 9.2
Size on evenly woven linen with approximately 30 threads to 2½ cm: 18 cm. Scale: One square equals 3 threads. See Plate 9.30. The motif can be used in various ways. Embroider it, e.g. on a white tea cloth in different shades of one colour, like blue or pale pink, or repeat the motif for a border. Place 5 motifs together for the centre-piece on a tea cloth as shown in Fig. 9.2

One motif on a cushion cover will be striking especially on a coarse linen as in Plate 9.30.

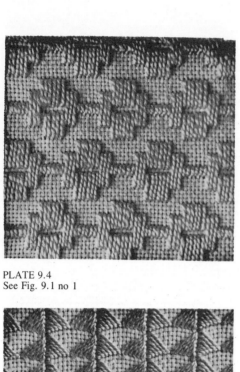

PLATE 9.4
See Fig. 9.1 no 1

PLATE 9.7
See Fig. 9.1 no 4

PLATE 9.5
See Fig. 9.1 no 2

PLATE 9.6
See Fig. 9.1 no 3

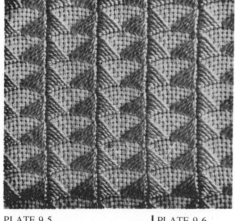

PLATE 9.8
See Fig. 9.1 no 5

PLATE 9.9
See Fig. 9.1 no 6

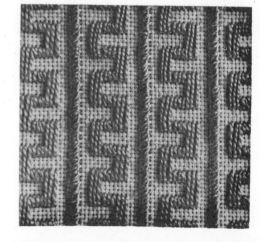

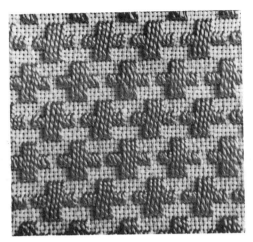

PLATE 9.10
See Fig. 9.1 no 7

PLATE 9.13
See Fig. 9.1 no 10

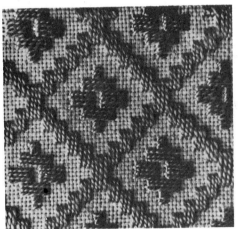

PLATE 9.11
See Fig. 9.1 no 8

 PLATE 9.12
See Fig. 9.1 no 9

 PLATE 9.15
See Fig. 9.1 no 12

PLATE 9.14
See Fig. 9.1 no 11

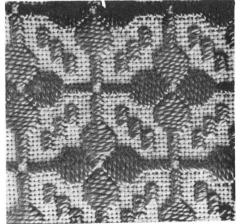

PLATE 9.16
See Fig. 9.1 no 13

PLATE 9.19
See Fig. 9.1 no 16

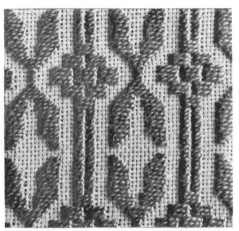

PLATE 9.17
See Fig. 9.1 no 14

PLATE 9.18
See Fig. 9.1 no 15

PLATE 9.20
See Fig. 9.1 no 17

PLATE 9.21
See Fig. 9.1 no 18

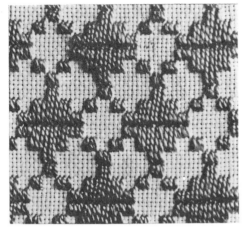

PLATE 9.22
See Fig. 9.1 no 19

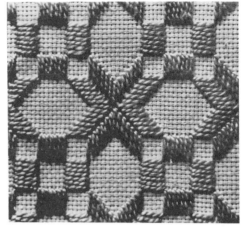

PLATE 9.25
See Fig. 9.1 no 22

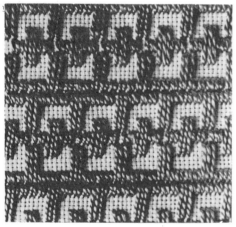

PLATE 9.23
See Fig. 9.1 no 20

PLATE 9.24
See Fig. 9.1 no 21

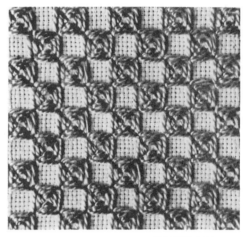

PLATE 9.26
See Fig. 9.1 no 23

PLATE 9.27
See Fig 9.1 no 24

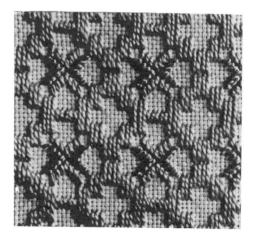

9.2 Cross stitch

Cross stitch is a very old, popular and gay type of embroidery in which bright colours may be used without reserve.

Decorate many articles in the home, like cushion covers, chairbacks, chair — and stool -covers, table linen, wall panels, bedspreads, handbags, children's clothes, pockets on skirts and jackets, etc, with cross stitch. There is a large variety of related stitches, but the ordinary cross is the most popular. Holbein stitch is most commonly used with cross stitch for a more delicate result. The Chinese method is the ideal one for working cross stitch as all the stitches fall in parallel lines at the back of the work. It takes a little more time and patience but the exceptional neatness makes it worth while. This method is discussed here.

General rules for cross stitch
1. The top threads of all the crosses must lie in the same direction, viz. from the bottom left to the top right.
2. When cross stitch is worked correctly, all

PLATE 9.29
A runner in Hardanger work and geometric satin stitch executed in white, grey and black on red linen. D: Author, M: Mrs. Margo Dodson

D 9.2

the stitches at the back of the work will lie parallel and not diagonally or at right angles. See Plate 9.32.

Figure 9.2

3. Finish the thread off on the wrong side in the same direction as the stitches. A thread must be split and each part finished off in a different direction with a sharp-pointed needle.

4. Never use a transfer for cross stitch. It must always be done on the counted thread so that each cross is perfectly square and they all meet in the same hole on the corners.

5. For this reason a fairly firm and evenly woven material must be used. Etamin from Greece is particularly suitable. Generally the thread used must be slightly thicker than one

245

PLATE 9.30
Two small cushions (28 cm x 28 cm) embroidered with blue and white on the blue linen. Left: Motif D 9.2; Right: Geometric satin stitch filling.

PLATE 9.31
Section of a cross stitch border. M: Mrs. Alletta Wessels

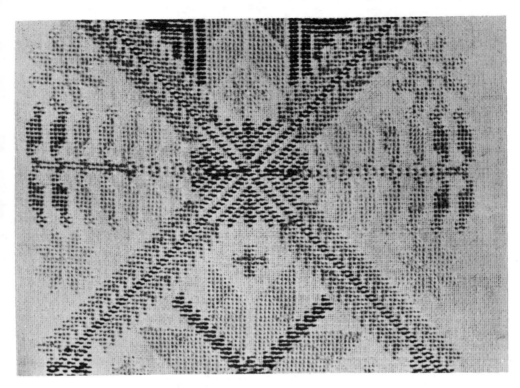

PLATE 9.32
The wrong side of the runner, illustrating the Chinese method

thread of the material. If the stitches are too large or the thread too thin, the work will appear sparse instead of rich and colourful.

Cross stitch from Greece often has a little gold thread mixed with the other colours.

6. Preferably choose bright colours that harmonise.

The Chinese method

To illustrate this method, the following design, easily developed into a border, will be explained. See Fig. 9.3

Scale: One square equals 2 or 3 threads.

General principles of this method:

The first route:

1. Commence the work in the lower right-hand corner of the design, working only one half of each cross right up to the top of the design. In the process, however, some of the crosses will have to be completed when proceeding from one row to the next.

2. It often happens that the needle emerges in the middle of the next row of crosses and then the shortest section of the new row must be completed first and after that only one half of the crosses of the rest of the row.

3. In intricate patterns it often happens that a whole cross is left unworked on the first route. In that case both stitches of the cross will be made on the second downward route.

4. It will be noticed that parts of the design often branch out from a central motif and these branchings are then worked in one direction and also completed by returning towards the central motif. This is clearly shown in nos. (viii), (ix) and (x) of the diagram where the leaf on the right-hand side has been completed with the needle back at the main stem. In (xi), (xii) and (xiii) a similar section is worked to the left. In (xiv) and (xv) the 2 smaller parts are completed and in (xvi) the first half of every cross is worked to the top.

The second route:

Now it is very simple to finish the crosses

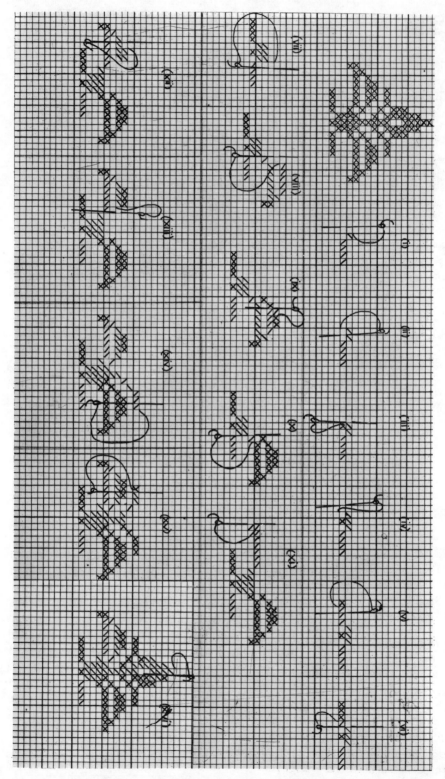

Figure 9.3

from top to bottom, completing the half crosses almost automatically. If the first route has been worked correctly, the second route is child's play. Sometimes it is necessary to pass the needle underneath the first stitch so that the top thread will not lie in the wrong direction. Remember that the real purpose of this method is to have all the stitches at the back of the work lying vertically. Should a deadlock be reached, unpick a small part and follow a different route. The Chinese method is most successful in most cases, and is impractical only in exceptional instances. In the latter case the design could be changed.

A cross stitch design for the pocket of a skirt or jacket
D 9.3
See Plate 9.33.
Scale: One square equals one cross.
Key: A: Tan; B: Black; C: White; D: Green.

Two cross stitch motifs.
D 9.4 and D 9.5
Keys:
D 9.4: A: Turquoise; B: Yellow; C: Black; D: Tan.
D 9.5: A: Green; B: Black; C: Blue; D: Red.

Three allover patterns.
See Fig. 9.4

D 9.3

PLATE 9.33
Design D 9.3

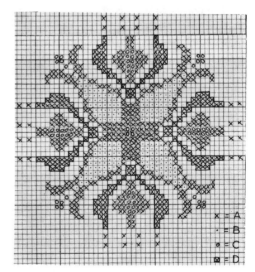

D 9.4

Scale: One square equals 2 or 3 threads.
Key:
1. The open cross: Pale blue.
   The outlined cross: Dark blue.
   The spot: Red.
2. The open cross: Pale green.

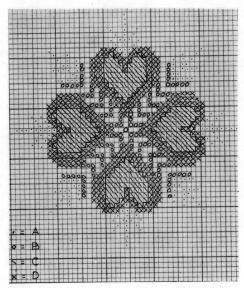

D 9.5

The outlined cross: Dark green.
The spot: Yellow.
3. The open cross: Royal blue.
   The outlined cross: Red.
   The spot: Black.

Cross stitch designs can also be used for two other types of embroidery, viz. Sorbello stitch and plait stitch and all three may be combined on one article. Plait stitch is flatter than cross stitch, which in turn is flatter than Sorbello stitch.

9.3 Sorbello stitch

Sorbello stitch originated in Italy and is especially effective on cushion covers, tea cosies, serviette bags, table runners, etc. Use a thread of the same thickness as one thread of the material, the latter being evenly woven. Any cross stitch design is also suitable for Sorbello stitch. The wrong side of the work can be kept very neat if the worker proceeds to the next row along the right side of the work, and Sorbello stitches then worked over that thread.

Sorbello stitch
See Fig. 9.5 and Plate 9.36
Scale: One square equals 3 or 4 threads. Keep

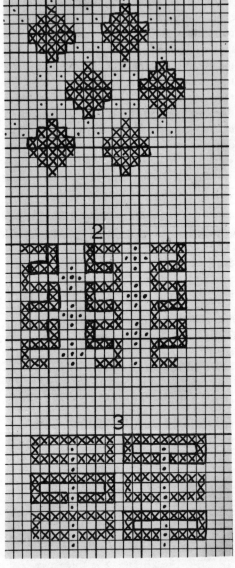

Figure 9.4

the tension slack throughout.

(i) Work a small stitch at the top of the square and bring the needle out in the lower left-hand corner.

(ii) (iii) and (iv) Work 2 or 3 buttonhole stitches over this stitch only (not through the material).

(v) Insert the needle in the lower right-hand corner of the square and bring it

PLATE 9.34
Blue cross stitch on white linen. M: Mrs. Aletta Wessels

out at the top left-hand corner of the next square.

(vi) Similar to (i),

The loops of this stitch must preferably all lie in the same direction except in borders where it is prettier when they face the edge of the article.

If the material is fairly fine only 2 instead of 3 buttonhole stitches may be worked.

9.4 Plait stitch

This stitch has a beautifully smooth texture and is more successful in solid patterns than in sparse ones in which single stitches occur. Choose an evenly woven material and a thread of the same thickness as one thread of the material. See Plate 9.37 on which the lower border and 2 squares in plait stitch have

PLATE 9.35
Sorbello work on a cushion cover. D: Author, M: Mrs. Lena Steyn

251

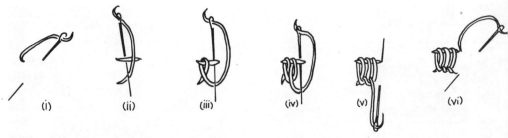

(i)   (ii)   (iii)   (iv)   (v)   (vi)

Figure 9.5

PLATE 9.36
Sorbello work motifs in the corners of a small cloth look very attractive. DM: Author.

been worked on etamin linen. See also Plate 9.38.

Any fairly solid cross stitch pattern is also suitable for plait stitch.

Extremely durable and attractive floor rugs can be made with this stitch.

Plait stitch
See Fig. 9.6. Scale: One line equals one thread.

(i) and (ii) These 2 stages show the method of working this stitch clearly. Note that the starting position is one thread higher at a and ending one thread lower at b for evenly woven linens. But on squared material like binca, or jute for rug-making, the stitch starts at a and ends at b. It is better to work the rows to and fro instead of always in one direction. The back of the work looks neat because the

PLATE 9.37
A sampler. The centre panel and two motifs and the border at the bottom are made in plait stitch. Bright colours on ecru etamine linen. DM: Author

stitches all lie vertically. Finish off in the same direction as the stitches and split the thread if necessary.

A bag in plait stitch
D 9.6
See Plate 9.38. Scale: One square equals one

cross.

Green, tan orange, black and white were used here on ecru material. This design can be used for many other purposes, e.g. on curtains in a child's bedroom, on a breakfast cloth or on a cushion cover for the stoep, etc. Suggested colour-scheme: Work in 3 colours; grey, black and white on royal blue material.

9.5 Holbein stitch

As a result of the technique this stitch is sometimes called double running stitch. When done in black on white, it looks delicate and resembles a drawing in Indian ink. In colour, however, it is just as striking if the colour of the thread contrasts well with that of the material. The most successful combinations result when a dark thread, e.g. dark blue, dark brown, dark red or dark green is used on white or ivory material, but white on black or on red is also attractive.

Holbein stitch can be used on its own but it is often combined with cross stitch and its related stitches, with geometric satin stitch, blackwork, needleweaving and always with Assisi work.

Use a firm, evenly woven material so that the stitches will remain in position. The

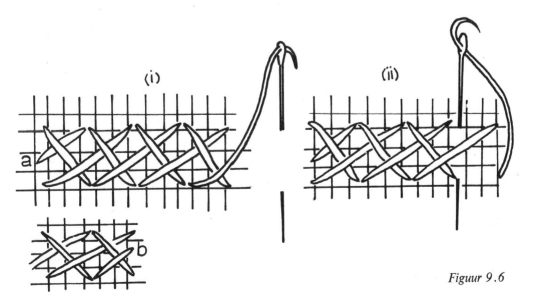

Figuur 9.6

253

thread must be slightly thinner than one thread of the material.

General rules

The first route:

Work the design or motif in running stitch over 2 threads on coarse linen and over 3 threads on fine linen, according to the design. All parts of the design branching out of the main motif must be completed on the first route. Eventually only the main motif is completed on the return journey.

D 9.6

The second route:

It is very important that all the stitches be worked as in Fig. 9.7 (i).

Note that the needle goes in at one side of the stitch and comes out at the other side. This gives a continuous line and prevents the untidy effect shown in(ii). The work is reversi-

branching.

(ii) Insert the veins of the leaf and then work anti-clockwise around the leaf and back.

(iii) Complete the branching and then the base to where the main stem begins. Proceed with the main stem up to the

PLATE 9.38
Design D 9.6. Plait stitch in brown, green, rust, white and black on coarse cream material

ble as it is exactly the same on both sides except where the threads have been finished off. This must be done as invisibly as possible, by splitting the thread and finishing off the 2 parts separately.

A border.
Holbein stitch is explained by means of the following design.
D 9.7 No. 1
See Fig. 9.8. Scale: One square equals 2 threads.

(i) Commence at a and work running stitch as shown up to the top end of the

scroll forking out to the left, which is then worked and completed back to the main stem.

(iv) Work the part to the left of the main stem from b to c and then from b to c to the right of the main stem. Then proceed with the main stem up to c. Now work the branch d to the left and back to the main stem to c and the part to the right to e and back. Continue working the main stem and anti-clockwise around the centre leaf with all its detail and back before going down the main stem to complete it. Proceed with the

255

PLATE 9.39
A sampler in Holbein work

base to where the other branching begins again and continue in this way.

Work on the same principle as described
for No. 1.

Three more borders.
D 9.7 nos 2, 3 and 4

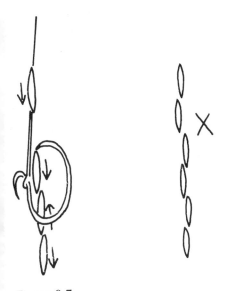

Figure 9.7

Three motifs.
D 9.8 nos 1, 2 and 3
Scale: One square equals 2 or 3 threads.

These motifs may be combined to form larger motifs or allover patterns.

Plate 9.40 shows No. 3, which was used on a serviette bag.

9.6 Assisi work

After a visit to the picturesque little town of Assisi on the slope of the hillock in Italy, the visitor will always have a soft spot for everything connected with it. Above all there will be the lasting impression of numerous gay little embroidery shops along a grey cobbled street. On the outside against the stone walls and the door frames, dozens of articles hang, embroidered in the typical style known as Assisi work.

It is colourful and gay in blue, red, brown, gold and black on white, cream or coloured linen. A large variety of articles is displayed, bibs and little collars for children, serviette bags, cushion covers, towels, all kinds of household linen, handbags, and finally the large tablecloths, the most beautiful of all. The monastery of the great patron of animals,

D 9.7

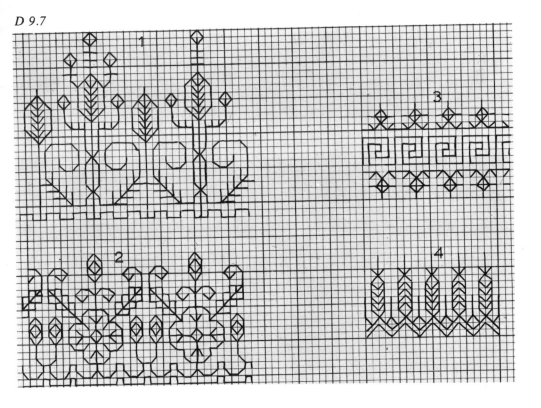

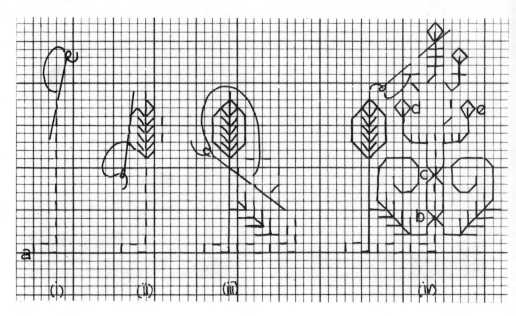

Figure 9.8

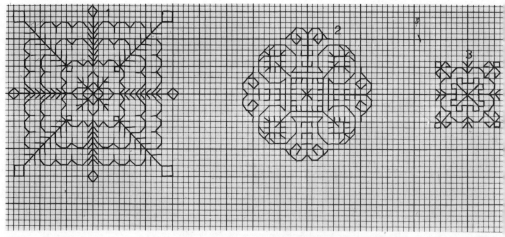

D 9.8

St. Francis, and everything related to him, dominates the little town and his doctrine is portrayed in the designs of animals, birds and dragons found in Assisi work.

What is Assisi work? Briefly it can be described as a combination of Holbein work and cross stitch as the design is outlined in the former in a larger framework of both and the background between the framework and the design is filled in with cross stitch.

The material must be evenly woven and fairly close. The thread must be of the same thickness or slightly thicker than one thread of the material. The Holbein stitch is usually worked in a dark colour, e.g. black or dark brown and the background of crosses in one colour only, blue and red being most popular.

It is not necessary to use the traditional

designs of animals and dragons for Assisi work, as any idea, even abstract motifs, will be suitable.

General rules
1. Complete all the Holbein stitch first.
2. Then work all the additional motifs.
3. Work the background in cross stitch in horizontal rows by working one half of the crosses from right to left and then the second half from left to right. The Holbein work often cuts into the crosses so that only a ¼ or ½ a cross can be worked. Every little part must, however, be filled in right up to the Holbein stitch to make the background complete. If the Holbein stitch lies over half a cross, only a quarter of a cross can be worked as at a and b in Fig. 9.9.

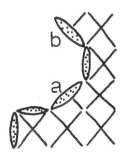

Figure 9.9

A circular table cover
D 9.9
Scale: One square equals 2 or 3 threads. Size: 61 cm diameter.

Plate 9.41 shows the design worked in wool on a coarse cotton material with 20 threads to 25 mm . It is double hemstitched round the edge, the material cut away 3 cm to the outside, and unravelled. The long threads formed thus, are cut off evenly.

PLATE 9.40
Design D 9.8 no 3. A serviette bag

D 9.9

Two designs for borders
D 9.10
Scale: One square equals 2 or 3 threads.

9.7 Canvas work

This type of embroidery is usually done in wool or silk on canvas, using either one stitch throughout or a variety of stitches. This kind of embroidery dates from the 13th century and reached its peak in England in the 17th and 18th centuries. The canvas must be covered completely: In a good piece of canvas embroidery the canvas must never be visible in the least. The choice of canvas, of stitch or stitches and working thread is most important so that the relation between canvas and stitch and thread will be exactly right. It is wrong to use too thin wool or silk which cannot cover the canvas completely, and just as wrong to use too thick a thread as that will give an untidy, forced and uneven appearance to the work and might even cause the canvas to tear.

There are many kinds of canvas available but the easiest to work on is one with a double thread. It is obtainable in qualities ranging from a very fine one (35 and 40 threads per

PLATE 9.41
Design D 9.9. A round cloth in Assisi embroidery, in blue wool on coarse cream material.

D 9.10

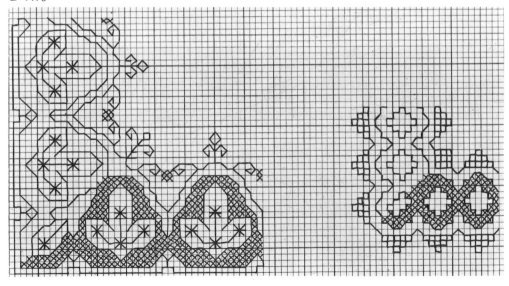

PLATE 9.42
Section of a wall panel worked in a great variety of canvas stitches in wool. Size: 94 cm x 61 cm . DM: Author.

25 mm) for evening bags to a very coarse one (4 threads per 25 mm) suitable for rugs. A canvas with 10 to 12 threads per 25 mm is the common one used for panelling.

Various kinds of special embroidery wool are also available for canvas work. Some kinds can be split when a thinner thread is required. Even Crewel wool meant for wool embroidery may be used on finer canvas, but the result will not be as even because it is too tightly spun. For fine canvas work, one or 2 or more threads of stranded cotton may be used. When a variety of stitches is used on one article, there is no reason why the working thread may not also be varied. On the other hand, when only one stitch is used throughout, only one type of thread should preferably be used to ensure an even surface.

Use tapestry needles No.'s 22 and 24.

Many beautiful shades of colours are avail-

able in wool and silk and the most elegant combinations are easily planned. Large pieces of work must be done on a frame to prevent it from pulling out of shape. Canvas embroidery is used for upholstery fabric on chairs and stools, (especially popular in the 17th and 18th centuries,) as well as for murals, rugs, handbags and evening bags, etc.

The design may vary from an authentic antique one taken from the early periods when the work was so popular, to a modern, abstract and geometric idea. But the rule that it is never in good taste to copy nature slavishly with needle and thread, is valid for canvas embroidery also.

The working thread must be reasonably short as the canvas is inclined to wear it off and make it dull and especially wool becomes much thinner towards the end of the thread. The work must never be commenced with a

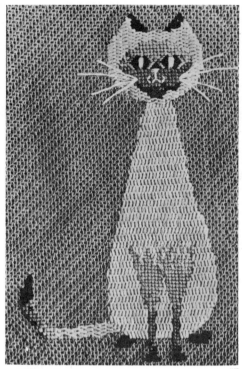

PLATE 9.43
A picture in canvas work. Stranded cotton on fine canvas.
M: Mrs. Zannie Mostert

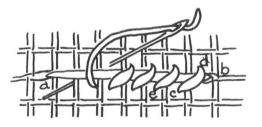

Figure 9.10

knit in the thread. Some needlewomen, however, make a temporary knot and insert the needle about 25 mm away from the beginning from the right side to the wrong side and then work over this thread, cutting off the knot when the work has progressed up to it.

Canvas work stitches
The following are a few known and unknown stitches. It is a good idea to make a sampler of all the stitches. Many will be found most attractive and the next piece of canvas work

attempted will very likely display an interesting variety instead of only one stitch.
Scale throughout: One line equals one thread.

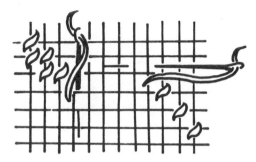

Figure 9.11

PLATE 9.44
Tent stitch — the two methods

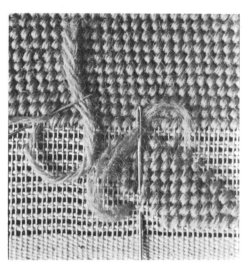

1. Tent stitch. See Fig. 9.10, Fig. 9.11 and Plate 9.44

This is probably the best-known stitch and in its finest form it is called petit point. It is usually done on a single thread canvas, but looks just as pretty on a coarser double thread canvas. In the latter case it must be tramméd

263

PLATE 9. 45
An evening bag in petit point. DM: Author.

PLATE 9.46
Long and short cross stitch.

as follows:

Work from right to left. Bring the needle out at a, just to the left of where the last stitch is to be worked and between 2 horizontal threads. Take the thread across to b, to the right where the first stitch is to be worked and again between 2 horizontal threads. Bring the needle out at c, insert at d, out at e, etc. Note that the diagonal stitch will be longer at the back of the work than in front. It is not possible to trammé on single canvas and one must take great care that the canvas does not show.

This stitch is inclined to pull the work askew and it should therefore always be done on a frame. Another method, especially for large areas and for large articles like chairs and stools, is to work the tent stitch diagonally. This method is more suitable as it makes

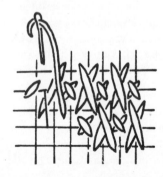

Figure 9.12

264

PLATE 9.47
Rice stitch

PLTE 9.48
French stitch

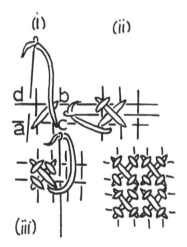

Figure 9.13

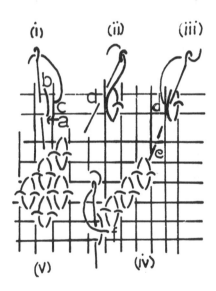

Figure 9.14

the work more durable, does not pull askew and has a smoother appearance. Fig. 9.11 shows the working method. Note that the needle passes horizontally under 2 threads going up and vertically under 2 threads coming down.

2. Long and short cross stitch. See Fig. 9.12 and Plate 9.46
The diagram shows the working method clearly.

3. Rice stitch. See Fig. 9.13 and Plate 9.47.
(i), (ii) and (iii) clearly show the stages in which the stitch is worked by making a large cross over 2 threads a b c d first, which is in turn crossed with 4 small stitches diagonally across one thread, first over the corner at the top left, then below left, then the corner at the top right and the lower righthand corner last.

PLATE 9.49
Hungarian stitch

PLATE 9.50
Knitting stitch (Kelim stitch)

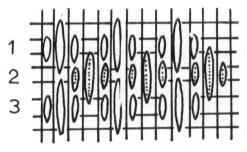

Figure 9.15

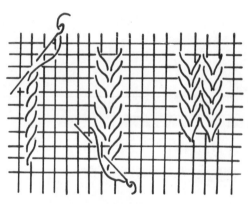

Figure 9.16

4. French stitch. See Fig. 9.14 and Plate 9.48.

   (i) Commence at a, insert the needle 2 threads higher up at b and bring it out diagonally over one thread to the right at c. Insert in between and in a line with a and b. Bring the needle out at a again.

   (ii) Insert at b and bring the needle out diagonally over one to the left at d.

   (iii) Insert again in between and in a line with a b and bring it out 2 threads below d at e.

   (iv) Repeat from e to d as from a to b. (The position f of the 2nd stitch is in the same hole as a of the previous stitch)

   (v) Here the rows follow successively. This stitch was used for the back-ground in Plate 9.43.

5. Hungarian stitch. See Fig. 9.15 and Plate 9.49

1. The first row: Work one upright stitch over 2 threads, then next to it one stitch over 4 threads, one thread longer than the first one at the top and the bottom. Again one over 2 threads, skip 2 vertical threads and repeat.

2. The second row: Work in the same way and note the way in which the long stitch fits into the previous row.

3. The third row: Same as the first row.

266

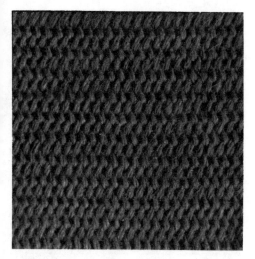

PLATE 9.51
Plaited Gobelin stitch

PLATE 9.52
Fern stitch

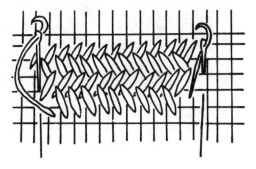

Figure 9.17

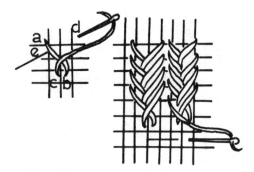

Figure 9.18

6. Knitting stitch (Kelim stitch). See Fig. 9.16 and Plate 9.50

The diagram clearly shows the method of working this stitch and the way in which the rows follow each other. The stitch can also be worked on the diagonal and horizontally, e.g. when working the outlines of designs for Kelim rugs.

7. Plaited Gobelin stitch. See Fig. 9.17 and Plate 9.51

These 4 rows are worked to and fro. Each stitch lies vertically over 2 threads, but one thread to the right or left, and each row lies halfway over the previous row and gives a plaited effect.

8. Fern stitch. See Fig. 9.18 and Plate 9.52

Bring the needle out at a and insert at b, 2 threads to the right and 3 threads lower than a. Bring it out at c, one thread to the left of b and insert at d, 3 threads to the right of a. Bring the needle out at e, one thread below a and repeat.

9. Fishbone stitch. See Fig. 9.19 and Plate 9.53

Bring the needle out at a and follow the method as on the diagram.

10. Knotted stitch. See Fig. 9.20 and Plate 9.54

The diagram shows the method clearly. Note the way in which the rows interlace.

PLATE 9.53
Fishbone stitch

smart evening bag. Use a gold thread for the motif on a white or black background or a white motif on a black background.

Scale: One square equals one hole in the mesh.

A mural in canvas work
D 9.11
Schematic diagram: See Fig. 9.24
Size: 43 cm by 53 cm . Scale of diagram: 25 mm equals 160 mm .

PLATE 9.54
Knotted stitch

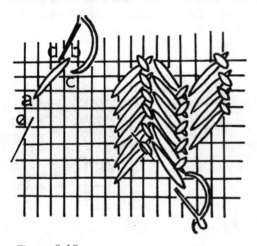

Figure 9.19

11. Oblong cross stitch. See Fig. 9.21 and Plate 9.55

The cross is over 2 threads lengthwise and over one breadthwise, joined in the centre by means of a straight horizontal stitch over one thread.

12. Rococo stitch. See Fig. 9.22 and Plate 9.56

This is a particularly pretty stitch which should be worked on a fairly open canvas, or, if a finer canvas is used, the thread must be thin. The diagram shows the method clearly. Work the motifs diagonally from the top right to the lower lefthand corner. Fig. 9.23: Use this allover pattern in Rococo stitch for a

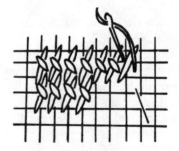

Figure 9.20

Different shades of green, turquoise, blue and yellow will be suitable for this panel. Only one canvas stitch, or a variety may be used, as preferred, on a canvas of 10 to 12 threads per 25 mm . Use wool. To transfer the design onto the canvas: Trace the design on transparent paper, using ink. Lay it on a white surface, put the canvas over it. Now use a fine paintbrush or pen to draw the design onto the canvas.

The following stitches may be employed with success:

Key: A. Let A end more or less on the dotted line on the diagram. Use stitch No. 6 worked horizontally.

PLATE 9.55
Oblong cross stitch

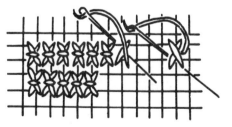

Figure 9.21

B. Work the rest of the background in stitch No. 4.

C. Stitch No. 1.

D. Stitch No. 12.

E. Stitch No. 1.

F. Stitch No. 1.

G. Stitch No. 8.

PLATE 9.56
Rococo stitch.

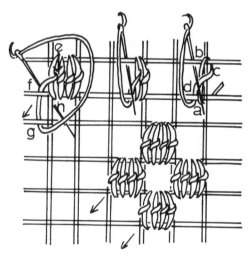

Figure 9.22

H. Stitch No. 1. (Work the outline in a contrasting colour first and then fill in).

I. Stitch No. 1.

Work al the remaining stems and lines in Stitch No. 1.

Design D 8.1 is also suitable for canvas work.

Figure 9.23

Figure 9.24

Every embroideress reaches a stage in her career when she seeks a wider horizon which will be absolutely her own interpretation of embroidery. This stage is reached after she has mastered all the well-known stitches and media and will find satisfaction only in something quite original. She will have developed a feeling for composite work where the one medium accentuates the other but still forms a harmonious whole and thus she can experiment to her heart's content.

Some of the most beautiful pieces of work are those where different media are combined on one article. This can however, only be done within limits as the methods must all be suitable for the specific article and material, they must be complementary and form a pleasing whole. Hardanger work, e.g., is not successful on a loosely woven linen and if it is to be used with other media, it will decide the choice of material and the rest of the work will have to be adapted accordingly. Various combinations have already been discussed in the preceding chapters, e.g. white and blackwork, and the following are a few more examples.

Composite work

10.1 A tea cloth in hardanger and drawn fabric work

D 10.1

Schematic diagram: See Fig. 10.1. Size: 152 cm by 152 cm .

Scale of diagram: 25 mm equals 30 cm . Scale of design: One square equals 2 threads. See Plate 10.3

Use other fillings described in Chapter 7 Par. 7.2 if preferred. The experienced needlewoman may use more than one filling in one motif, e.g. Hardanger flowers and picots in the open diamond-shaped motifs.

Key: Fold the material carefully to find the centre, X, as on the design. Use black sheen and tack over and under 2 threads from the centre in all 4 directions on the straight of the fabric out towards the edge.

A. The kloster blocks are easily recognised and must be worked first. Tack from one group of kloster blocks to the next in a dark thread to eliminate faulty counting.

B. Hardanger faggot stitch.

C. Four-sided stitch. Cut the square in the middle of the 4 kloster blocks at the end of the lines in four-sided stitch.

D. Eyelets.

E. To work this motif, see Par. 7.3 No. 2.

F. See Fig. 10.2.

The large satin stitch stars: Use No. 5 Pearl cotton, commence at a and work No. 1 first. Keep the stitches level below and work one stitch over 2 threads, one over 3, 4, 5, 6, 7 and then 3 stitches over 8 threads. Now keep all the stitches level at the top and work one stitch over 7, 6, 5, 4, 3 and 2 threads. Pass the needle through the back of the work back to a. Work No. 2 as a mirror-image and right up against No. 1. Repeat right around so that an open square in the centre is formed.

G. Using No. 5 cotton work a satin stitch band around the stars. Outlining the lower 2 stars: Commence one thread to the inside of the corner-position and work one stitch over one thread, one over 2, over 3 and over 4 threads. Work the required number of upright stitches over 4 threads and decrease at the next corner by working over 3, 2 and over one, ending one thread from the corner position. Complete the square and note that on 2 occasions on the top side 5 stitches are worked over 2 instead of over 4 threads to make room for the 2 kloster blocks.

PLATE 10.1
A cloth with a combination of handmade filet lace, drawn fabric work, geometric satin stitch, Reticella lace, needleweaving and surface darning. D: Author M: Miss Rita Grobbelaar

Outlining the top star: Commence at the lowest point and work a diagonal row of satin stitches over 4 threads so that each stitch is one thread higher than the previous one. Work over 8, 6, 4 and over 2 threads at the ends on the right and on the left, ending one thread shorter than the position on the design. Work the other diagonal lines at the top in the same way.

H. Weave half a wheel on two sides of each square. Quarters of wheels also appear on the design. See Par. 7.2 II No. 12.

I. The satin stitch leaves: Work on the same principle as described for star A in Par. 7.2 II No. 1, from * to *, except that the stitches lie over only 8 threads instead of 10. (Work 3 stitches over 8 threads).

J. The filling of the cross motif in the centre: Weave all the bars and work the diagonal leaves with 2 picots as indicated to form a flower shape. See Par. 7.2 IV No. 14.

K. The filling of the 2 diamonds: Weave all the bars and work Hardanger flowers in the specified alternate spaces. See Par. 7.2 IV No. 2.

L. The V-shaped open motifs: Work as described in Par. 7.4 No. 1.

M. The large diamond shaped motif: See Par. 7.2 II No. 1B

for the method but work over 4 instead of over 6 threads and 9 stitches altogether on each of the 4 sides. Outline each star with 2 rows of Hardanger double faggot stitch. Use No. 12 or No. 8 cotton, and work 4 stars in the spaces

272

PLATE 10.2
Section of a cloth of grey linen worked in white geometric satin stitch, drawn fabric and chain stitich. D: Author M: Mrs. Lulu Heyns

on each side.

N. Use No. 8 cotton and work bands of needle-weaving strengthened with double hem-stitching. See Chapter 6.

Further uses for this design
1. See Fig. 10.3
Construct a border in this way and add a small motif if it seems too sparse.

2. See Fig. 10.4
Take X as centre and enlarge the design to both sides for a chairback or tray cloth.

3. See Fig. 10.5
A lovely tea cosy.

4. See Fig. 10.6
Use this part reversed alternately for a border and add a small diamond in Hardanger work to fill the space.

10.2 A border in cross stitch, Holbein work, drawn fabric work and geometric satin stitch

D 10.2 See page 277 for the design.
Scale: One square equals 3 threads. Separate motifs may very easily be taken from this design. Used as a border, it will be most effective on any table-linen.
Suggested colour-schemes:

1. Material: Red Hardanger material.
   Cross stitch: White No. 8 Pearl cotton.
   Holbein stitch: Black No. 8.
   Drawn fabric work: White No. 12.
   Satin stitch: The same shade of red as the material in No. 5 Pearl cotton.

2. Material: Ivory evenly woven linen with approximately 20 threads to 2½ cm.
   5 Pearl cotton.
   Holbein stitch: Black No. 8.

Figure 10.1

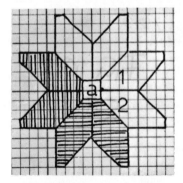

Figure 10.2

Drawn fabric work: Ecru (No. 644 D.M.C.) No. 8.

Satin stitch: The flowers in white No. 5, the leaves in ecru (No. 644) No. 5.

Work the outlines in Holbein stitch in black around the white satin stitch.

3. Material: White or ivory evenly woven linen with approximately 30 threads to 2½ cm. Cross stitch Blue (No. 799, D.M.C.) Pearl cotton No. 8.

Holbein stitch: Black No. 8.

Drawn fabric work: White No. 12.

Satin stitch: Blue (No's 797, 799 and 800,

PLATE 10.3
A section of design D 10.1. Showing the following: Hardanger fillings nos 2, 14, border Fig. 7.27 no 1, satin stitch star, surface darning. Hardanger single faggot stitch, four-sided stitch and eyelets.

Figure 10.3

Figure 10.6

Figure 10.4

Figure 10.5

D.M.C.) No. 5 Pearl cotton.
Key: A. Cross stitch. B. Holbein stitch. C.

Four-sided stitch. D. Geometric satin stitch. E. Mosaic stitch. F. Eyelets. G. Detached buttonhole bars.

10.3 A christening robe in shadow work and broderie anglaise

*D 10.3
Schematic diagram: See Fig. 10.7

The material for this christening — robe must be semi-transparent to do justice to the shadow work. Beautiful terylene cambric is obtainable, crease-resistant and most suitable for this purpose. Broder Spécial in No. 35 is the correct thread to use, but as it is unavailable, use one or two threads of stranded cotton.

Key:
A. Use carbon paper and trace the whole design, except line A, very lightly onto the wrong side of the material, so that line A is

PLATE 10.4
A cream old Glanis linen tea-cloth worked in red geometric satin stitch, sorbello, and different drawn fabric stitches. D: Author, M: Mrs. Lulu Heyns.

the raw edge is about 13 mm over line A. Tack. Now trace line A lightly on the right side of the hem so that it is in the right position. Work small running stitches on this line through both layers of the material. Work small firm buttonhole stitches over this with the loops away from the hem and use a guiding-thread of No. 5 Pearl cotton as well. Cut off the superfluous 13 mm on the wrong side right up against the stitches. The whole hem will be double with a pretty scalloped edge.

B. Shadow work. Work the veins and stem of the leaves in backstitch after the leaves have been completed.

C. Stem stitch on the wrong side which will result in backstitch lines on the right side.

D. Eyelet-holes.

E. The bodice of the robe may be decorated with the border shown in brackets on the design.

PLATE 10.6
Geometric satin stitch, Holbein stitch and Hardanger work in white and black on grey material D: Author, M: Mrs. Valerie Saunders

D 10.2

PLATE 10.5
A fine exambple of drawn fabric embroidery in ecru and cross stitch in pastel shades. D: Author, M: Mrs. Fienie Olivier

PLATE 10.7
Blue linen was used for this runner, and different blues, black and white for the counted thread embroidery. D: Author, M: Mrs. Zannie Mostert

PLATE 10.8
Corner of a table-cloth of pure silk organza richly embroidered in shadow work, satin stitch, eyelets, cutwork, etc. DM: Author

Figure 10.7

PLATE 10.9
Combinations of shadow work, drawn fabric embroidery and Reticella lace. D: Author, M: Mrs. Cupie Wessels and Mrs. Elize Stockenström

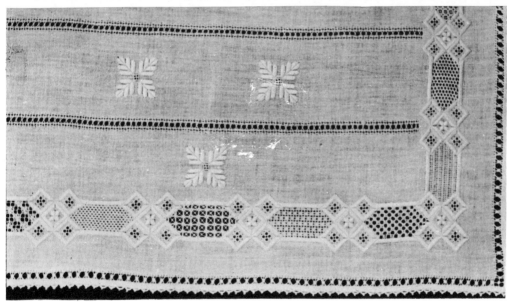

PLATE 10.10
Section of a cloth showing a combination of drawn thread work, drawn fabric work and geometric satin stitch. D: Author. M: Mrs. Aletta Wessels

10.4 A motif in drawn thread work and bullion work

D 10.4

Use carbon-paper and trace the design on the material. This motif will be most effective on a reasonably coarse Irish linen in ivory or ecru. Broder Spécial in Nos. 25 and 30 is the correct thread to use, but as it is unavailable,

PLATE 10.11 AND PLATE 10.12
Two sections of a round cloth worked in drawn thread work, drawn fabric work, Old Hedebo work and surface stitchery. DM. Author.

use No. 8 pearl cotton shade 644, sharp-pointed needles with small eyes for the bullion work and stranded cotton in a colour similar to that of the ground for the drawn thread work filling and band. The worker must decide for herself whether to use one or two threads of the stranded cotton depending on her choice of material.

Key: A. Outline the square with buttonhole stitch and the typical ring bullion picots in every 6th stitch.

B. Use any drawn thread filling in the square.

C. Bullion work. D. Drawn thread work band.

PLATE 10.13
Here geometric satin stitch, needleweaving and drawn fabric embroidery are used as an all-over pattern in pale blue on cream linen. D. Author, M: Mrs. C. B. Steyl

PLATE 10. 14, PLATE 10.15, PLATE 10.16
Three delicate motifs in Russian drawn thread and black Holbein work. D. Author, M: Mrs. B. Cohen

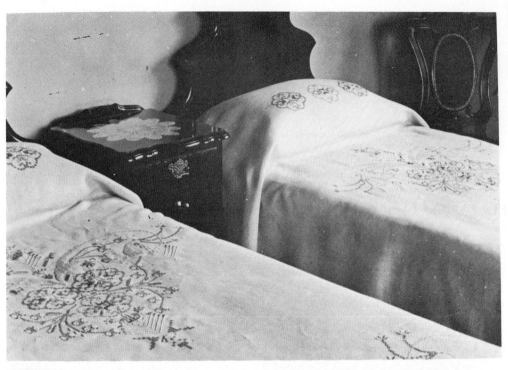

PLATE 10.17
Blue and white bedspreads for a blue bedroom! A variety of drawn fabric stitches, canvas stitches and geometric satin stitch were used on cream linen. D: Author, M: Mrs. Valerie Saunders

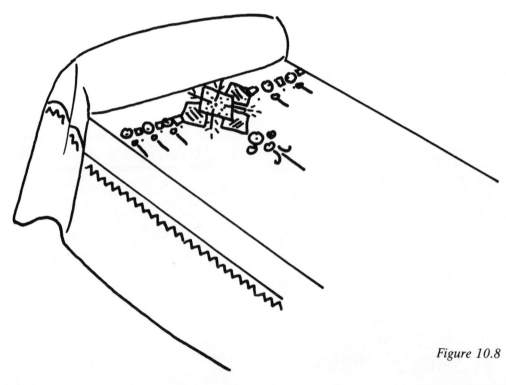

Figure 10.8

PLATE 10.18
A rich border combining geometric satin stitch, drawn fabric embroidery, needleweaving, drawn thread work, blackwork and Holbein stitchery. DM: Author.

10.5 A bedspread in cross stitch, geometric satin stitch, Holbein stitch, canvas work stitches and backstitch wheels

D 10.5

Schematic diagram: See Fig. 10.8
Scale: One square equals 3 threads.

Use an evenly woven, reasonably coarse material with about 25 threads per 25 mm . If the material is too narrow for a bedspread, join on the 2 long sides. (See Par. 1.6 for method of joining). Decorate this seam with any of the stitches used in the design. Place the design just below the pillow in the middle of the bed. The choice of the colour of the material and thread will depend on the colour-scheme of the room in which the bedspread will be used.
Suggested colour-scheme:
Material: Pale pink reasonably coarse even-weave linen.

Thread: No. 5 or No. 3 Pearl cotton in white, black and 3 shades of pale pink.
Key:
A. Cross stitch. B. Geometric satin stitch. The method of working all these motifs will be found in the chapters on drawn fabric work. In this case all the satin stitch is outlined in Holbein stitch. C. Holbein stitch. D. Rice stitch. E. French stitch. F. Backstitch wheel.

Index

The following diagrams are in the envelope at the back of the book:
D 3.1, D 3.2, D 4.5, D 4.6, D 4.7, D 4.8, D 4.9, D 5.2, D 5.4, D 5.5, D 5.9, D 5.11, D 5.13, D 5.14, D 6.1, D 7.2, D 8.1, Fig. 9.1, D 9.11, D 10.1, D 10.3, D 10.4, D10.5

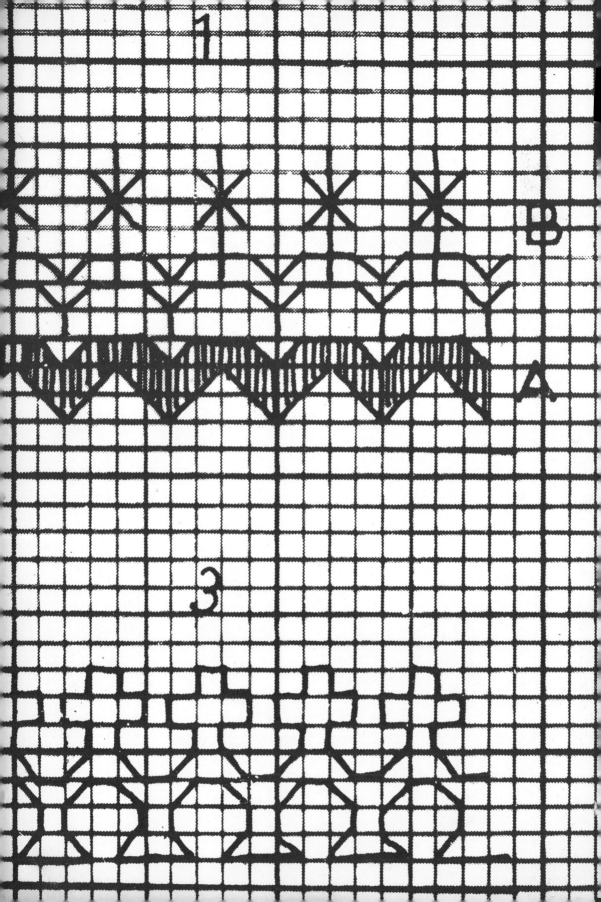